Putnam's School Series.

LANDMARKS

OF

GENERAL HISTORY

IN THE

CHRISTIAN ERA.

BY THE

REV. C. S, DAWE, B.A.,

ST. MARK'S COLLEGE, LONDON.

NEW YORK:

G. P. PUTNAM'S SONS,

182 FIFTH AVENUE.

PREFACE.

This little book, as its title implies, is designed to set before the reader such a record of the great events in the Christian era, as may guide him along the highway of historic truth, enabling him to know the most memorable events, their sequence and connection, and to become acquainted with the men who have played the most prominent part in shaping the destiny of nations. In carrying out this design, the author has endeavoured to write a book that may be read with pleasure and studied with profit. He has, accordingly, avoided anything approaching to that most hateful of all books in a school library, "a synopsis of universal history;" and has attempted to describe the chief events in a clear and interesting style, omitting all minor details of a dry and unattractive character, and giving to the narrative a biographical complexion. Facts, related in general and abstract terms, seldom enrich the mind or dwell in the memory; but when grouped around some central human figure, they generally command the attention of the reader, and find a permanent place in his memory.

As a school-book, this little work is intended for pupils

who are already familiar with the outlines of English history; and, therefore, events relating more particularly to our own nation are purposely omitted. It is hoped that the student will find in the following pages a valuable introduction to the study of modern history, and a store of such information, respecting events in the Christian era, as is indispensable for the due appreciation of even the most ordinary works of literature.

C. S. D.

July, 1874.

CONTENTS.

CHAPTER V.

Dissolution of the Western Empire.

CHAPTER VI.

The Age of Justinian.

CHAPTER VII.

Christianity from Constantine to Gregory.

CHAPTER VIII.

Mohammed and the Saracens.

CHAPTER IX

Charlemagne and the Franks.

CHAPTER X.

Europe in the Tenth Century.

CHAPTER XI.

Rise and Progress of the Turks.

CHAPTER XII.

The Crusades.

CHAPTER XIII.

Europe in the Fourteenth Century.

CHAPTER XIV.

Mongols, Turks, and Moors.

CHAPTER XV.

Discovery and Conquest of America.

CHAPTER XVI.

Age of the Reformation.

LANDMARKS OF GENERAL HISTORY

IN THE CHRISTIAN ERA.

CHAPTER I.

THE ROMAN EMPIRE UNDER AUGUSTUS.

JULIUS CÆSAR, the great Dictator of the Roman republic, ended his career on the Ides of March, B.C. 44, in the Senate-house at Rome, where he fell a victim to the daggers of Brutus, Cassius, and other conspirators, in the name of liberty.

The citizens at first knew not whether to applaud or condemn the "patriots," who boldly paraded the streets of Rome, holding up in proud defiance their blood-stained weapons, and reiterating their cries of "Liberty!" But on the next day deep sympathy for the fallen Cæsar spread throughout all ranks on hearing the recital of his will, by which he bequeathed to every Roman citizen 300 sesterces, a sum equal to more than £2 of our money, and directed his splendid gardens beyond the Tiber to be thrown open as a public park. Devotion to the memory of the Dictator, and hatred for his murderers, from this moment visibly increased.

These feelings were wrought to their highest intensity by the funeral oration pronounced by Mark Antony over the mangled corpse of Cæsar, as it lay in the Forum upon its ivory bier. The orator recited the chief acts of Cæsar's life, recounted his deeds of bravery, generosity, and patriotism, and then drew a vividly mournful picture of his tragic fate. To render his speech still more effective, he displayed a waxen image marked with three-and-twenty ghastly wounds, and then spread before the eyes of the excited spectators the very robe in which Cæsar had met his death, now rent and red with blood. The infuriated crowd, after burning, according to ancient custom, the corpse of their hero, rushed from the blazing pyre with torches in their hands to the houses of the assassins to avenge his death. But all the conspirators had fled. Brutus and Cassius, a year or two afterwards, sought death from the swords of their own friends, to avoid falling into the hands of Mark Antony, after their defeat at Philippi.

ANTONY AND OCTAVIAN.

The death of Cæsar left Antony master of Rome. But a rival soon appeared in the person of Octavius, Cæsar's nephew and heir. This youth was destined to reign as the first emperor of Rome. He showed from the first a prudence beyond his years. As Cæsar's heir he demanded from Antony the property bequeathed by Cæsar's will, but he could only obtain the shreds of his inheritance. Octavius then sold all he had, and, having raised money besides on his own credit, gained great popularity by paying all the legacies of Cæsar's will. Antony soon discovered that in this beardless boy he had a formidable competitor for the supreme power in the state.

After the defeat and death of Brutus and Cassius at Philippi (B.C. 42), Mark Antony and his rival divided the Roman world between them, Antony taking for his share the eastern provinces, and Octavius (now called Octavian) the western provinces.

Antony at once proceeded to make a tour through his dominions. At Tarsus he received a visit which proved his utter ruin. This was from Cleopatra, queen of Egypt, who had so long exercised her sway over the heart of Cæsar. She now came to meet Antony at Tarsus, resolved to conquer by her beauty. The galley which carried her up the Cydnus was of more than Oriental gorgeousness: the sails of purple; oars of silver, moving to the sound of music; the raised poop burnished with gold. She gracefully reclined upon a splendid couch, shaded by a spangled canopy; her attire was that of Venus; around her flitted attendant Cupids and Graces. The queen invited the Roman ruler to her ship, and he complied. From that moment he was her slave, and lent his power to execute all her caprices. Occasionally he broke the silken cord of the enchantress, and took the field as a veteran warrior. It is remarkable how this brave soldier, amid the hardships of war, could shake off his luxurious habits, and how cheerfully he would share with the meanest soldier all the toils and privations of the most disastrous campaign. At length he sunk into an indolent voluptuary, and whiled away his time in silly amusements. He gave the Romans great offence by stamping Cleopatra's head with his own upon the coins he issued as the ruler of the East. He disposed of kingdoms by his own arbitrary will. Herod was made king of Judæa to the exclusion of the rightful heir; and Polemo, his own illegitimate son by Cleopatra, was seated on the throne of Armenia.

While Antony was rapidly losing the respect of the Romans by his worthless, frivolous life, under the influence of Cleopatra's fascinating wit and manner, Octavian was winning golden opinions by his patient industry and resolute perseverance in the administration of his government. Before the close of B.C. 32, Octavian, with the sanction of the senate, declared war nominally against Cleopatra, but with the intention really of crushing his rival. A sea-fight off Actium in the following autumn left Antony a fugitive without a fleet and without an army. He escaped to Alexandria with his enchantress, who had fled at a critical part of the battle with a squadron of sixty Egyptian ships. Octavian, secure of his prey, followed at his convenience, and it was not until August 1, B.C. 30, that the conqueror entered Alexandria.

Cleopatra then withdrew to her mausoleum with two of her maidens, through whom she sent a message to Antony that she was dead. Believing the information to be true, he called upon a faithful attendant, named Eros, to kill him. Eros drew his sword as if he designed to obey his master; but suddenly turning about, he plunged it into his own breast. "This, Eros, was nobly done," said Antony; "thy heart would not permit thee to kill thy master, but thou hast taught him what to do by thy example." He then stabbed himself, and, while dying, was taken at his request to Cleopatra's retreat, where he ended his wasted life.

The queen then tried her arts and blandishments upon Octavian; but she saw neither pity nor passion in the icy looks he turned upon her. She perceived that his fair words were only intended to disarm her suspicion, and that his real intention was to conduct her to Rome to grace his triumph, and to gratify the people with the sight of that princess whose charms had subdued the great Cæsar, and enslaved his friend and avenger. She soon resolved, at the cost of her life, to disappoint his expectation. When his soldiers came to remove the royal captive, they found her in queenly attire lying dead upon her golden bed. The manner of her death is uncertain; but the popular belief ascribed it to the bite of an asp, brought by a peasant in a basket of figs.

THE FIRST EMPEROR OF ROME.

After the victory of Actium, the fate of the Roman world depended on the will of Octavian, surnamed Cæsar by his uncle's adoption, and afterwards Augustus by the flattery of the senate. The conqueror was at the head of forty-four veteran legions devoted to the house of Cæsar, and ready to do the bidding of their chief. A century of civil war had inclined the Romans to welcome peace at any price. Since the tyrant Tarquinius, in B.C. 509, had been deposed and expelled from Rome, the Romans had adopted the republican form of government. Instead of a king ruling for life, two chief magistrates, called *consuls*, were annually elected to govern the state. But now, on the return of Octavian from Egypt, Rome again became in all respects, except in name, a monarchy under the sovereign rule of its chief citizen, Augustus.

Augustus dated his reign from the day of the battle of Actium; but it was not until two years afterwards (B.C. 29) that he established himself in Rome as emperor. He inaugurated his reign by a magnificent triumph of three days, and at the same time closed the temple of Janus in sign of universal peace, being the first time since the year B.C. 235. The Romans, sick of war and civil discord, gladly submitted to the rule of the only man that could maintain peace. Augustus was too prudent to assume the regal name and diadem, but he exercised, by universal consent, an authority more than regal.

The reign of Augustus was chiefly passed in works of peace. The city was so vastly improved under his directing hand, that he could justly boast at the end of his reign, that "he had found Rome of brick and left it of marble." The buildings at Rome were repeated on a smaller scale in every large town and colony of the empire. Wherever the Roman went he carried with him his art of building: for roads, bridges, canals, aqueducts, and other engineering works of public utility, the Romans have gained an imperishable name.

Whilst the most civilised nations of the globe were united under the sceptre of the first Roman emperor, the Redeemer of our race was born. This momentous event happened three or four years before the time erroneously fixed as the commencement of the Christian era. "The fulness of the time" had come, for men had outgrown their old superstitions, and the noblest among them were longing for a purer faith. The need of a revelation from heaven was never greater; for beneath the veil of outward decency, which Augustus had in part made fashionable, the morals of the nation were utterly corrupt. Even the emperor's own daughter Julia, and her daughter of the same name, became so notorious in Rome for profligacy, that he was obliged to banish both of them at different times to secluded islands off the Italian coast.

Augustus died in A.D. 14, after an illustrious reign of forty-three years, a period remarkable for the splendour of Latin literature and the arts of peaceful industry.

LITERATURE OF THE PERIOD.

Latin and Greek divided the Roman world between them; the former prevailed in the west, and the latter in the east. The Romans endeavoured to extend, with the progress of their arms, the use of the Latin tongue. In the western provinces they were successful, for the barbarians whom they subdued were ready to exchange their own rude dialects for the more polished language of their conquerors; but in the eastern provinces, Greek held its ground as the popular language. Latin, however, was universally employed in the administration of government and of justice.

The Greek literature formed the fountain head, whence flowed the stream of Latin poetry, philosophy, and oratory.

The greatest of Roman orators was Cicero, who flourished in the days of Julius Cæsar, and soon after the death of the Dictator fell a victim to the wrath of Antony, whom he had stung by those invective speeches, known as Philippics. By Antony's express desire, the orator's head, and the hands which had written the Philippics, were cut off, and brought to Rome, and nailed to the Rostra in the Forum. Fulvia, the wife of Antony, stuck her hair-pin through the silent tongue that had denounced in burning words her husband's iniquities.

The greatest of the Roman poets were Virgil and Horace, both of whom adorned the reign of Augustus. The chief poems of Virgil are the *Georgics* and the *Æneid*, the former being a picture of peaceful industry and simple home happiness in the days of the ancient Romans, and the latter an epic or heroic poem designed to magnify to the eyes of Romans the greatness of their origin and destiny. The gay Horace is chiefly famous for his *Odes* and *Satires*, in which he holds up a mirror reflecting the manners of the day, and endeavours by his cheery wit to reform, whilst seeming to amuse. Contemporary with Virgil and Horace was the historian Livy, who wrote a history of Rome from the earliest times. He took the dry chronicles of his nation, and clothed them in forms of heroic life and poetic beauty, so that the great Romans of former ages lived again in the hearts and minds of their countrymen. These three writers have thrown a splendid lustre over the Augustan age of literature.

IMPERIAL ROME AND ITS PEOPLE.

Rome, on the accession of Augustus, had become too small for its population, and too mean for its imperial position. Under this emperor and his immediate successors, it was almost rebuilt and greatly extended. In the meantime, its narrow streets and winding alleys were almost impassable; neither shops nor bazaars had as yet become common, so that a vast amount of retail trading was transacted by itinerant vendors in the streets, which resounded with their multitudinous cries. Obstructions were frequently caused by crowds of spectators, with eyes intent upon conjurors, buffoons, and athletes while they exhibited their tricks and feats. The passage of the thoroughfares was so difficult that the Roman of quality preferred his palanquin to his carriage.

The Romans in ancient times were simple and frugal in their tastes and manners, but now they had become luxurious and self-indulgent. The cold plunge in the Tiber which had braced the sinews of the old Romans, now made way for an elaborate system of tepid and vapour baths, in which the rich idler languidly spent his vacant hours, listening to soft strains of music, or exchanging the small gossip of the day. At mid-day every door was closed, and every citizen, at least in summer, withdrew to his bed-chamber to enjoy his *siesta*. The great meal of the day was the *cœna* or supper. The Romans no longer sat at table like their forefathers, but reclined on couches arranged along the three sides of a square. In the open space between, the slaves, moving noiselessly about, anticipated every wish of their master and his guests. They carved, and supplied each person's plate with such fragmentary viands as he could raise to his mouth with his fingers only, and poured water upon his hands at every remove.

In the days of imperial Rome, every household of any pretension was managed by a host of slaves, who had lost their freedom by capture in war, who had been born in slavery, or who had been sold when children by their parents. The first question asked respecting a person's fortune was, *Quot pascit servos*, How many slaves does he keep? Slaves were employed not only to discharge menial offices, but as musicians, secretaries, and physicians.

The Roman citizens must have had much leisure time; and, accordingly, we find ample parks and gardens devoted to their recreation. The circus and amphitheatre, however, supplied the Romans with their favourite amusements. Chariot racing was the chief sport in the circus. Four chariots, each drawn by four fiery steeds, with the reins passed round the bodies of the drivers, started together on the fall of a white napkin from the hand of the president. Seven times they madly whirled around the course amid clouds of dust and storms of excited uproar. Both in the circus and the amphitheatre were exhibited vast crowds of wild beasts, which were let loose in the arena to fight frantically with one another, or to be transfixed with arrows and javelins from the hands of condemned criminals or captives. But the most brutal of all Roman sports were the combats of the gladiators in the amphitheatre. These men were slaves trained to fight with adroitness and skill. On the appointed day of the exhibition, hundreds, or even thousands would be marched into the arena, and matched in pairs.

At first, there was generally a kind of sham fight with wooden swords; but at the trumpet signal the real battle began. The fate of each wounded gladiator depended on the verdict of the spectators, who answered his appealing looks for pity with down-turned thumbs, if they wished to spare his life, or with up-turned thumbs if they sentenced him to die.

The first stone amphitheatre was built at the command of Augustus. In the reign of Vespasian arose that stupendous edifice known as the Colosseum, the noblest existing monument of all ancient architecture. This amphitheatre was capable of containing about 87,000 spectators. Here the emperor Trajan, on his return from the conquest of Dacia, exhibited 10,000 gladiators at once.

EXTENT OF THE ROMAN EMPIRE.

The Roman empire, in the age of Augustus, extended from the Euphrates on the east, to the Atlantic on the west, from the Rhine and Danube on the north, to the deserts of Arabia and Africa on the south, being in breadth about 2000 miles, and in length above 3000 miles. The Roman empire, therefore, comprised mainly those countries around the Mediterranean, having Rome for its centre as well as its capital.

The Romans fondly thought their empire to be almost co-extensive with the world, yet, in truth, there are at the present day four empires (the British, the Russian, the American, and the Chinese), each of which exceeds in size the dominions of Rome at the period of their greatest extension, and of which one only comprises a few square miles of all the regions over which Augustus held sway. The empire was enlarged after the death of Augustus by Agricola's conquest of Britain, and a little later by the addition of Dacia, a province between the Lower Danube and the Dniester.

CHAPTER II.

THE ROMAN EMPERORS FROM AUGUSTUS TO CONSTANTINE.

FROM the death of Augustus (A.D. 14) to the accession of Constantine (A.D. 306), more than forty emperors ruled over the Roman empire. Their history, with a few brilliant exceptions, is a dark register of crimes and follies. The senate claimed the right of installing the new ruler in his office, but the election was virtually in the hands of the soldiery, especially the Prætorian or Imperial Guard. Very frequently, however, the emperor nominated his successor, and invested him with a share of the government during his own lifetime. A few only of the emperors ended their days in peace: the sword of an assassin, or a self-inflicted wound, most commonly opened up a way for a new competitor for the perilous purple of a Roman emperor.

The history of the three centuries intervening between the reign of Augustus and that of Constantine will be most conveniently treated in four periods.

I. AN AGE OF TYRANNY. (14-68).

Augustus was succeeded by four despots — Tiberius, Caligula, Claudius, and Nero. These four monarchs belonged to the house of Cæsar, but they were all unworthy to bear his name. The records of their reigns abound in deeds of cruelty and bloodshed, and reveal a sad picture of debauchery and profligacy. The empire, meanwhile, was free from desolating wars, and, except in Rome, suffered but slightly from the tyranny of these despots.

Tiberius (14–37) reigned at first with much ability and industry. Had he died at the end of ten years, he would have left the reputation of being a good sovereign, though sour and morose in disposition. During this time he never quitted the din and dust of Rome. He lived a simple and frugal life, and endeavoured to reform the luxurious and dissolute life of his subjects. He checked the adulation of the senate, and declared that "a good and useful prince should be the servant of his people."

Towards the middle of his reign he became insanely moody and suspicious, fancying every moment that his throne was tottering under him. This led at length to his withdrawal from Rome. For eleven years he lived in retirement in the lone isle of Capreæ, leaving his favourite, Sejanus, at Rome to carry out his behests.

The name of this minister is infamous. Sejanus had set his heart on the imperial sceptre, and he was ready to steep his hands in blood, however deep, so that he might grasp it. He once risked his life to save his royal master's, by throwing his Herculean frame, as an arch, over the prostrate body of the emperor, to shield it from the falling ruins of a roof that had suddenly collapsed. But he ended his career as a traitor to his friend and sovereign. The fallen minister saw the Romans exultingly pulling down his statues, as he passed through the Forum on his way to death. His hated corpse was trampled under foot and abandoned to beast and bird.

The discovery of his favourite's plot left the emperor no peace of mind by day or night. At length he sought, in a moment of madness, to drown his apprehensions in bloodshed, and in one frightful massacre all perished, without distinction of age, sex, or condition, who were reckoned the friends or relatives of Sejanus. Death came to the relief of the nation A.D. 37.

Caligula (37–41), the youngest son of Germanicus, received his nickname from the *caligæ* or military boots he wore, when a boy among his father's legions. A dangerous mutiny was once quelled by showing to the troops their young pet and playfellow. The boy became a favourite of Tiberius, and contrived by consummate hypocrisy and servility to retain the tyrant's special favour till his death. His chief companion, when a youth, was that Agrippa before whom St. Paul afterwards pleaded his cause. One of the first acts of Caligula's reign was to present Agrippa with a chain of gold equal in weight to the iron fetters from which the death of Tiberius had released him. The crown of Samaria was afterwards added to this gift. From his Jewish friend, Caligula had learnt the part of an oriental despot—a part he soon began to play when installed emperor of Rome.

At first he dazzled the people by his magnificence, and gratified them with splendid spectacles and exciting games in the circus and amphitheatre. The flattery of his subjects turned his brain, and he fancied himself a god; at least he claimed divine worship, and ordered his statue to be placed in the temples. It was only his premature death that saved the Jews from the profane introduction of the emperor's image into their temple at Jerusalem.

The records of his reign are full of the fantastic freaks of a madman. His lavish expenditure could only be supported by cruel despotism. While fondling his wife's neck, he said, "Fair as it is, how easily I could sever it." This was no vain boast, as is obvious from the number of wealthy citizens who on some frivolous pretext were deprived of life, that he might fill his coffers with their gold. At times he delighted to enter his treasury, and wade in the heaps of gold with bare feet, or throw himself down and roll frantically among them. As long as he gained his gold by striking off the heads of the nobles, the populace looked on unmoved; but when he proceeded to wring new taxes out of the people, all Rome turned against him as one man. It was then he expressed to his headsman that diabolical wish—"Would that the people of Rome had but one neck!"

The story of his pretended conquest of Britain is almost incredible. Having drawn up his troops on the northern shores of Gaul, with the fleet ready for embarkation, he suddenly ordered his soldiers to pile arms and fill their helmets with shells; then with these *spoils of the ocean* he returned in triumph to Rome as a conqueror.

This imperial madman was in the fourth year of his notorious reign, when his career of blood and folly was closed by the daggers of a band of conspirators.

Claudius (41–54), the uncle of Caligula, warned by the fate of his predecessor, took Augustus for his model, and endeavoured, though very imperfectly, to imitate his virtues. The chief military exploit of his reign was the partial conquest of Britain. Claudius himself passed over into Britain, but the real work of this war fell to Vespasian, the future emperor. When the British chief, Caractacus, was led in chains before Claudius, he was so struck with his undaunted bearing that he generously spared his life.

Claudius married as his second wife, Agrippina, who had by a former husband a son, known in history as Nero. Claudius gave to his stepson his daughter Octavia in marriage, and declared him his heir and successor. To make sure of the speedy succession of her son, Agrippina poisoned a dish of mushrooms, the favourite delicacy of the emperor's supper table. The treacherous morsel was swallowed, but as it only caused a fit of retching, the royal physician, who was in the secret, under pretence of aiding the sufferer to vomit thrust a poisoned feather down his throat.

Nero (54–68) by his fiendish crimes has gained above all other miscreants the pre-eminence in infamy. "Evil, be thou my good" seems to have been the maxim of his life. For five years, however, whilst acting under the direction of his tutor, Seneca, he ruled prudently and prosperously. In the meantime his vices were secretly striking their roots deeper and spreading their branches wider.

His first great crime was the murder of his rival Britannicus, the son of Claudius. The black deed was achieved before the eyes of the tyrant at a banquet in the palace. The warm wine-cup was tasted as usual by the attendant and presented to the young prince. He found it too hot, and in the drop of cold water which was poured into it so deadly a poison had been infused, that the child, on swallowing it, fell back lifeless. The murderer next proceeded to rid himself of his mother, the notorious Agrippina. She was induced when at Baiæ to enter a vessel so constructed as to fall to pieces on withdrawing certain bolts. The stratagem, however, failed, as his mother was picked up by a boat and taken to her villa; but she only escaped the waves to die by the swords of assassins. The self-accuser was fain to fly from the scenes which could not change their faces like the courtiers to flatter him. But change of place left him unchanged. The exile and murder of his wife Octavia, to make way for Poppæa Sabina, the fairest woman of her time, formed a natural sequel to these unnatural crimes.

The servile patience of the senate in the face of such enormities, and the glowing reception from the populace which the matricide received on his return to Rome, clearly prove that the Romans of that time were not deserving of a better master, than the sanguinary tyrant who held the sceptre of death over them.

A great fire, lasting for six days, laid the greater part of the city in ashes (A.D. 64). The emperor was supposed to have been the author of the calamity, and so to clear himself from the imputation he set on foot a fearful persecution against the Christians, as the cause of the disaster. In rebuilding the city, the emperor took care to beautify and enlarge his palace, and that to such an extent as to give point to the saying, that "Rome was reduced to a single house."

Whilst Nero was busy with his plans for building, conspirators were planning his death. But the plot was discovered and all concerned in it, including the philosopher Seneca, and the poet Lucan, were condemned to die, but allowed to open their own veins and bleed to death.

The hour of retribution was only postponed. Within three years a general, named Galba, raised the standard of revolt, and was saluted as emperor by the army. The timid tyrant slunk away in disguise from his capital, and tried to conceal himself from his pursuers; but on hearing the tramp of horsemen at hand, he placed a weapon to his breast, and the slave Epaphroditus drove it in (A.D. 68).

In less than two years from Nero's ignoble end, three generals—Galba, Otho, and Vitellius—successively wore the purple and stained it with their blood. Meanwhile a veteran general was at his post of duty in the East, to whom all eyes now turned to save the empire from anarchy. This was Vespasian, who had gained his first laurels in Britain, and was now preparing to besiege Jerusalem. His reign began in A.D. 69.

II. GOLDEN AGE OF THE EMPIRE. (69-180).

The period inaugurated by the accession of Vespasian and closed by the death of Marcus Aurelius (A.D. 180), was distinguished by the prosperous administration of the government, by the tranquil obedience of the people, and, with a single exception, by the virtue and wisdom of the rulers. This epoch embraces the reigns of eight monarchs, of whom one only, Domitian, was a debauchee and a tyrant. Gibbon, the great historian, says: "If a man were called to fix the period in the history of the world, during which the condition of the human race was most happy and prosperous, he would without hesitation name that which elapsed from the death of Domitian to that of M. Aurelius. The vast extent of the Roman empire was governed by absolute power under the guidance of virtue and wisdom."

Vespasian and his Sons.—Vespasian and his two sons, Titus and Domitian, were successively appointed to rule over the destinies of the great empire. The father was a plain homely man, of frugal, industrious habits, sternly bent on doing his duty. By his example and authority the voluptuous luxury of the Romans was restrained, and a simpler style of living made fashionable. The demolition of Nero's "golden house," and the conversion of some of his other palatial buildings into public baths for the people, indicate that the good of the people rather than his own aggrandisement was the highest aim of this emperor. Vespasian also built the Colosseum, the most magnificent of the Roman amphitheatres, within the limits of the vast Neronian palace, and probably with the spoils of that labyrinth of masonry. At the age of seventy, full of toils and honours, he was called at last to his rest by mere natural decay, after a reign of ten years.

The chief event of his reign is associated with the name of Titus, his eldest son and successor. A rebellion of the Jews had broken out in the reign of Nero, and it was resolved, by the utter destruction of their capital, to put an end to their existence as a nation. Jerusalem was protected by three walls and two citadels. The siege began in April 70, and at that time the city contained at least a million souls. On the approach of the Roman legions a small band of Christians, mindful of our Lord's prediction, withdrew to the little town of Pella.

Never was a city more obstinately defended. After forcing the outer wall, the Romans thought it more prudent to blockade the city, so as to reduce it by famine. Thousands who attempted to escape were captured, and suspended on crosses round the walls, until there was no wood left for the crosses, nor space on the walls to fix them. The famine in the city was so horrible, that a mother was discovered with the mangled limbs of her own infant in a dish before her. The siege had lasted four months, when the impatient Romans stormed the temple. On the evening before the day fixed for the final assault, a soldier, climbing on a comrade's shoulders, flung a blazing torch through an open window. The flames shot up, and soon devoured the doomed edifice in spite of the frantic efforts of Titus to save it. The last stronghold was taken in the sixth month of the siege, and when Titus had finished his task, Jerusalem was a heap of smoking ruins. Most of the inhabitants perished in the siege; the survivors were sold as slaves, or treated as criminals.

Titus, on his return to Rome, was associated with his father in the government, and succeeded him as emperor (A.D. 79). He won golden opinions from both the nobles and the populace, and was styled "Delight of the human race." Nero, however, might have left as fair a name had he reigned like Titus for only two years.

It was in this short reign that the slumbering fires of Vesuvius awoke, and by their terrific energy sent forth torrents of melted lava, and showers of burning cinders, which overwhelmed in rapid ruin the towns of Pompeii and Herculaneum, reposing in fancied security in the plain below. The elder Pliny, famed as a naturalist, in approaching too near fell a victim to his scientific curiosity.

Titus was succeeded (A.D. 81) by **Domitian,** his cruel and hateful brother. In this reign Agricola completed the conquest of Britain. But the superior merit of this general soon occasioned his recall to Rome, and when he died (A.D. 93), the rumour spread that Domitian had poisoned him. "Nevertheless the emperor assumed," says Tacitus, "all the outward signs of grief; for it was easier for Domitian to dissemble his joy over a dead enemy, than his fear of a living one." From this time the best blood of Rome, which had hitherto trickled, under his hand, in a few intermittent drops only, like the first drops of a thunder shower, now poured forth in a copious and unceasing stream until his own assassination (A.D. 96).

Domitian was cruel even in sport: in youth one of his chief amusements was maiming and killing flies, and there is a story told of him, when emperor, which illustrates the wanton delight he took in causing pain. He invited a select number of the highest nobilty to a banquet. The guests arrived at midnight, and were ushered into a chamber hung with sable drapery, with ceiling and floor jet-black. As each guest arrived he was conducted to a funereal couch, and at its head he might see by the dim lamp a column, like a tombstone, on which his own name was graven. Presently there entered a troop of naked boys, with blackened skin, who danced around with horrid movements. The nobles, paralysed with fear, expected every moment to be put to death; but the tyrant was in sportive mood, and when he had sufficiently enjoyed the jest, the guests were introduced into the banquet hall.

Nerva and Trajan.—The senate elected, as Domitian's successor, the mild and gentle Nerva (A.D. 96). His excessive leniency drew upon him a stinging rebuke from a distinguished senator: "It is ill," he said, "to have a prince under whom no one may do anything; but worse to have one who lets every one do as he will." Nerva, having discovered that his feeble age was unable to stem the torrents of disorders, had the sagacity to choose, as his colleague, Trajan, the resolute chief of the army on the Rhine. The death of Nerva a few months afterwards left Trajan in the possession of the imperial sceptre.

The accession of Trajan (A.D. 98) was hailed with delight by the soldiers. Confident of their fidelity and his own integrity, he could boldly say, on handing to the prefect of the Prætorians the poniard which was the symbol of his office, "Use this for me, if I do well; if ill, against me." This virtuous and active prince had from early youth been trained as a hardy soldier, and had acquired the skill of a noble general. His first exploits were against the Dacians, who dwelt between the Dniester and the Lower Danube, and whose king, Decebalus, in the reign of Domitian, had received tribute from the imperial treasury as the price of peace. After a severe contest, lasting five years, Dacia became a province of the empire. This success of Trajan's arms has been immortalised by the erection of a splendid column, named after the conqueror, which still stands in Rome in all its pristine majesty.

Trajan was a great builder: Rome grew larger and more beautiful under his hand; and throughout the provinces innumerable bridges, aqueducts, and temples, long served as monuments of the splendour and vigour of his reign.

The last years of Trajan's reign were thrown away in a useless war with Parthia, whose capital was Ctesiphon on the Tigris. Though the emperor was everywhere victorious, and though he entered the Parthian capital in triumph, the conquered province was too remote for permanent possession. The conqueror died on his way home A.D. 117. His charred remains were placed in a golden urn and deposited at the foot of his own triumphal column.

Hadrian and the two Antonines.—Hadrian, who wore the purple after Trajan, was the *Beauclerc* among the emperors. His memory was prodigious, his application incredible. But though learned he was no mere dreaming bookworm. The greater part of his reign was passed in incessant travelling throughout the length and breadth of his vast empire; for the emperor was resolved to make himself personally acquainted with the condition and needs of his subjects. In A.D. 119 he crossed over into Britain, and left an enduring monument of his visit in the great rampart he constructed between the Tyne and the Solway. Rome was not neglected in his care for the provinces: the edifices, indeed, which arose in Rome at the command of Hadrian, surpassed in magnificence the works of his predecessors.

In this reign the Jews again rose in arms to assert their national existence. Under their leader, Barcochebas, they fought with marvellous valour; but after a hopeless struggle the remnants of the unhappy nation were finally dispersed.

When Hadrian died of dropsy, in A.D. 138, he was succeeded by his adopted son, **Antoninus**, surnamed **Pius**, on account of his dutiful affection towards him. The new emperor shared his power with his own adopted son, **Marcus Aurelius.** The two Antonines (as these two princes are called) governed the Roman world forty-two years with almost the same invariable spirit of wisdom and virtue. Marcus revered the character of his elder colleague, loved him as his parent, obeyed him as his sovereign, and, after he was no more, regulated his own administration (with one important exception) by the example and maxims of his predecessor. Under the elder Antonine the Christians enjoyed protection, but the younger Antonine deemed it his duty to inflict heavy punishments upon them for their neglect and contempt of the national religion. Both of these princes detested war as the disgrace and calamity of the human race. They acted on the principle, "It is nobler to save a single citizen than to slay a thousand enemies." But they knew as well how to draw the sword at the call of justice, as to sheathe it at the plea for mercy. Each of these princes was severe in judging himself, whilst indulgent to the faults of others. Their united reigns are, by the common consent of antiquity, the only period of Roman history in which the happiness of the people was the sole object of the government.

III. DISASTROUS CONDITION OF THE EMPIRE (180-268).

In an absolute monarchy, like the Roman empire, it is in the power of the ruler to ruin the state, but it is not always in the power of his successor to repair its shattered fortunes; for it is easier to throw down than build up. It was an evil day for Rome when **Commodus,** the unworthy son of Marcus Aurelius, assumed the reins of government (A.D. 180). Commodus seems to have taken Nero as his model: he coveted, as his highest object of ambition, a famous name as a gladiator; and he shed the blood of the noblest in Rome to fill his coffers with their gold. His cruelty at length recoiled on his own head, and he expired in the arms of a wrestler hired to strangle him (A.D. 192).

For eighty-six days the virtuous **Pertinax,** who was now proclaimed emperor, threw a transient gleam of happiness over the unhappy city. But Rome was now under the armed heel of the Prætorian guards, who missed the licence of the former reign. They assassinated the emperor, and shamelessly proclaimed that the Roman world was to be disposed of to the best bidder by public auction. Julianus, the purchaser, found himself on the throne of the empire without a friend or a single adherent. In sixty-six days his nominal reign ended in his execution as a common criminal.

The avenger of Rome and the restorer of order to the convulsed empire was **Septimus Severus,** the iron chief of the legions in Pannonia, who began his successful reign A.D. 193. Severus ruled as a military despot, but he used his power for the general good, and as long as his arm wielded the imperial sceptre, the soldiers were kept within due bounds. Severus passed the last two years of his life in Britain. He had chastised the Caledonians for their invasion of Southern Britain, and was preparing to lead a larger army against them for their complete subjugation, when death put an end to his project. Severus died at York (A.D. 211).

The next half century brought the empire to the brink of ruin. In that short period about a dozen princes were set up to rule, by the choice of the army or the clamour of the populace; and such was the deplorable condition of the empire that not one of them ended his days in peace. The Goths and other barbarians took advantage of the internal disorders of the state. In A.D. 249 they crossed the Dniester and overran Dacia, and two years later gained a decisive victory over the Romans under the emperor **Decius,** who perished in a morass in his attempt to escape.

A still worse fate befell the emperor **Valerian,** who, in a war with Persia, was taken prisoner by Sapor, the Persian king (A.D. 260). We are told that Valerian, in chains, but arrayed in imperial purple, was exposed to the gaping crowds in the cities of the East, a constant spectacle of fallen greatness; and that whenever the Persian monarch mounted his horse, he placed his foot on the neck of the captive emperor. When Valerian sunk under the weight of shame and grief, his skin was stuffed with straw and formed into the likeness of a human figure, and this was preserved for ages in the most celebrated temple of Persia. The unfortunate Valerian was the only emperor of Rome that had ever fallen into the hands of the enemy.

The empire was passing through one of the blackest epochs of her history. The night of shame and degradation lasted for nearly twenty years, from the invasion of the Goths in the reign of Decius. During that calamitous period, every province of the Roman world was afflicted by barbarous invaders and military tyrants. On the death of Gallienus (A.D. 268), the shattered empire seemed on the eve of dissolution.

IV. RESTORATION OF THE EMPIRE.

The ruined empire was saved from destruction by a series of great princes, who derived their obscure origin from the martial province of Illyricum. Within the space of thirty years, Claudius, Aurelian, Probus, and Diocletian, triumphed over the foreign and domestic enemies of the state, re-established with the military discipline the strength of the frontiers, and deserved the glorious title of *Restorers of the Roman world.*

By **Claudius** the Goths were swept out of the empire, but on the renewal of the invasion in the reign of his successor, **Aurelian,** it was deemed prudent to relinquish Dacia to their use. Aurelian, by his valour and discipline, staunched the wounds of the bleeding state, and bound up its dismembered limbs. His last achievement was the recovery of Egypt, Syria, and Asia Minor out of the hands of Zenobia, the celebrated queen of Palmyra and the East.

Zenobia was esteemed the most lovely as well as the most heroic of her sex. She was of a dark complexion, her teeth were of a pearly whiteness, and her large black eyes sparkled with uncommon fire, tempered by the most attractive sweetness. Her masculine understanding was strenthened and adorned by study. She gave her hand to Odenathus, who by the aid of her incomparable prudence and fortitude raised himself to the sovereignty of the East. After the assassination of Odenathus by his nephew, Zenobia filled the vacant throne, and ruled in Palmyra over the surrounding nations above five years. Palmyra or Tadmor was a city on the borders of Syria and Arabia, in the heart of a sandy desert. Its splendid ruins of temples and palaces in the midst of a sea of sand are still the objects of wondering curiosity to modern travellers. Palymra was the last stronghold of the heroic queen. After an obstinate defence the city fell into the hands of Aurelian, and Zenobia was taken to Rome to grace the triumph of the conqueror (A.D. 274).

Since the foundation of Rome, no general had more nobly deserved a triumph than Aurelian; nor was a triumph ever celebrated with superior pomp and magnificence. The spectacle was opened by twenty elephants, four royal tigers, and two hundred of the most curious animals from every climate. They were followed by sixteen hundred gladiators, meet companions for the fierce beasts that preceded them. The spoils of the East were next paraded in all the gorgeousness of oriental splendour. The ambassadors of the most remote parts of the earth, all arrayed in rich or singular dresses, displayed the fame and power of the Roman emperor. The presents he had received, including a vast number of crowns of gold, were likewise exposed to the public gaze. The victories of Aurelian were attested by the long train of captives who reluctantly attended his triumph. But every eye, disregarding the crowd of captives, was fixed on Zenobia, who preceded on foot the triumphal car of the conqueror. Her beauteous figure was confined by fetters of gold, but a slave was permitted to support the gold chain which encircled her neck. The emperor's magnificent chariot was drawn by four stags. The most illustrious of the senate, the people, and the army, closed the procession. So long and so various was the pomp of the triumph, that, although it opened with early dawn, it was already dark when the emperor returned to his palace.

Aurelian's career was brought to an untimely end through the revengeful treachery of his secretary (A.D. 275).

The strength of Aurelian had crushed on every side the enemies of Rome. After his death they seemed to revive with redoubled fury and force. They were again vanquished by the active vigour of **Probus,** whose short reign of six years was almost the duplicate of Aurelian's. It may here be observed that the authority of the senate, which had long been rather nominal than real, expired with the emperor Probus (A.D. 282).

The reign of **Diocletian,** who was invested with the purple in A.D. 285, is remarkable for the partition of the empire, and the abdication of the emperors after a brilliant administration, lasting twenty years. In the year after his accession, Diocletian raised Maximian to an equal share of power and dignity with himself. These two princes played the part of Jupiter and Hercules: Diocletian with his wise head and clear foresight directed and planned, whilst Maximian with his invincible arm was the ready instrument to execute his will. Rome was no longer the real centre of government. Diocletian made Nicomedia in Bithynia his royal seat, and Maximian held his court at Milan. On the same day, in A.D. 305, the two emperors abdicated the imperial throne, after appointing as their successors Galerius and Constantius.

Diocletian passed the remainder of his days in honourable repose and quiet contentment, employing his leisure hours in simple rural labours. When solicited by Maximian to reassume the reins of government, he observed, that if his old colleague could see the fruit trees he had planted with his own hands, he would no longer urge him to exchange happiness for power.

Their abdication was succeeded by eighteen years of civil discord, ending in the sole sovereignty of Constantine, the famous son of the emperor Constantius (A.D. 323).

ROMAN EMPERORS FROM AUGUSTINE TO CONSTANTINE.

I. AGE OF TYRANNY.

	A.D.		A.D.
Tiberius, . . .	14—37	Claudius, . .	41—54
Caligula, .	37—41	Nero, . . .	54—68
		Galba, Otho, Vitellius,	68—69

II. GOLDEN AGE OF THE EMPIRE.

Vespasian, . .	69—79	Trajan, . .	98—117
Titus, . . .	79—81	Hadrian, . .	117—138
Domitian, . .	81—96	Antoninus Pius,' .	138—161
Nerva, . . .	96—98	M. Aurelius, .	161—180

III. DISASTROUS CONDITION OF THE EMPIRE.

Commodus, . .	180—192	Maximin, . .	235—238
Pertinax, . .	193—193	Gordian, . .	238—244
Julian, . . .	193—193	Philip, . . .	244—249
Severus, . .	193—211	**Decius**, . . .	249—251
Caracalla, . .	211—217	Gallus, . . .	251—253
Macrinus, . .	217—218	Emilianus, . .	253—253
Elagabalus, . .	218—222	**Valerian**, . .	253—260
Alex. Severus, .	222—235	Gallienus, . .	260—268

IV. RESTORATION OF THE EMPIRE.

Claudius II. . .	268—270	{ Carinus, . .	283—285
Aurelian, . .	270—275	{ Numerian, . .	283—284
Tacitus, . .	275—276	{ **Diocletian**, . .	284—305
Probus, . . .	276—282	{ **Maximian**, . .	285—305
Carus, . . .	282—283	{ **Constantius**, .	305—306
		{ **Galerius**, . .	305—311

CHAPTER III.

THE EARLY CHRISTIAN CHURCH.

Our Lord was born in the reign of Augustus, and suffered death when Tiberius was emperor. His disciples in the first century of the Christian era almost universally enjoyed the protection of the Roman magistrate. In the two centuries that followed, the Church passed through many vicissitudes of fortune. By some emperors the Christians were left in the enjoyment of peace; by others they were submitted to severe penalties. The sufferings of the Christians were not always due to the cruelty of tyrannical monarchs, but often to the mistaken policy of some of the wisest and best rulers. In cloud and sunshine the Christian Church gradually grew and spread. At length it embraced within its fold the emperor, Constantine the Great, and under his auspices Christianity became the national religion of the Roman empire (A.D. 324).

PROGRESS OF THE CHRISTIAN RELIGION.

The conquests of Rome prepared and facilitated those of Christianity. Under the sceptre of Augustus the most civilised provinces of Europe, Asia, and Africa were united; and under his rule and that of his successors these various nations gradually assimilated in laws, manners, and language. The writings of the apostles, when translated from Greek into Latin, were perfectly intelligible, in one or the other of these languages, to nearly all the subjects of Rome. The public highways, which had been made for the use of the legions, opened an easy passage for the Christian missionaries throughout the whole extent of the empire. Nor had the first preachers of the gospel to contend against the armed opposition of the Roman government; for it was the recognised policy of the early emperors to tolerate all religions, so long as they were not subversive of social order, nor inimical to civil authority. Thus the Christian religion rapidly spread, and long before the reign of Constantine, the faith of Christ had taken root in every province, and gained thousands of converts in all the great cities of the empire. Probably by the end of the third century the Christians formed about one-fifth of the entire population, and in Syria and Asia Minor the proportion was very much higher.

The chief centres of Christendom in this early period were Jerusalem, Antioch, Alexandria, Ephesus, Corinth, and Rome. After the destruction of Jerusalem by Titus (A.D. 70), that city never regained the high position which it had once held in the primitive church; whilst Rome, from its importance as the seat of empire, gradually became the chief centre of all Christendom. The Church of Rome was believed to have been founded by the labours and adorned by the martyrdom of St. Peter and St. Paul; it became strong in the number of its members, and was in easy communication with all other Christian churches. Hence it necessarily became pre-eminent, and its bishops the most influential in the whole Church of Christ.

PERSECUTIONS OF THE EARLY CHRISTIANS.

Notwithstanding the purity of the Christian religion, the excellence of its precepts, and the virtuous life of its adherents, its dissemination was violently opposed by many of the Roman emperors, from Nero downwards. The first and chief cause of the persecution of the Christians was owing to their efforts to proselytise. They could not tolerate the idolatrous faith and worship of their fellow-citizens, nor omit any opportunity of subverting the false religion prevailing around them. Hence there sprung up an antagonism between the Christians and their pagan countrymen in every city of the empire. The tongue of slander soon became busy, and the most incredible stories, respecting the practices of the Christians, in their secret religious assemblies, were maliciously invented, industriously circulated, and eagerly believed. Eleven persecutions of greater or less severity and extent afflicted the Christian Church before the end of the third century of the Christian era. We proceed to narrate the chief events connected with the more disastrous of these persecutions.

Persecution under Nero.—The first persecution of the Christians, which involved the sacrifice of many lives, took place at Rome in the reign of Nero (A.D. 64). It was occasioned by the great fire that broke out in that city in the tenth year of his reign. The voice of rumour accused the emperor of being the incendiary of his own capital. The tyrant, who had killed his own mother and his own wife, was readily believed to have hired ruffians to set the city on fire, that he might feast his eyes on the leaping flames, and watch with fiendish delight their destructive progress, as street after street fell a prey to their devouring fury, and family after family became homeless and destitute. To avert suspicion from himself, and to satisfy his thirst for blood, Nero laid the blame upon the Christians of Rome, and inflicted on them the most exquisite tortures. From the writings of Tacitus, a contemporary historian, we learn how fearful was the persecution which they had to endure. They died in torments, and their torments were embittered by insult and derision. Many were nailed on crosses and exposed to the jeers and scorn of the cruel crowd; some were sewn up in the skins of wild beasts, and then brought into the arena of the amphitheatre to be worried to death by fierce dogs, for the amusement of thousands of applauding spectators. The ingenuity of the imperial tyrant was taxed to invent such modes of death as might serve to gratify his cruel passions, and impart a keener interest to the spectacles of the theatre or circus. The most fiendish of these modes of torture was reserved for the royal gardens, where chariot races were often held, in which the emperor himself sought applause from the assembled thousands by lashing his horses furiously round the course in the dress and attitude of a charioteer. The Christian victims were turned to account by the inhuman monster to lend a horrid charm to his favourite pastime. Smeared with pitch and other highly inflammable substances, they were stationed at intervals around the race-course, and destined to serve as torches at the nightly sport of this imperial demon. This persecution was probably confined to Rome, and its intensity served to shorten its duration, as the infliction of such tortures created a general feeling of pity.

Persecution under Domitian.—Thirty years later a new persecution, wider in its reach, but of less severity, was instituted by Domitian (A.D. 95). The banishment of St. John to Patmos, where he saw the visions of glory and mystery recorded in the last book of Holy Scripture, is supposed to have occurred in consequence of this persecution. Two grandsons of St. Jude, the "brother" of our Lord, were brought before the emperor charged with plotting against the Roman government. But on showing their hands, rough and horny with labour, and giving such answers as proved them to be simple peasants, they were dismissed without punishment. The Christians were not long subject at this time to cruel treatment. Domitian, before his assassination (A.D. 96), had stayed the hand of the executioner, and recalled the Christians who had been banished. Under the gentle rule of Nerva, his successor, the Christians were restored to their rank and fortune, and the Church was everywhere at rest.

Persecution under Trajan.—It was not only tyrants, like Nero and Domitian, who persecuted the Christians, but such great and virtuous princes as Trajan and Marcus Aurelius could punish this unoffending class of their subjects with imprisonment, exile, and death. The persecution, however, in the reign of Trajan was probably confined to a single province in Asia Minor, including Bithynia and Pontus.

The governor of that province, Pliny the younger, was uncertain how to act towards the Christians, who, he found, presistently refused to observe the national religion. In his perplexity he writes to the emperor Trajan (A.D. 110), and in his letter he affirms that the temples were almost deserted, that the sacred victims scarcely found any purchasers, and that the superstition (as he calls Christianity) had not only infected the cities, but had even spread itself into the villages of his province. Suspecting that the Christians in their private assemblies were guilty of some immoral or illegal practices, he had put some of them to the torture, but the only confession he could extort was to this effect—that they were accustomed to meet before dawn on certain days and sing alternately a hymn to Christ as God; that they bound themselves by an oath to abstain from crime, and that they partook in common of a simple meal. Trajan in his answer directs the governor not to seek out the Christians, nor to admit any anonymous information against them, but to punish the offender if the "crime" is clearly proved, and the accused refuses to recant.

Under Trajan took place the martyrdom of Ignatius, a famous bishop of Antioch for nearly half a century. When the emperor visited that city, the venerable bishop was brought before him and by his orders carried to Rome to be exposed to wild beasts. In an epistle which Ignatius addressed to the Christians at Rome after his condemnation, this aged servant of Christ expresses an eager desire for the crown of martyrdom, and entreats that the Romans will not through mistaken kindness attempt to prevent his fate. "Rather," he says, "do you provoke the beasts that their bodies may become my tomb."

Hadrian, who succeeded Trajan (A.D. 117), was induced to defend his Christian subjects from the hatred and violence of the heathen populace; for it had become common, in some cities of the empire, for the mob to raise a clamour in the amphitheatre, and demand the sacrifice of some eminent Christian living peaceably among them. Hadrian accordingly published an edict, forbidding Christians to be arrested on mere rumour, or to satisfy a popular cry, and ordering all false informers to be heavily punished. This state of comparative security lasted throughout the reign of Hadrian and his successor, Antoninus Pius.

Persecution under Marcus Aurelius.—On the accession of Marcus Aurelius, an emperor celebrated for his benevolence, justice, and wisdom in the general government of his people, the persecution of the Christians was revived with great severity (A.D. 161). His reign was a period of great public disasters and calamities, which the superstitious people ascribed to the wrath of the gods on account of the neglect of their worship by the Christians. Hence it was thought necessary to sacrifice the "atheists," as as they deemed the Christians, to propitiate their gods.

The most eminent martyr of this reign was Polycarp, a disciple of St. John, by whom he was appointed to the see of Smyrna. In his old age he fell a victim to popular clamour. A low, muttering cry was one day heard in the amphitheatre of his city, which soon grew into a universal yell, "Polycarp to the lions." The bishop prudently retired to avoid the storm; but on being pursued and discovered, he calmly said, "The will of God be done." He ordered food to be set before his captors, whilst he withdrew to pray. The venerable bishop on being offered his life, if he would renounce his faith, firmly replied, "Fourscore and six years have I served Christ, and he hath done me nothing but good; how can I now blaspheme my Lord and Saviour?" Amidst the yells of the enraged spectators a fire was kindled around this veteran of the cross; but the flame, instead of devouring him, swept around him "like the sail of a ship filled with wind." As the fire seemingly refused to do its office, one of the executioners stabbed the martyr with his sword.

Ten years later in the same reign many Christians of Southern Gaul were put to the test, by fire and sword, by torture and death. One of the first to suffer was Pothinus, bishop of Lyons, an old man bending beneath the load of ninety years. He was beaten, kicked, and pelted by the crowd; after which he was thrown almost lifeless into a dungeon, where he died within two days. Those Christians who claimed the privilege of Roman citizens were generally beheaded, whilst slaves were crucified, and all others exposed to wild beasts. Among the Roman citizens who were "faithful unto death" was a young man of Autun, named Symphorian. As he was on the way to the block, he heard the voice of his mother, saying, "My son, my son, be strong and play the man; lift your eyes to Him who dwells in heaven; the sword cannot cut off thy life, but only raise it to a better." The friends of the victims were seldom allowed the consolation of burying their bodies. These were cast to the dogs, and the fragments left uneaten were burnt to ashes, and then scattered upon the rapid Rhone, in mockery of the doctrine of the resurrection.

Persecution under Severus.—This stern monarch issued an edict, forbidding any of his subjects to embrace Judaism or Christianity (A.D. 202). Under cover of this edict a terrible persecution was carried on in Africa. Of the African martyrs the most celebrated is a lady named Perpetua. She was noble and wealthy, a young mother with an infant at her breast. After her arrest she was visited in prison by her heathen father, who urged her to deny Christ, and to save her life for the sake of her infant and himself. She was deeply affected by his tears and by the thought of her helpless babe, whose presence she said "turned her prison into a palace;" but she remained firm in her determination to die and to leave all for Christ's sake. When taken before the magistrate, her father appeared below the dock with her infant in his arms, and again implored her to recant. She said, "Can I call this child other than mine own?" "No," he replied. "Neither, then, can I call myself other than a Christian." When condemned, she was brought into the arena with many of her companions. The male victims were exposed to lions, bears, and leopards; the women were tossed by a furious cow, and afterwards stabbed with a sword.

But the laws which Severus had enacted expired with their author; and the Christians, after this passing tempest, enjoyed a calm of thirty-eight years (A.D. 211–249), only interrupted by the brief reign of the savage Maximin, the

Thracian giant. Till this period they had usually held their assemblies in private houses and sequestered places. They were now permitted to erect and consecrate convenient edifices for the purposes of religious worship, and to elect their officers in a public manner. Many eminent Christians were admitted into the palace, and held honourable offices there. This prosperity had a damaging effect upon the spiritual well-being of the Church; but a fiery ordeal was at hand to purge away the dross from the silver.

Persecutions under Decius and Valerian.—Decius is memorable as the first emperor who attempted to extirpate the Christian religion by a general persecution of its professors (A.D. 249). His hostility was especially directed against the bishops and clergy; and, accordingly, we find the bishops of Rome, Antioch, and Jerusalem among the victims. The chief object, however, was not the death of the Christians, but their recantation. All could purchase life and liberty by offering sacrifice to some heathen god, and multitudes of Christians in every city proved ready to fulfil this condition. Thus the Church was purged of her unworthy members. The death of Decius in battle (A.D. 251) put an end to these violent measures for a time.

But in the fourth year of Valerian (A.D. 257), the policy of Decius was revived. An edict was issued in these plain terms: "Let bishops, presbyters, and deacons, at once be slain." Thus it was hoped the Church would receive its death-blow. But the death of the martyrs became a source of life to the Church, and even those who avoided martyrdom by flight planted the seeds of the gospel in other lands, and thus enlarged its boundaries. The most distinguished victim of this persecution was Cyprian, bishop of Carthage. This eminent bishop heard his doom with an expression of thankfulness to God. He was surrounded by his loving people, many of whom exclaimed, "Let us go and be beheaded with him." Cyprian was without delay conducted to the scene of execution, a level space surrounded by trees, the branches of which were soon bowed down by members of his flock, who had eagerly climbed up to witness their bishop's triumph over death. His blood, as it dripped from his severed neck, was caught in hankerchiefs, and treasured up as a sacred relic.

The capture of Valerian by the Persian monarch (A.D. 260) brought peace to the Christians, who from this time enjoyed the free exercise of their religion for more than forty years.

Persecution under Diocletian and Maximian.—This was the last, and the most terrible, which the Christians were called upon to endure. It was ushered in by an attack on the church of Nicomedia, situated near the palace of Diocletian (A.D. 303). The church was ransacked, and the sacred bocks were burnt. The consecrated edifice was then given over to the soldiers, by whom it was soon demolished. Next day an imperial edict directed that this example should be followed throughout the empire. No sooner had the edict been posted, than it was torn down by a bold Christian hand and trampled under foot. The intrepid man was seized and roasted at a slow fire. Very soon fires of destruction were burning over the whole empire, their flames being fed by the sacred books and buildings of the proscribed Christians. But in many places the Holy Scriptures were effectually concealed, and the churches merely shut up or converted to secular uses. The fury of the persecutors next fell upon the clergy, who were thrown into the dungeons of the vilest criminals, and tortured in every conceivable way to make them turn traitors. The rage of the persecutors waxed fiercer as they witnessed the constancy of their victims, and another royal edict exposed all Christians without exception to the most savage treatment. The storm fell unequally in different parts of the empire; but for two years it raged more or less throughout Christendom. On the abdication of Diocletian and Maximian (A.D. 305), there was a sudden lull of the storm in the West, where the authority of Constantius prevailed; but in the East, where Galerius ruled supreme, the cruel work went on for four or five years longer. During this reign of terror the rack and the scourge, red-hot beds and hooks of steel, blood-thirsty lions and tigers, the mutilation of limbs and the gouging out of eyes, were the means adopted for stamping out the Christian religion.

TRIUMPH OF CHRISTIANITY.

Before his death in the year 311, Galerius in view of the grave tried to atone for his past errors and cruelties by publishing an edict of toleration, in which he permitted the Christians to worship God in the way they deemed right. Two years later, when Constantine and Licinius divided the Roman world between them, there appeared the celebrated edict of Milan, which henceforth remained a fundamental law of the empire. It was enacted that Christians should enjoy the same rights and privileges, whether religious or civil, as their pagan countrymen; and a free and absolute power was conceded to every man to follow the religion which his own conscience might approve.

A still further triumph for Christianity was at hand. In A.D. 324, when Constantine became sole emperor, he immediately exhorted all his subjects to imitate without delay the example of their sovereign, and to embrace the divine truth of the Christian religion. Christianity may be regarded henceforth, except in the short reign of Julian the Apostate, as the established religion of the state.

CHAPTER IV.

CONSTANTINE AND HIS SUCCESSORS.

DIOCLETIAN had introduced a new system of government into the empire. He not only shared his authority with Maximian, a colleague of equal rank, and designated like himself *Augustus*, but he also delegated to two subordinate rulers, each bearing the inferior title of *Cæsar*, a substantial portion of sovereign power. On the abdication of Diocletian and Maximian (A.D. 305), the two Cæsars, Galerius and Constantius, were promoted to the rank of Augustus, and two others were raised to the dignity of Cæsar. Eighteen years of discord and confusion ensued, ending in the sole sovereignty of Constantine, son of Constantius. But the policy of division, inaugurated by Diocletian, again prevailed on the death of Constantine, and led to the final division of the Roman world into the eastern and western empires (A.D. 364).

HOW CONSTANTINE BECAME EMPEROR.

Constantine the Great was born at Naissus, in Dacia. His mother, named Helena, was the daughter of an innkeeper. He was about eighteen years old when his father, Constantius, was appointed as *Cæsar* over the western provinces (A.D. 292). Instead of following his father to the west, he remained in the service of Diocletian, and gained a great name as a warrior in the wars with Egypt and Persia. The fame of Constantine preceded him to the west, so that on the death of Constantius at York (A.D. 306), his son was hailed as his successor by the acclamations of his legions. In the following year he married Fausta, daughter of Maximian, and received from the old emperor the title of *Augustus*.

For six years the empire of Constantine was confined to the territory west of the Alps and the Rhine; but in the year 312 he carried his arms into Italy, where Maxentius, the profligate and incapable son of Maximian, was playing the tyrant with the aid of his Prætorian guards. The virtues of Constantine seemed more illustrious by contrast with the vices of Maxentius. Whilst Italy had been groaning under the dominion of an odious tyrant, the Gallic provinces had been thriving under the government of a wise ruler. Constantine, with the resolution of delivering Italy from tyranny, led his legions across the Alps by way of Mont Cenis. On reaching Susa, at the foot of this mountain, his soldiers set fire to the gates and ladders to the walls, and mounting to the assault amid a shower of stones and arrows, they entered the place sword in hand. In the plain of Turin a pitched battle was next fought with the troops of Maxentius. The skilful evolutions of Constantine completely baffled and broke up the massive columns of mail-clad cavalry, on which the Italian monarch mainly relied. Another battle, fought by the light of the moon and stars, under the walls of Verona, left the way to Rome quite clear. A third victory at Saxa Rubra, nine miles from Rome, opened the gates of that city to Constantine and his victorious troops. In that battle the brave Prætorians fell where they had been posted by their general; the other troops of the beaten army rushed by thousands into the deep and rapid Tiber. There also Maxentius was carried by the crowd of fugitives, as he was attempting to cross the Milvian bridge, and there he sank down under the weight of his armour into the muddy bed of the river. The sight of his head on the following day filled all Rome with joy.

Constantine was now (A.D. 312) the undisputed emperor of the West, that is, of Italy and the provinces west of that country, both in Europe and Africa. For ten years Constantine ruled the Western Empire with wisdom, and defended its frontiers with vigour.

In the tenth year he crossed the Danube, penetrated

into the strongest recesses of Dacia, then occupied by the Goths, took a full revenge for the havoc they had caused, and gave peace to the suppliant barbarians on condition that, whenever required, they would supply the Roman armies with 40,000 of their bravest men.

Constantine now thought that the time had come for reuniting all the provinces of the empire under one master. He accordingly declared war against Licinius, who had become emperor of the East soon after the death of Galerius. The plains of Hadrianople were soon filled with the troops of the rival emperors. In the great battle that was here fought (A.D. 323), the military genius of Constantine and his personal bravery won the day. Licinius retired to Byzantium, but the destruction of his fleet by the skill and prowess of Crispus, his rival's eldest son, induced him to withdraw from that fortress, and to try his fortune once more in the open field. A final defeat at Chrysopolis, now Scutari, left Constantine master of his empire, his liberty, and life. The fallen emperor was promised his life, but some specious excuse was soon invented for his execution. By this victory of Constantine (A.D. 324), the Roman world was again united under the sway of one master.

CONSTANTINE AS A CHRISTIAN.

Constantine was the first Roman emperor, who professed Christianity. He is said to have been converted by a miraculous vision (A.D. 312) on his march against Maxentius. Soon after mid-day, he saw in the sky a luminous cross, and inscribed upon it in glittering letters, "By this conquer." While perplexed with the vision, the emperor fell asleep; when he saw the Saviour with the cross in his hands, and received from him the command to adopt it as his standard in war. Constantine's army marched henceforth under the shadow of the *labarum*—a consecrated banner with the figure of the cross, and the initial letters of the Redeemer's name blazoned on it. The sight of this banner in battle animated the soldiers of Constantine, and paralysed their opponents with terror and dismay.

Constantine, on becoming sole emperor (A.D. 324), publicly declared in favour of Christianity. He delayed his baptism, however, till his death, to obtain, as he hoped, at the last moment of his life, remission of all his sins. In the meantime, he proclaimed to the world that neither his person nor image should again be seen within the walls of a heathen temple. He joined regularly in public worship as a Christian, and listened, standing, to the longest addresses of his bishops.

Under the powerful patronage of Constantine, the ranks of the Christians became crowded with new converts; not only were thousands of Roman subjects ready to follow the example of their emperor, but even the barbarians on the frontiers learned to esteem a religion which had been embraced by the greatest monarch, and the most civilised nation of the globe. In every city Christian churches were repaired, and new ones built, at the expense of the national treasury. But whilst the church gained in numbers, wealth, and dignity, it lost much of its ancient purity and devotion; for many of its new members were but spurious Christians, who had joined the church in the hope of imperial favour.

Constantine, while fostering the Christian church, respected the religious freedom of his pagan subjects. He merely prohibited such heathen festivals and sacrifices as had formerly been celebrated in the name of the state. He also closed a few temples that were notorious for indecency, or that contained mechanical contrivances for imposing on the credulity of the ignorant.

FOUNDATION OF CONSTANTINOPLE.

On becoming sole emperor, Constantine proceeded to lay the foundations of a city, destined to perpetuate the name of the founder, and to rival, or even partially eclipse, the glory of Rome. Since Diocletian had made Nicomedia his seat of government, the ancient capital had lost much of its pristine splendour and importance.

When Constantine entered Rome, after the aefeat of Maxentius, the citizens hailed him as their patron and deliverer; but their hopes were doomed to disappointment, for during his entire reign he passed no more than two or three months in Rome, which he visited only twice during the remainder of his life. Indeed, by disbanding the Prætorian guards, which for three centuries had been stationed at Rome, he dealt a fatal blow to the dignity and power of the senate and people.

Constantine selected as the sight of his new capital, the ancient Byzantium, situated on a tongue of land at the south-western entrance of the Bosphorus. An arm of the Bosphorus here forms a splendid port, known in ancient times as the *Golden Horn*, from the rich cargoes which every wind wafted into it from distant shores. On the day appointed for the foundation of the city, Constantine, on foot, with a lance in his hand, led the solemn procession, and traced out the boundary of the destined capital. To his attendants, who observed with astonishment the growing circumference, he replied, "I shall advance, till the invisible guide who marches before me thinks right to halt."

The space thus marked out measured more than ten miles round. On this favoured spot the imperial city soon appeared resplendent in white marble. The cities of Greece and Asia were ransacked and robbed, that their art treasures might adorn their upstart sister. Whatever could beautify the city, or contribute to the well-being of its inhabitants, was provided without stint from the imperial treasury. The city was dedicated (11th May, 330) with the title of New Rome; but this name was soon exchanged for Constantinople, in honour of its founder.

The site of Constantinople appears to have been formed by nature for the centre of a great monarchy. For beauty, safety, commercial convenience, and political importance, the spot selected could not have been surpassed. The imperial city, that crowned its seven hills, stood on the highway from Europe to Asia, as a gate between the two, where they approach within 600 yards of each other.

It also commanded the passage between the Euxine and the Propontis (Sea of Marmora), as the barbarians of the Euxine speedily found when they attempted, as before, to pour their piratical swarms into the heart of the Mediterranean. The climate was healthy, the soil fertile, the harbour secure and capacious, and the approach on the land side of small extent and easy defence. The new capital could boast that it was the only city in the empire not polluted by a heathen temple. Within a century after its foundation it contained fourteen magnificent churches, and in population and wealth was unsurpassed by Rome itself.

CONSTANTINE AND HIS SONS.

The emperor had been twice married. His first wife had left him only one son, who was called Crispus. By Fausta, he had three sons, named Constantine, Constantius, and Constans. At the age of seventeen, Crispus was invested with the title of Cæsar, and soon gained renown for his prudence and valour in war. He became such a favourite with the people and the army as to provoke the jealousy of his father, by whose orders he was at length executed on a charge of treason. On the death of Crispus the three sons of Fausta received the title of Cæsar, but the emperor retained the sole authority in his own hands. And when, in 332, the Goths invaded his dominions, the aged emperor took the field in person and gained a great victory. Indeed, from the beginning to the end of his reign, the same fortune invariably attended the arms of this fortunate emperor. Constantine completed the thirtieth year of his reign (A.D. 335); an event which none of his predecessors, since Augustus, had been permitted to celebrate. Two years later he ended his memorable life at a palace in the suburbs of Nicomedia. According to his last request his corpse was carried to Constantinople. Here it was adorned with the purple and diadem, and laid on a golden bed in an apartment splendidly furnished and illuminated. Every day, at the usual hour, the various officers of the court came to bend the knee before the lifeless form, as if in mockery of the formal homage they had long been wont to offer.

Constantine was succeeded by his three sons, but not a page of their history can be read with pleasure or profit. **Constantius**, the second son, outlived his brothers, and reigned as sole emperor till his death in A.D. 361. He inherited the defects, without the abilities, of his father.

JULIAN THE APOSTATE.

Julian, who succeeded Constantius II., was the last survivor of the imperial house of Constantine. Julian had gained great distinction in the reign of his predecessor by his victories over the Franks and other barbarians, who had devastated the fields and cities of Gaul. Before the throne was vacant, he had been hailed as *Augustus* by the legions stationed at Paris. They came at midnight to his palace, raised him aloft on a shield, and crowned him with a circlet formed on the spot of a standard-bearer's chain. The death of Constantius in the following year (A.D. 361) saved the empire from civil war.

Julian had hitherto professed the Christian religion, in which he had been educated from early childhood. On assuming the imperial diadem he threw off the mask which he had so long worn, and declared himself a pagan, and thus acquired the obnoxious surname of *Apostate.* He was a great student of Grecian literature; whilst he measured the worth of heathenism from the lives of its heroes as they were represented in books, he estimated Christianity by the imperfections of the actual men and women around him.

The Apostate resolved to undo the work of Constantine in favour of Christianity, and to restore paganism as the religion of the state; but his brief reign, which lasted only two years, defeated the hopes of his heathen subjects. He had only time to begin the execution of his design. His first care was for the temples, which had been levelled in the dust by the zeal of the Christians in the last reign. The emperor decreed that those who had pulled down should build up, and as the Christians mostly refused to obey, either from poverty or conscientious unwillingness, they were subjected to tortures, imprisonment, and death. The case of Mark, bishop of Arethusa, who is believed to have saved Julian's life, when a child, is especially noted. The magistrates required the full value of a temple which had been destroyed; but, as they were satisfied of his poverty, they desired only to bend his inflexible spirit to the promise of the slightest compensation. They apprehended the aged prelate, they inhumanly scourged him, they tore his beard; and his naked body, anointed with honey, was suspended in a net between heaven and earth, and exposed to the stings of insects, and the rays of a Syrian sun. From this lofty station, Mark still persisted to glory in his *crime*, and to insult the impotent rage of his persecutors. He was at length rescued from their hands by the emperor, in consideration, perhaps, of the service he had rendered him in infancy.

Julian's attempt to revive the old religion was like galvanising a corpse. The utter decay of the old religion in Antioch, the Syrian capital, is an indication of the senility which at this time was creeping over the pagan system of the Roman world. The emperor himself tells us that, on repairing to the temple of Daphne, near that city, on the day of a great festival, he found, instead of the splendid ceremonial and the crowd of worshippers which he had expected, that only a single old priest was in attendance, with no better sacrifices than a goose, which the poor man had been obliged to provide at his own cost. But in some parts of the empire, the pagans were cheered with the grateful prospect of flaming altars, bleeding victims, the smoke of incense, and a solemn train of priests and soothsayers. The sophist Libanius tells us with glee, that "the sound of prayer and music was again heard on the tops of the highest mountains; and the same ox afforded a sacrifice for the gods, and a supper for their joyous votaries." This festive feature of paganism was, probably, its chief attraction to most of its adherents.

In a spirit of defiance to the Christian religion, the

apostate emperor resolved on rebuilding the temple of Jerusalem. At the call of their great patron, the dispersed Jews assembled from all quarters to forward the undertaking with their pious labour, and their hoarded wealth. Spades and pickaxes of silver were not deemed too precious for the work, and even women of high birth thought it not degrading to remove the rubbish in their mantles of silk and purple. The decree had gone forth from a great monarch that the temple should be built, and a whole people were eager to do his bidding; but, in trying to set up what the Most High had cast down, they soon found themselves fighting against God. It is related by Marcellinus, a pagan and a contemporary, that "whilst they urged with diligence and vigour the execution of the work, horrible balls of fire, breaking out near the foundations from time to time, rendered the place inaccessible to the scorched and blasted workmen, and so the undertaking was abandoned."

Meanwhile, Julian was marshalling his forces for the conquest of Persia. The greatness of the enterprise may be imagined from the fact, that 1100 ships were launched on the Euphrates laden with supplies for the Roman army. It was found necessary to dig a canal, 500 miles in length, to transport this vast fleet to the river Tigris. After this had been accomplished at an immense expense of toil and treasure, the emperor, acting according to the specious counsel of a Persian nobleman who had come into his camp as a deserter, in one night burnt his ships and nearly all that they contained. He then set out on a disastrous march into the heart of Persia, through an extensive region of rich meadows and fields of ripe corn. But on the approach of the Romans this fair prospect was turned by its inhabitants into a black, smoking, and naked desert. Day after day the army toiled on, but everywhere the same scene of desolation presented itself. The desponding army at length received the tardy signal of retreat. With provisions growing more scanty from day to day, they had to fight their way back step by step.

In one of these encounters an arrow pierced the emperor's side, and at midnight he expired, after a remarkable reign, compressed into the small space of one year and eight months (A.D. 363). The corpse of Julian was conveyed to Tarsus, and there buried in a stately tomb. It was an ancient custom, in the funerals, as well as in the triumphs of the Romans, that the voice of praise should be corrected by that of satire and ridicule. This custom was practised at the funeral of Julian; whilst his heathen admirers were gratified with an oration recounting his virtues, his faults and follies were humorously depicted with the applause of a Christian audience.

PARTITION OF THE EMPIRE.

Jovian, who was elevated to the vacant throne by the army, reigned only eight months; but under that brief reign Christianity obtained an easy and a lasting victory.

Valentinian, the next emperor, shared his authority with his brother **Valens**; and soon afterwards the two emperors executed the solemn and final division of the Roman empire (A.D. 364). Valentinian reserved for himself Illyricum, Italy, and the other provinces of the West. When this important business had been amicably settled, the two brothers embraced for the last time. The emperor of the West established his temporary residence at Milan, and his brother Valens withdrew to Constantinople to assume the sovereignty of the East.

EMPERORS FROM CONSTANTINE TO VALENTINIAN.

	A.D.		A.D.
CONSTANTINE THE GREAT, ...	306	Sole Emperor, ...	324
{ CONSTANTINE II., ...	337	Died, ...	340
{ CONSTANS, ...	337	,, ...	350
{ CONSTANTIUS II., ...	337	,, ...	361
JULIAN THE APOSTATE, ...	361	,, ...	363
JOVIAN, ...	363	,, ...	364
VALENTINIAN, ...	364	,, ...	375

CHAPTER V.

DISSOLUTION OF THE WESTERN EMPIRE.

THE ruin of the Western Empire dates from the passage of the Danube by the Goths (A.D. 376), on their obtaining from the Emperor Valens permission to settle in Thrace. The old iron empire, with an enemy in her midst, was no longer able to withstand the repeated attacks of her barbarian assailants. The iron had become more and more mixed with clay; the Romans had become enervated by luxury, corrupted by vice, and weakened by disunion. The iron-clay fabric was, in consequence, shattered into fragments by the terrible blows of the fierce invaders, that came from the woods and morasses of Germany, the steppes of Russia, and the wilds of Asia. Exactly one hundred years after the Goths crossed the Danube and found a home on Roman soil, Romulus Augustulus, the last emperor of Rome, resigned his sceptre into the hands of a Goth, named Odoacer (A.D. 476). The old empire of the West had by the time of Odoacer's accession shrunk within the confines of Italy, whilst new kingdoms, full of wild vigour, were founded on the ruins of the shattered empire, by her barbarian conquerors.

MIGRATIONS OF THE GOTHS.

Of all the barbarians who contributed to the fall of the Western Empire, the most famous were the **Goths.** They came originally from Scandinavia, where Gothland is still a familiar name. In the second century we find them settled on the shores of the Baltic, west of the Vistula, in three divisions, *Visigoths* (West Goths), *Ostrogoths* (East Goths), and *Gepidæ* (Laggards). It is said that the first colony that crossed the Baltic came over in three ships, and that the third being a heavy sailer lagged behind, and that, in consequence, the name of Laggards was applied to them and their descendants. In the beginning of the third century a second migration carried the Goths from the Baltic to the Euxine. Both in numbers and spirit, these hardy warriors of the north were equal to the most perilous adventures. The use of round bucklers and short swords made them formidable antagonists in any close engagements, whilst the manly obedience they paid to their hereditary chiefs gave decision to their counsels and union to their strength. The Goths accordingly fought their way without much difficulty to the warm and fertile shores of the Euxine, and established themselves between the Dneister and the Dneiper, on the borders of the Roman Empire. They were soon tempted by the rich harvest fields of Dacia (between the Danube and the Dneister), to turn their arms against the Romans. The Emperor Decius was defeated and slain (A.D. 251). Twenty years later the Romans withdrew from the northern bank of the Danube, formed a new Dacia on the southern side of that river, and left the old province of that name in the hands of the Goths (A.D. 270). In the course of the next century the Goths became, in a great measure, civilised and converted to Christianity. At the close of that period, when Valens was emperor of the East, their territory was invaded by fierce hordes of savages, named Huns.

The **Huns** were a Scythian or Tartar race from Central Asia. These savages were remarkable for their ugliness; their wide cheek-bones, small deep-seated black eyes, and little flat noses looking like two breathing holes in the middle of their dirty, swarthy, beardless faces, all gave a most hideous aspect to these stunted, broad-shouldered, bandy-legged savages. These hitherto unknown warriors had been dwelling for some time on the eastern shores of the Volga. On crossing this river (A.D. 376), they seem to have advanced with lightning speed over the sandy steppes to the banks of the Tanais (Don). Joined by the

Alans, whom they found in this region, they precipitated themselves on the Goths. The Goths fled in terror before the irresistible rush of these pitiless, fearless, ugly savages. In their extremity the Visigoths of Dacia appealed to the pity of Valens, and implored him to give them an asylum. Their petition was granted on condition of surrendering their arms, and the children of their chief men into Roman hands. They were willing to submit to any conditions. There was no time to lose; the swift foe would soon be upon them. The Danube, for many days and nights, was covered with a large fleet of boats and canoes, each sunk to the water's edge by its crowded freight of fugitives. Wives and children, arms and jewels, household goods and gods were rowed by strong willing hands across the broad stream, in that part of its course at least a mile wide. In this tumultuous passage many were swept away and drowned, but all the rest got safely across before the Huns and their allies, with their utmost speed, could arrive to dispute the passage.

When the Goths ranged themselves under their respective chiefs on the Roman side of the Danube, they numbered 200,000 warriors; and these with their wives, children, and slaves, amounted to a million persons. The greedy avarice of the Roman officers had allowed the refugees to redeem their swords and spears with their gold and silver. Thus the Romans had introduced into the heart of their empire a nation of armed warriors destined to sack Rome, and pave the way for the overthrow of the Western Empire.

Two years later the emperor attempted to repair his error in a great battle with the Goths near Hadrianople. The Goths well knew that their existence as a nation was at stake; and under their able leader, Fritigern, they fought with the energy of desperation. The Roman cavalry fled, the infantry were surrounded and cut to pieces. Valens, covered with wounds, sought refuge in a cottage not far from the scene of battle. Here he perished in the flames kindled by his pursuers. The conquerors could now roam at will over the open country, and burn and destroy without stint or stay; but the fortified towns were safe from their unskilled attacks.

REIGN OF THEODOSIUS.

The further progress of the Gothic arms was checked for a time by the great **Theodosius**, who succeeded Valens as Emperor of the East. By prudence, rather than by valour, he saved his empire from ruin. The opportune death of Fritigern left his enemies without any effectual bond of union, and conscious of this they willingly listened to fair proposals of peace. Whilst Theodosius lived, the Goths fairly observed the terms of the treaty, and used their swords in defence of his empire; but on his death there was no hand that could restrain them.

The reign of Theodosius is remarkable for the vigorous measures he took for the abolition of paganism. "It is our will and pleasure," decrees the emperor, "that none of our subjects shall presume in any place to worship an inanimate idol by the sacrifice of a guiltless victim." The act of sacrificing was even declared an act of high treason, and, as such, to be expiated by the death of the guilty. Theodosius also shut up the pagan temples, or converted them into Christian churches. But the zeal of the Christians outran the emperor's decree, and in many places the temples were demolished. The destruction of the celebrated temple and idol of Serapis, at Alexandria, was accomplished by the express command of Theodosius. The idol of Serapis was a colossal image adorned with jewels and plates of gold and silver. There was a popular belief that if it were injured by an impious hand, immediately heaven and earth would go to wreck; and even Christians looked on with anxiety when a soldier, mounting a ladder, raised his axe against the figure. But when it was seen that with impunity he first struck off a cheek, and then cleft one of the knees, the spell was broken. Then the head of the god was thrown down, and a swarm of rats rushed forth from it, exciting the disgust and derision of the crowd. On examining the temple, a discovery was made of tricks by which the priests had imposed on the credulity of the worshippers; and in consequence of this exposure many became Christians.

The reign of this wise and pious prince was stained by an act of cruelty, worthy of such miscreants as Nero and Domitian. A popular outbreak in Thessalonica had occasioned the murder of Botheric, and several of that unhappy general's chief officers. Theodosius, being of a hasty and choleric temper, on receiving intelligence of this wanton cruelty, immediately resolved on an indiscriminate slaughter of the Thessalonians. A general massacre accordingly took place in the amphitheatre of their city, and at least 7000 persons were slain (A.D. 390). Theodosius at this time resided at Milan, and there also the famous Ambrose was living as archbishop. When the emperor went as usual to the great church of Milan, he was stopped in the porch by the archbishop and requested to withdraw. When Theodosius tried to excuse himself by the example of David, the undaunted Ambrose replied, "You have imitated David in his crime, imitate then his repentance." The emperor submitted and retired, and for eight months lived in penitential seclusion. At the end of that time, on entering the church, he prostrated himself on the pavement, with every sign of the deepest grief and humiliation.

The empire of the West was about this time thrown into confusion by the murder of the emperor, Valentinian II., who had succeeded his father, Valentinian I., when a mere infant (A.D. 375). The young emperor had long been a cipher in the hands of Arbogastes, the master-general of his forces. But on reaching manhood, he resolved to throw off his golden chains, and to dismiss Arbogastes from his service. On reading the paper which deprived him of his high office, Arbogastes remarked with insulting coolness, in the presence of the emperor, "My authority does not depend on the smile or the frown of a monarch." A few days afterwards the unfortunate young prince was found strangled in his palace (A.D. 392).

Theodosius resolved to avenge his death; but it was not until the autumn of the year 394 that retribution overtook the murderer. Arbogastes, finding his cause desperate, turned his sword against his own breast. The whole Roman world now cheerfully acknowledged the authority of Theodosius; but four months later he expired (A.D. 395), leaving his sons, **Arcadius** and **Honorius**, to reign over the East and West respectively. As Honorius was only a boy in the 11th year of his age, the real ruler of his empire was Stilicho, the master-general of his forces.

ALARIC THE GOTH.

The death of Theodosius was speedily followed by the revolt of the Goths under **Alaric**, who by his military genius and success in war, insensibly united the whole nation under his victorious standard. With the unanimous acclamations of the Gothic chieftains, Alaric was elevated on a shield and proclaimed King of the Visigoths. Late in the year 402, Alaric crossed the Alps, and appeared under the walls of Milan. Honorius fled to the impregnable fortress of Ravenna, which became for some time the seat of government in Italy. Stilicho, a general worthy of the best days of Rome, saved Italy from destruction. By him the Goths were defeated at Pollentia, and induced to withdraw from Italy.

After the retreat of the Goths, Honorius celebrated a triumph at Rome, memorable as the last occasion on which gladiators stained their swords with human blood for the fiendish delight of Roman citizens. The abolition of this horrid spectacle was due to Telemachus, a Christian monk, who leaped into the arena and endeavoured to separate the combatants. The spectators, provoked at his interference, overwhelmed him with stones; but he was regarded as a martyr, and the inhuman practice was never again permitted.

Alaric had retired from Italy, but he secretly aspired to plant the Gothic standard on the walls of Rome, and to enrich his army with the spoils of that famous city. Stilicho alone stood between him and his fair prize; and this obstacle was removed by the senseless and ungrateful Honorius, who signed a warrant for his execution (A.D. 408). Alaric soon appeared before the gates of Rome, encompassed the walls, shut out all supplies of food, so that in a few months bread was scarcer than gold. Ambassadors went out to Alaric offering to surrender the city on honourable terms, and declaring, that unless they were granted, he must be prepared to give battle to all the thousands of Rome. "The thicker the hay, the easier it is mowed," was the barbarian's concise reply. He then mentioned the ransom he would accept, as the price of his retreat from Rome; but his demands were so exorbitant, that the ambassadors in amazement exclaimed, "If such, O king! are your demands, what do you intend to leave us?" "Your lives," was the instant reply. However, he ultimately agreed to retire from the city on receiving most of the gold, silver, silk, and scarlet cloth in Rome.

Through the weak obstinacy of Honorius, the storm thus averted fell two years later with redoubled fury on the devoted city. On Alaric's return to Rome (A.D. 310), the city was betrayed into his hands. At the hour of midnight the Salarian gate was silently opened by some slaves, and the inhabitants were roused from sleep by the blast of the Gothic trumpets. For six days the city was given up to slaughter and pillage. On the sixth day the conquerors withdrew from the scene of havoc, and, with the spoils of the richest city in the world, proceeded along the Appian way to the fertile fields and fair cities of the south. Fire and famine marked the progress of the invaders. The extreme limit of Italy had been reached, when Alaric's dreams of future conquests in Sicily and Africa were rudely dispelled by that universal conqueror — death. The river Basentius was diverted from its course, and a sepulchre was constructed in the vacant bed. After the funeral, the waters were restored to their accustomed channel; and the captives, who had been employed in the work, were inhumanly slain, that no one might know where the conqueror of Rome was laid.

The Goths, or more precisely the Visigoths, under their

new king Adolphus, entered into the service of Honorius, and turned their arms against his enemies. The alliance was cemented by a marriage between the Gothic king and Placidia, the daughter of the great Theodosius. The Visigoths under Adolphus settled in the south of France, and the successors of Alaric fixed their royal residence at Toulouse.

ATTILA THE HUN.

In the reign of **Attila** (A.D. 440-453), the Huns again became the terror of Europe. He ruled over all the barbarians from the Volga to the Rhine, and from the Baltic to the Danube. This terrible monarch used to boast that a blade of grass never grew where his horse had trod. He excelled even his own countrymen in the hideous aspect of his countenance; and he had a habit of fiercely rolling his eyes, as if he enjoyed the terror which he inspired. This savage hero was commonly spoken of by the Romans as the *scourge of God.* His capital was situated in Hungary; but it was little better than a huge village of wooden houses, built and adorned with rude magnificence. Attila himself in his dress, arms, and furniture adhered to the simplicity of his Scythian ancestors. The royal table was served in wooden cups and platters; the royal palate was a stranger to any food but flesh, and even bread was an untasted luxury. But his warriors delighted in the display of their barbaric splendour; their swords were studded with gold and gems, and their tables were profusely spread with plates, goblets, and vases of gold and silver.

We have a curious picture of the barbarian king in his capital, from the account given by certain Roman ambassadors who visited him there. As the king entered the royal village with his guests, a numerous troop of women came out to meet him, and marched in long files before him, chanting hymns in his honour. As he passed the door of one of his favourite soldiers, the wife of the latter presented wine and meat for his refreshment. He did not dismount, but a silver table was raised for his accommodation by his domestics, and then he continued his march. The ambassadors were received by the queen reclining on a soft couch, with her ladies round her working embroidery. Afterwards they attended the king's council, held according to Oriental custom in the gate of the palace, a custom that is perpetuated to this day in the title of the "Ottoman Porte."

Attila spent the first ten years of his reign in desolating the Eastern Empire. Such was the extent of his resources, that he could bring half a million of warriors into the field. Constantinople itself was able to set him at defiance, but more than seventy cities of the empire were erased from the earth.

In 450, we find the king of the Huns preparing to invade Gaul. Theodoric, son of the great Alaric, was at that time king of the Visigoths, in the south of Gaul. The Gothic king threw in his lot with the Romans. The fate of the West was decided in the plain of Chalons. The battle fought here is one of the most memorable in the history of the world. The victory was won by the skill of Aëtius, the Roman ambassador, and by the valour of the Visigoths. Attila's host was only saved by the approach of night from total defeat. Attila sullenly withdrew from Gaul, and in the ensuing spring (A.D. 452), appeared on the south of the Alps. Rome was saved by the generous boldness of Leo, its celebrated bishop. While the Hunnish king was on the road to Rome, he was confronted by Leo, and overawed by his majestic aspect. On the offer of a large ransom, Attila consented to withdraw from Italy. Shortly afterwards he died in his wooden palace beyond the Danube. His gigantic empire immediately fell to pieces, and left no lasting monument of its existence.

GENSERIC THE VANDAL.

Rome had been saved from the ravages of the Huns, but it had only escaped from one host of barbarians to fall into the hands of another. The **Vandals** hastened across from Africa to devour the prey that the Huns had spared.

These rapacious barbarians in the beginning of the fifth century, pressed on by the torrent of Huns from Asia, had swept across Germany; and, after taking into their ranks Burgundians and Suevians in their passage westward, had entered the defenceless provinces of Gaul (A.D. 406). The Vandals and their allies speedily overran the whole country, drove before them a promiscuous crowd of the mean and noble, and carried off the spoils of hearth and altar. The Burgundians found a home in the south-east of Gaul; whilst the Vandals and Suevians crossed the Pyrenees and revelled in the riches of Spain. The Suevians finally settled in the north-west corner of the peninsula; but the fierce, restless Vandals, bequeathing their name to the province of Andalusia (formerly Vandalos), sought their fortunes in Africa. Under their king **Genseric**, the Vandals landed in Africa (A.D. 429) and proceeded to pillage, burn, and massacre all that came in their way. Ten years later Carthage was taken, and the Roman province of Africa was a Vandal kingdom.

On the retreat of the Huns from Italy, Genseric resolved to try his fortune in that unhappy country. On approaching Rome, the barbarian was surprised to see, issuing from one of the gates of the city, an unarmed and venerable procession of the Roman clergy, with Leo, their bishop, at its head. The king of the Vandals promised to spare the lives of the citizens, but he proved either unwilling or unable to redeem his promise. After a fortnight spent in stripping the city of all its wealth, the robbers returned with a prosperous voyage to their port of Carthage (A.D. 455), leaving the Goths to invest with the imperial purple any puppet they chose. In the course of the next twenty years, eight emperors were set up and pulled down, and then the farce was played out. Romulus Augustulus, the last emperor of Rome, was pensioned off; and a bold Goth, named Odoacer, who had been for some time the virtual ruler, assumed the title of King of Italy (A.D. 476).

NEW KINGDOMS OF THE WEST.

Whilst Honorius was reigning in security at Ravenna, and Alaric was trampling down the corn fields and vineyards of Italy, the ties which had long bound the western provinces to Rome began to slacken.

Britain, being the most remote of the provinces, was the first left to take care of itself. When Alaric entered Rome (A.D. 410), Britain was an independent nation. Forty years later the Saxons gained a footing in the island, and after a hard struggle, lasting a century and a half, established the seven kingdoms called the Heptarchy.

In the meantime, the Franks made themselves supreme in **Gaul.** In the beginning of the fifth century, as we have stated, the Burgundians settled in the valley of the Rhone and Saone, whilst the Visigoths founded a kingdom in the south of France, which they afterwards extended northwards as far as the Loire. Ten years after the extinction of the Western Empire (A.D. 486), Clovis, king of the Franks—a tribe of Germans that had seated themselves along the Belgic rivers—invaded Gaul, and began at Soissons a career of victory, ending in the subjugation of the entire country, which henceforth took the proud name of France. Clovis is, therefore, the true founder of the French kingdom, and his name, under the softened form of Louis, has accordingly been borne by many of her kings. This prince was converted to Christianity by his wife, the fair Clotilda; he was followed to the font in the cathedral of Rheims by 3000 of his warriors (A.D. 496). The last conquest of Clovis was that of the Visigoths. At the battle of Poitiers (A.D. 507) their king Alaric was slain by the hands of Clovis himself, and their power in Gaul completely destroyed. Clovis made Paris his capital, and there he died (A.D. 511).

The Visigoths, resigning to Clovis most of their territory in Gaul, crossed the Pyrenees, and ruled in Spain till the final overthrow of their monarchy by the Saracens at the beginning of the eighth century.

Meanwhile, the Ostrogoths became the dominant people

in Italy. Under the long and peaceful reign of Theodoric the Ostrogoth, Italy revived and flourished. Theodoric succeeded Odoacer (A.D. 493), and ruled 33 years with wisdom and justice. Guided by his wise counsellor, the learned Cassiodorus, he ruled over Goths and Italians to their mutual advantage; to the former he assigned the service of war, and to the latter the arts of industry. Under the shadow of peace agriculture revived, and Italy again became the land of purple grapes and golden corn. Such was the security of the country, that the city gates were not shut either by day or night; and it was commonly said, that a purse of gold might be left in the fields without being lost to its owner. On the death of Theodoric (A.D. 526), the transient happiness of his reign vanished from Italy as a dream.

CHAPTER VI.

THE AGE OF JUSTINIAN.

Justinian ascended the throne of the Eastern or Byzantine Empire (A.D. 527), and reigned thirty-eight years. There was nothing heroic in his character, but his reign was rendered illustrious by the martial exploits of Belisarius and Narses, and by the useful labours of the great lawyer, Tribonian.

THE EMPEROR AND HIS CAPITAL.

The first act of Justinian was to share his throne with a beautiful actress, named Theodora, whose influence over the emperor remained paramount until her death, twenty-one years after her marriage. Throughout this reign, Constantinople was often the scene of disastrous riots. It is difficult to ascertain the cause that originally divided the whole populace of the capital into two hostile factions, distinguished by blue and green respectively. The hippodrome was the chief scene of their tumults, and here in A.D. 532 commenced a most destructive riot, called *Nika* (victory), from the watchword of the rioters. For five days the city was in the hands of the mad mob; the wealthy citizens withdrew to the Asiatic side of the Bosphorus, and even the emperor would have deserted his palace but for the courageous firmness of Theodora. It is computed that 30,000 persons were slain before order was restored. The cathedral of St. Sophia, with many other splendid edifices, became a black heap of smoking ruins. The cathedral was rebuilt by Justinian on a magnificent scale, and still stands after thirteen centuries a stately monument of his fame. It is, however, no longer a Christian temple, but the principal Mohammedan mosque.

Among many other memorable events which signalised this reign, the introduction of silk-worms into Europe is not the least important. Two Persian monks had gone to China as Christian missionaries. Having contrived to conceal a number of the eggs of the silk-worm in a hollow tube, they eluded the vigilance of the Chinese authorities, and returned in triumph with their treasure, which they presented to Justinian. Under their direction the eggs were hatched, and the first colony of silk-worms established in Europe.

LEGISLATION OF JUSTINIAN.

The greatest glory of Justinian's reign was the simplification and orderly arrangement of the Roman laws. These had become so numerous and contradictory, that the most upright judges were often at variance in their decisions. Justinian accordingly undertook, with the aid of Tribonian, and other learned lawyers, to reduce the laws to a simple and harmonious system.

The work was executed with incredible speed and diligence. First appeared the *Code*, containing in twelve books a condensation of all systems extant. Under the name of *Institutes*, was published a manual for the use of law-students, in which the principles of Roman law were clearly and briefly stated. Shortly afterwards appeared the *Pandects* or *Digest*, comprising in a digested form the decisions of the wisest judges in the law courts, and the opinions of the ablest lawyers in their commentaries. This abstract was published in fifty volumes, giving the essence of twenty thousand treatises. To these three parts of the Justinian system was afterwards added a fourth, called the *Novels*, which comprised the new laws made by Justinian himself.

VICTORIOUS CAREER OF BELISARIUS.

At the time of Justinian's accession to the Byzantine empire, the Vandals ruled in Africa, with Carthage as their capital, and Gelimer as their king. Justinian aspired to deliver the countries of the West from the barbarians, and he resolved to begin with the re-conquest of the Vandal kingdom. The emperor sent **Belisarius** with a powerful army into Africa (A.D. 533). Gelimer awaited his approach at a place ten miles from Carthage, and there his army was beaten and dispersed. The conqueror on the next day entered Carthage, which blazed with torches of joyous welcome. Gelimer, after losing another battle, became a fugitive and then a captive. By these disasters the power of the Vandals was effectually broken. Belisarius, leaving a governor at Carthage with the title of Exarch, returned to Constantinople, and enjoyed the honours of the first triumph ever celebrated in that city. Instead of ascending a triumphal car drawn by four horses or elephants, the modest conqueror marched on foot at the head of his companions in arms. Gelimer was clad in a purple robe, and still maintained the majesty of a king in his fallen fortune. Not a tear escaped his eye, not a sigh his troubled breast; but, as he slowly advanced, he repeatedly exclaimed — VANITY! VANITY! ALL IS VANITY! Among the spoils displayed were the holy vessels of the Jewish temple, which had been carried by Titus to Rome, and from thence to Carthage by Genseric, the Vandal king. They were soon afterwards deposited in the Christian church of Jerusalem.

Justinian next turned his arms against the Ostrogoths, who ruled in Italy. Belisarius gained possession of Sicily (A.D. 535), and in the following spring crossed the Strait of Messina, and advanced along the shores until he reached Naples. This strong city was surprised in the darkness of night by 400 soldiers, who found an entrance into the city through the dry channel of an aqueduct. A rope attached to an olive tree having enabled them to rise into the garden of a solitary matron, they surprised the sentinels, sounded their trumpets, and gave admittance to their companions, who on all sides scaled the walls and burst open the gates of the city. The humane general restrained the licence of his soldiers: "The gold and silver," he repeatedly exclaimed, "are the just rewards of your valour. But spare the inhabitants, restore the children to their parents, and the wives to their husbands." The conqueror then advanced on Rome, before Vitiges, the Gothic king, could muster sufficient force to oppose him, or even to dispute his entrance into the city. Next spring, however, Vitiges laid siege to Rome with 150,000 men (A.D. 537).

This siege is one of the most remarkable in history, and has placed Belisarius in the foremost rank of the world's great military captains. In the first contest, which took place outside the walls of Rome, the Goths were nearly successful. The fate of Italy that day depended on the life of one man, who rode conspicuous on a bay horse with a white face. "Aim at the bay horse," was the constant cry, many a bow was bent, many a javelin was hurled, at that central figure; but the great general, after beating back the enemy, retired in safety behind the walls of Rome. After many days of active preparation, the Goths advanced with confidence to the assault. Belisarius, standing on the ramparts, aimed an arrow at the foremost barbarian and pierced his heart. A second shaft from the same true hand was also a messenger of death; and then followed a flight of arrows from a thousand bows, which laid low the oxen that were drawing the siege-engines to the walls. The fierce contest lasted from dawn to twilight, but the Goths were repulsed on every side, with the loss of 30,000 killed and as many wounded. This perilous day was the most glorious in the life of Belisarius. So hard pressed were the defenders at times throughout the day, that many a peerless statue was torn from its lofty pedestal, broken into fragments, and hurled on the heads of the assailants below. The Goths lingered before the city in the hope of reducing it by famine; but after one year and nine days they burnt their tents, and hastened for shelter behind the fortifications of Ravenna.

The Goths offered to surrender this impregnable town

to Belisarius, if he would accept their services in his army and rule as king of Italy. But, as soon as his standard was planted on the walls of Ravenna (A.D. 539), he declined to wear the crown.

Thus both Italy and Africa were wrested out of the hands of the barbarians, and added to the empire of the East, in the short space of six years, by the valour, virtues, and genius of Belisarius. He was the idol of the soldiers; and yet so strict was his discipline, that not an apple was gathered from the trees, not a path could be traced in the fields of corn, around his camp. He was daring without rashness, prudent without fear, hopeful in misfortune, and modest in success.

END OF THE OSTROGOTHS.

Belisarius was recalled from Italy to the defence of the East, which was endangered by the ambition of the Persian king. Taking advantage of his absence, the Ostrogoths chose Totila as their king, and under his skilful command soon reduced the whole country to obedience except Rome, Ravenna, and some other strongly fortified towns. Rome was taken and retaken; but in the year 549 it was betrayed to Totila, who, by that time, had made himself master of nearly all Italy. His kingdom, however, was of short duration.

The eunuch Narses was sent by Justinian with a numerous and gallant army to recover Italy. His body, though feeble and diminutive, concealed the soul of a statesman and a warrior. In his first battle with the Goths he was victorious, and Totila was slain as he fled from the field (A.D. 552). This victory was followed by the capture of Rome and the recovery of Italy. The Ostrogoths from this time ceased to be a nation: some of them evacuated the country, others mingled with the Roman people. Narses was appointed viceroy of Italy, with the title of Exarch, and ably ruled that kingdom above 15 years, with Ravenna as his seat of government.

LAST EXPLOITS OF BELISARIUS.

Belisarius had long reposed on his laurels, when he was summoned from his retirement to save, by a last crowning victory, the emperor and the capital from ruin (A.D. 559).

At this time there ranged over Poland and the central parts of modern Russia many savage tribes, known to the old Romans as Sarmatians, but appearing in later history as Sclaves or Sclavonians; whilst in the southern part of Russia were the remains of the Huns, then called Bulgarians, whose name is derived from the Volga, and still lives in the word Bulgaria. The Bulgarians, true to their Tartar origin, were bold and dexterous archers, who drank the milk and feasted on the flesh of their fleet and fiery horses, whose flocks and herds in their search for pasture guided the movements of their roving camps. The Sclavonians are the ancestors of the Russians and Poles, and of the Bohemians, Croats, and other races of Austria. In the sixth century they were still in a very barbarous condition. They dwelt in rude wooden huts collected in small villages in the depths of some forest, on the bank of some river, or on the edge of some morass. The fertility of the soil rather than the industry of the natives supplied the rustic plenty of the Sclavonians. Each tribe or village acknowledged no master but its own chief. They fought on foot, and among their weapons of offence was a long rope with a running noose. A river or a lake often concealed a band of these warriors: they would dive and remain under water, breathing through a hollow cane, until their unsuspecting enemy came within reach.

The Bulgarians and Sclavonians sometimes united their forces for the plunder of the rich provinces south of the Danube. In the thirty-second winter of Justinian's reign, the Danube was deeply frozen (A.D. 559). The Bulgarian cavalry, with a host of Sclavonians in their rear, crossed the frozen highway and advanced to the walls of Constantinople, which in many places had been thrown down by a recent earthquake. Justinian trembled at their approach, and the unwarlike citizens were bewildered at the danger. The eyes of prince and people turned instinctively to one man, now a feeble veteran, who had plucked Carthage out of the hands of the Vandal and defended Rome against the Ostrogoth. The spirit of old and young was roused by the name of Belisarius. Ten thousand men went out of the gates of Constantinople to encounter the dreaded enemy. Belisarius that day won his last victory, and saved his country from anarchy. He received but cold thanks from an ungrateful monarch, and so harshly was the aged hero treated by his envious master, that the fiction wears an air of truth, which represents the veteran chief as deprived of his eyesight, and reduced to beg his bread in suppliant tones, "Give a penny to blind Belisarius the general." The same year (A.D. 565) ended the memorable reign of Justinian and the life of the renowned Belisarius.

THE LOMBARDS IN ITALY.

Narses was the only exarch that ruled over all Italy. His government lasted until A.D. 568, and in that year a new flood of barbarians, called Lombards, swept down from the Alps, and reduced the exarchate to a narrow province.

The Lombards were originally called Langobards, from their long spears (*bardi*), and when first heard of by the Romans were living along the shores of the Baltic between the Elbe and the Oder. Thence they gradually descended southward, and by the reign of Justinian had reached the banks of the Danube. Here they came into contact with the Gepidæ, who, true to their name, had *lagged* behind in the plains of Hungary, while their kinsmen, the Visigoths and Ostrogoths, were seeking their fortunes in Spain and Italy. The crafty Justinian fomented the disputes that naturally arose between the Gepidæ and the Lombards, and dexterously contrived to protract the struggle between them throughout his reign. In the year succeeding his death, the Lombards formed a union with the Avars, a fierce race of barbarians lately come from Asia. The confederate forces under Alboin, the Lombard king, fell upon the Gepidæ and almost exterminated them. Alboin slew their King Cunimund with his own hand, and, according to the savage custom of the Lombards, fashioned his skull into a drinking-cup. In the division of the spoils, the fair Rosamond, daughter of Cunimund, fell to the share of Alboin, by whom she was married. The lands of the Gepidæ, according to the treaty between the allies, became the sole property of the Avars.

The Lombards, therefore, under their victorious leader resolved to seek a kingdom in Italy. Alboin crossed the Julian Alps, and descended upon the fruitful plains ever since called Lombardy (A.D. 568). Terror preceded his march, and desolation followed in his rear. The pusillanimous Italians made no attempt to resist the invader, but tried to hide themselves and some fragments of their wealth in the less accessible parts of their country. One city, however, namely Pavia, which had been strongly fortified by the Goths, kept the angry monarch waiting above three years before its gate. At length the conqueror entered the city with the avowed design of massacring all that the famine had spared; but as Alboin entered the gate his horse stumbled, fell, and could not be raised from the ground. This accident was regarded as a sign of the wrath of heaven: the conqueror paused and relented; he sheathed his sword, and proclaimed to the trembling citizens that they should live and obey. Pavia for some centuries was respected as the capital of the Lombard kingdom.

Alboin's career of victory was brought to an end through his own savage conduct and his wife's revengeful spirit. In a palace near Verona, the king feasted the companions of his arms. After draining many capacious bowls of Falernian wine, the drunken monarch called for the skull of Cunimund, his favourite wine-goblet. The cup of victory was handed round to the warriors, who drank with horrid acclamations. "Fill it again! fill it to the brim, and carry it to the queen." She recognised the fearful vessel, and shuddered with grief and rage, as she touched it with her lips. That night she vowed that the blood of Alboin should atone for the insult. Rosamond soon found a favourable moment for the execution of her vow. Helmichis, the king's armour-bearer, was the secret minister of her revenge. While the king, who had drunk to excess, was in a profound sleep, his faithless consort unbolted the chamber-door and ushered in her accomplice. On the first alarm the warrior started from his couch, and attempted in vain to draw his sword, for it had been fastened to its scabbard by the hand of his wife. A small stool, his only weapon, could not long protect him from the spear of his assassin (A.D. 573).

The queen became the wife of Helmichis, and the guilty pair fled to the court of Ravenna. Captivated with the prospect of marrying the exarch, Rosamond presented a poisoned cup to her husband, as he issued from the bath. Helmichis soon perceived that he was poisoned, and resolved that his wife should not profit by her crime, he pointed his dagger to her breast and compelled the murderess to drain the remainder of the cup.

Alboin had divided his dominion into many petty states or dukedoms, and for ten years after his death, Italy was oppressed by a ducal aristocracy of thirty tyrants. But on the invasion of the Franks, the dukes of Lombardy chose Autharis as their king, and not only defended what they had won, but extended their conquests to the south of the peninsula. At Reggio, the extreme point, Autharis rode his horse into the sea, and with his spear struck a column which had been erected there, exclaiming, "This is the boundary of the Lombard kingdom." Upon the death of Autharis without children, the Lombards desired his widow Theodolinda to choose another husband as their king. She selected Agilulf, Duke of Turin, who reigned over the Lombards for 25 years. The memory of Theodolinda is dear to the Catholic church, for by her influence Agilulf and many of his subjects became good Catholics. Pope Gregory is said to have presented to her the celebrated *Iron Crown* of the Lombards, so called from a circle of iron within it, which was supposed to have been forged out of one of the nails of the Cross.

None of the Lombard kings could ever establish the claim of sovereignty over all Italy. During the next two centuries the supremacy of the exarch of Ravenna was acknowledged by Rome, Naples, and Venice; whilst the rest of the country remained under the dominion of the king and dukes of Lombardy, with Pavia as the royal seat. The reign of the Lombard kings was often marked with virtue and ability; and their Italian subjects enjoyed on the whole a milder and more equitable government than any of the other kingdoms which had been founded on the ruins of the Western Empire.

CHAPTER VII.

CHRISTIANITY FROM CONSTANTINE TO GREGORY.

(A.D. 324–604.)

CONSTANTINE publicly declared in favour of Christianity in the first year of his sole sovereignty (A.D. 324). In the following year the emperor summoned a general council of the whole church, to be held at Nicæa, in Bithynia. The council drew up the Nicene Creed as the orthodox standard of faith, and condemned Arius as a heretic for denying that Christ was in all respects equal with God. The controversy, however, continued for some centuries to disturb the peace of the church; for the Arian doctrine found favour with many of Constantine's successors, and many of the barbarian nations first received the gospel from Arian teachers. The great champion of orthodoxy, as settled by the Nicene council, was Athanasius, who, from the age of thirty to that of seventy-six, held the see of Alexandria (A.D. 326-372). His mantle fell on Ambrose, bishop of Milan (A.D. 374-395), whose history illustrates the remarkable influence which the church was beginning to exercise over the mighty ones of the earth. (*Vide* p. 58.) The next great light of the church was Augustine, who for five-and-thirty years was bishop of Hippo, in Africa (A.D. 395-430). His theological writings are still extant, and held in high estimation by the majority of Christians. The history of Christianity from the time of its recognition by Constantine, as the national religion of his empire, to the close of the sixth century, is marked by three important events—the institution of monasticism, the conversion of the Teutonic barbarians, and the foundation of the papal authority.

I. MONASTICISM.

In the beginning of the fourth century, Christians who aspired to uncommon holiness began to withdraw from the business of the world and its pleasures, and to lead a life of seclusion and pious contemplation in some lonely desert. These exiles from civil society assumed the name of monks, of whom there were two classes: *anchorets*, who lived in an isolated cell; and *cœnobites*, who lived together as members of a community.

The monks at first were anchorets, and the first of these who gained a famous name, was an Egyptian hermit named **Antony.** After dwelling for some years among the tombs and the ruins of a castle, he finally found a sufficiently gloomy retreat in a wild desert near the Red Sea (A.D. 305). Here Antony lived for half a century, and long before his death a numerous colony of monks, settling round him, studded the desert with their cells. The hermit enjoyed the friendship of Athanasius, and he had the satisfaction just before his death (A.D. 356) of giving an asylum to that champion of the faith, when he withdrew from Alexandria to avoid the fury of his Arian foes.

The cœnobitic system originated with Pachomius, who founded a society on an island of the Nile called Tabenne. Before the founder's death (A.D. 348) it embraced eight monasteries with 3000 inmates. These monks were under a vow of absolute poverty, so that no one was allowed to speak of anything as his own, but like the primitive Christians, they had all things in common. They were also under a vow of absolute obedience to the chief of the monastery, who received the name of *abbot* (from a Syriac word meaning father). So blind an obedience was exercised, that a celebrated monk, on being commanded by this abbot to water a dry stick twice a day, for a whole year faithfully persisted in the work, toiling, whether sick or well, to fetch the water from a distance of two miles. The sister of Pachomius was the first woman who adopted the monastic life. She became the abbess of a large community of women styled *nuns.*

The monastic spirit was not long in exhibiting itself in extravagant forms, especially in Egypt and the East. A numerous sect of anchorets in Mesopotamia received the name of *boscoi* or graziers from their manner of life: they dwelt in mountains or deserts, without a roof to shelter them, and scarcely a rag to cover them, browsing on grass and herbs until, both in mind and body, they lost the likeness of human beings. And somewhat later appeared the *stylites* or pillar-saints. The most noted of these was **Simeon Stylites,** who established his aërial residence on a mountain about forty miles east of Antioch. Within a circle of stones to which he had confined himself by a ponderous chain, he ascended a column, which was successively raised from the height of nine to that of sixty feet above the ground. In this last and lofty station the ascetic hero resisted the heat of thirty summers, and the cold of as many winters. In praying he continually bent his meagre skeleton from the forehead to the feet; a spectator once counted 1244 repetitions of this movement and then lost his reckoning, and it is said that during the last year of his life he supported himself on one leg. Simeon's fame became world-wide. Pilgrims came from all quarters to crave his blessing, or in the hope of being cured by his prayers. Kings sent ambassadors and consulted him on the most important concerns of church and state, as if he possessed supernatural wisdom. After his death the smallest relic of this eccentric hermit was supposed to be endowed with miraculous power.

The monastic system, originating in Egypt, soon spread throughout the East, and before the close of the fourth century it had established itself in all parts of Christendom. It was introduced into Rome by Athanasius (A.D. 341), who in his visit to that city, was accompanied by some monks from the deserts of Thebais, in Egypt. The monastic life was greatly forwarded in Italy by the eloquence and reputation of Jerome, an austere monk, and the most learned man of his day, who settled in Rome A.D. 382; and it made great progress in the north of Italy under the fostering care of Ambrose, bishop of Milan. Meanwhile, monasteries were established in Gaul by Martin of Tours, who on his death was followed to the grave by 2000 of his disciples. Monasticism arrived in Britain before the Saxons, and after spreading throughout Ireland, was introduced into Scotland by Columba, an Irish abbot of royal descent, who built (A.D. 566) on the small island of Iona a monastery, long famous as a seat of religion and learning, and as a centre of missionary enterprise. But the revival and extension of monasticism in the West, after the desolating invasions of the barbarians, was principally due to the famous **Benedict**, who founded a monastery on Monte Casino (A.D. 530), which became the model for all kindred institutions in Western Europe. These Benedictine monasteries, during the dark centuries of the middle ages, were the schools, hospitals, inns, alm-houses, and centres of civilization in the several countries of the West.

II. CONVERSION OF THE BARBARIANS.

The barbarian nations, that dissolved the fabric of the Western Empire, had been to a certain extent converted to Christianity before they settled on Roman territory. As early as the year 300, the Christian religion had found its way among the Goths and some of the German tribes on the Rhine. The Visigoths were the first to embrace the gospel as a nation. It was introduced among them by captives, some of whom were bishops, and others, ladies of high rank and influential beauty. Ulphilas, the only missionary of the Goths whose name has come down to us, was a Goth by birth, but was descended from Cappadocian captives. When the Visigoths were distressed by the Huns (A.D. 376), it was Ulphilas who obtained permission for them to cross the Danube and settle in Roman territory. The refugees gradually adopted the religion of the Romans with whom they were then brought in close and continual contact.

Before the close of the fifth century nearly all the barbarians, whose kingdoms were founded on the ruins of the Western Empire, had assumed the Christian name. The Franks and Saxons were the last to disown the heathen gods of their ancestors. Clovis, king of the Franks, had married Clotilda, a Christian princess of Burgundy, and chiefly through her influence was converted. He was baptised at Rheims (A.D. 496) with 3000 of his warriors; and their example was imitated by the remainder of their countrymen, who now adored the cross they had burnt, and burnt the idols they had previously adored. Clovis and his warlike Franks henceforth became the champions of the orthodox faith, and, in the name of the Prince of Peace, turned their swords against the barbarians who had embraced the Arian form of Christianity.

The pagan darkness that overspread our own land, when the Saxons conquered it, was gradually dispelled by the light of Christianity. Ethelbert, king of Kent, married Bertha, a Christian princess of France; and she was accustomed to worship with her foreign attendants in the little chapel of St. Martin's at Canterbury. Thus the way was prepared for the mission of Augustine, who was sent by Gregory the Great with forty monks to convert the Saxons in England (A.D. 597). The Pope had first conceived the desire to engage in this good work on observing in the market-place, at Rome, three youths having blue eyes, flaxen hair, and ruddy faces, exposed for sale as slaves. On ascertaining that they were Angles, he declared that, if they were converted to Christ, they would not only be Angles but *angels*. Augustine and the other missionaries were courteously received by Ethelbert. They slowly advanced towards his throne singing psalms and litanies to some solemn Gregorian chant. The fierce, warlike people stood around their monarch's throne in silent awe, as the sacred strains of music fell on their ear. They saw with mingled surprise and astonishment the advancing procession, preceded by a crucifix and a banner having a picture of Christ painted on it. In a short time Augustine had the satisfaction of announcing to the pope, that he had baptized the king and ten thousand of his subjects.

III. FOUNDATION OF THE PAPAL AUTHORITY.

As the imperial power declined in the West, the papal authority gained strength. When Rome ceased to be the capital of the empire, it claimed to be the capital of Christendom. After the withdrawal of the emperor from Rome, the chief man in "the eternal city" was its bishop. The papal authority was founded mainly by three bishops of Rome—Innocent I., Leo I., and Gregory surnamed the Great.

While Honorius was cowering in the palace of Ravenna from the perils of the Gothic invasion under Alaric, **Innocent** was at Rome, the chief stay and counsellor of the citizens. The sack of Rome by Alaric was the extinction of pagan Rome; little had escaped but that which found shelter under the Christian name. Innocent was absent from the city, during its siege and capture, on a mission to the emperor's court at Ravenna in behalf of the beleaguered citizens. On returning to Rome he found it in ruins, but the ancient religion buried beneath them (A.D. 410). Henceforth Rome was an entirely Christian city, and the Pope of Rome its most influential citizen.

The next great name in the list of popes is that of **Leo. I.** (A.D. 440-461). During his pontificate, Leo was the only great name in the empire. By his extraordinary abilities, learning, and high character, Leo continued to rise, until his death, in estimation and reverence, and consequently in authority. It has already been related how he saved Rome from Attila, the fierce Hun, and how by his influence over Genseric, he mitigated the horrors attending the capture of the city by the Vandals. Leo raised the claims of the Roman bishop, as the representative of St. Peter, to a height before unknown. He procured from Valentinian III. a very remarkable law in favour of his pretensions, in which the emperor declares the bishop of Rome to be the rightful ruler of the whole church, and orders all bishops in the empire to submit to his authority.

The right of supremacy, which Innocent and Leo had claimed and exercised under the declining years of the senile empire, was finally established over all the new kingdoms of the West by **Gregory the Great.** He was a Roman of noble descent and ample wealth, with all the talents and virtues his age most admired. Early in life he distributed his wealth, and became a monk, devoting his whole time to prayer and study. Gregory himself was on his way to England as a missionary, when he was recalled to Rome, and on the death of the pope declared his successor (A.D. 590). His modesty shrunk from the proffered honour, and by the aid of some friendly merchants, who conveyed him in a basket beyond the gates of Rome, he concealed himself some days among the woods and mountains. As soon as the monk had become pope, he threw off at once the quiet habits of the cloister, and assumed the activity becoming a pastor and ruler of his people. He had a threefold mission to fulfil, as virtual sovereign of Rome, as primate of Italy, as apostle of the West. In the latter capacity, he reconciled to the Catholic or orthodox faith the Arians of Italy and Spain, and sent Augustine to evangelise the Saxons in England. As bishop, he gave to the ritual of the church greater solemnity and magnificence; he introduced a new mode of chanting, which still bears his name, and employed music as the handmaid of religion in his missionary enterprises. In the person of Gregory, the Pope of Rome first became in all except the name a temporal sovereign. He was obliged, through the absence and neglect of the emperor, to assume the government of Rome, or leave the city and the people to anarchy.

Owing to his influence and abilities, Rome was saved from the Lombards, who had overrun nearly all Italy, and by his care alone the citizens were preserved from famine. "The merits of Gregory," says Gibbon, "were treated by the Byzantine court with reproach and insult; but in the attachment of a grateful people, he found the purest reward of a citizen, and the best right of a sovereign." Gregory died A.D. 604.

CHAPTER VIII.

MOHAMMED AND THE SARACENS.

THE Christian religion had scarcely supplanted paganism within the limits of the old Roman empire, when a rival religion was promulgated in the deserts of Arabia by a remarkable man, named Mahomet or Mohammed, who appeared in the early part of the seventh century, with the sword in one hand and the Koran in the other, for the conversion and subjugation of the human race.

The Arabs had for ages consisted of various independent tribes, remarkable for their intrepid valour and their love of freedom; but before Mohammed welded them into one nation by the fire of religious enthusiasm, they were seldom formidable to any other nation except when their territory was invaded, and then all private feuds were postponed until the common enemy had been vanquished and expelled. Prior to Mohammed the Arabs were idolaters worshipping the sun, moon, and stars. All the tribes from time immemorial regarded Mecca as a sacred city, and Caaba, its temple, as peculiarly holy. On coming within sight of the sanctuary, pilgrims would cast away their garments, and with hasty steps seven times encircle the Caaba; and finally kiss a certain stone within the temple, supposed by them to be a petrified angel, once pure white, but in the course of ages blackened by the lips of sinners. The tribe of Koreish, from which Mohammed sprung, had acquired, by fraud or force, the custody of the Caaba and its wondrous relic.

MOHAMMED AND HIS CREED.

Mohammed, the son of Abdallah, was born at Mecca (A.D. 569). Left an orphan in early childhood, he grew up under the care of his uncle, Abu Taleb, and won all hearts by the beauty of his countenance and the eloquence of his tongue. At twenty-five he entered the service of Cadijah, a rich and noble widow, and soon won her hand and fortune. At the age of forty he proclaimed himself a prophet, after spending much time in religious contemplation in the caves and deserts around Mecca. One day, he says, while sunk in despondency, and on the point of destroying himself, he suddenly beheld between heaven and earth the angel Gabriel, who assured him that he was the prophet of God. From that moment Mohammed preached the religion called *Islam* (surrender), because the duty of ready submission to God's will formed one of its leading tenets. His disciples assumed the name of Moslems or Mussulmans.

The creed of Mohammed is embodied in the Koran, a book containing the pretended revelations made by the angel Gabriel to the prophet. The two chief articles of his creed were these:—there is but one God, and Mohammed is His prophet. He acknowledged the authority of Moses and our Lord, and asserted that he came to complete their work. He inculcated four great religious duties — pilgrimage, prayer, fasting, and alms-giving. Every Moslem is expected to make a pilgrimage to Mecca at least once in his lifetime, but this may be done by proxy. The believer is encouraged to hope, that prayer will carry him half-way to God, fasting will bring him to the door of His palace, and alms will gain him admittance. Five times a day the devout Moslem is directed to turn his face towards Mecca and pray, wherever he may be, or however he may be employed; and as cleanliness is supposed to be "the key to prayer," sundry ablutions are also enjoined as a suitable preparation thereto. A rigid fast is to be observed from sunrise to sunset during the month Rhamadan; pork and wine are prohibited at all times. A tenth of one's income is stated to be the true measure of charity. The prophet also revealed to his disciples the nature of rewards and punishments hereafter. Paradise is reserved for his own faithful Moslems, and they can only reach the golden gates by passing over the sharp and perilous bridge of the abyss, into which the guilty fall as they attempt with tottering steps to cross. Mohammed paints his paradise as a place of sensual delights, where the meanest believer will dwell in palaces of marble, clothed in robes of silk, and surrounded by every pleasure that can gratify the senses.

MOHAMMED'S CAREER AS A PROPHET.

When Mohammed had resolved upon assuming the prophetic office he assembled forty of his kinsmen, and, having explained to them the nature of his mission, he exclaimed "Who among you will be my vizier?" "O prophet," replied the youthful Ali, "I am the man; whoever rises against thee I will dash out his teeth, tear out his eyes, break his legs, and cleave his skull." These words breathe the spirit that long distinguished the disciples of the martial prophet. When Abu Taleb, Ali's father, tried to prevail upon Mohammed to relinquish his design, he replied—"If they should place the sun on my right hand, and the moon on my left, they shall not divert me from my course."

For ten years the new religion made slow and painful progress within the walls of Mecca. A plot was then formed against Mohammed's life, but flight saved the prophet from an assassin's sword. At the dead of night, accompanied by his friend Abu Beker, he silently escaped from his house, leaving Ali reposing on his bed, with the prophet's green vestment over him, to deceive the assassins watching at the door. Three days Mohammed and his friend were concealed in the cave of Thor, about a league from Mecca. His enemies, the Koreish, came to the mouth of the cave; but a spider's web across the entrance convinced them that the fugitive was not there. Soon afterwards Mohammed escaped to Medina, where he was received with faith and reverence (A.D. 622). This flight is called the *Hegira*, and forms the Mohammedan era, from which Moslems have since reckoned the years. At Medina the first mosque was built, and here began the public worship of the Moslems. The worshippers were summoned by a voice sounding from the minaret of the mosque, "God is great! God is great! There is no God but God. Mohammed is the apostle of God. Come to prayers, come to prayers." At early dawn it was added, "Prayer is better than sleep." Mohammed reigned supreme at Medina, but his kingdom was for some time confined within the walls of that city. Ere long the prophet became impatient of the slow progress made by persuasion, and determined to try the sharp argument of the sword. The prophet's white banner, hung over the gates of Medina, allured from all sides bands of roving Arabs, who readily embraced the new creed, and as readily propagated it with the sword. "The sword," they were taught, "is the key of heaven and hell; whoever falls in battle in the holy cause has all his sins instantly cancelled; and the loss of his limbs shall be supplied with a seraph's wings." The Arabs, who had always despised death, now regarded it as an object of hope and desire. No alternative was given to idolaters but conversion or death; and in this way the new religion rapidly spread. The death-blow was given to idolatry in Arabia by the capture of Mecca, and the destruction of the 360 idols of the Caaba. The conquest of the whole country soon followed, and before his death the prophet's empire extended from the Euphrates to the Red Sea.

Meanwhile, Mohammed was getting old. He had laid all his sons in the grave; his daughter Fatima, married to Ali, alone remained to him. At length, in the sixty-third year of his age, Mohammed gave permission, as he tells us, to the angel of death to take his soul. He tottered to the mosque, and for the last time preached

Islam to the people: "Everything happens," he said, "by the will of God, and has its appointed time, which is not to be hastened or avoided." A few days after this there was grief in every Arab tent. With faltering voice he uttered the last broken, though articulate, words: "O God! pardon my sins. . . . Yes, . . . I come, . . . among my fellow-citizens on high;" and thus peaceably expired on a carpet spread upon the floor of his house at Medina, where he was afterwards buried (A.D. 632).

CONQUESTS OF THE ARABS OR SARACENS.

On the death of Mohammed the Saracen empire embraced little more than Arabia; but in a hundred years after the Hegira, the caliphs, as the successors of Mohammed were styled, ruled from the Indus to the Pyrenees. Their empire included Arabia, Persia, Syria, Egypt, Africa, and Spain.

When Mohammed died, four candidates aspired to succeed him; *Abu Beker*, the father of Ayesha, the prophet's favourite wife; *Omar*, the father of another wife; *Othman*, his secretary and son-in-law; and *Ali*, who had married Fatima, his only surviving child. These four ruled in succession; they ascended the throne in advanced age, and conquered by their lieutenants. These early caliphs were remarkable for their ascetic habits, being more like Moslem monks than conquering kings.

The first caliph, **Abu Beker**, reigned only two years (A.D. 632-634). He sent a circular letter to the Arab tribes in these terms: "This is to acquaint you, that I intend to send the true believers into Syria to take it out of the hands of the infidels. And I would have you know that the fighting for religion is an act of obedience to God." An army assembled with great alacrity, and before setting out for the conquest of Syria, received this charge from their venerable caliph: "When you fight the battles of the Lord, acquit you like men, without turning your backs; but let not your victory be stained with the blood of women or children. Destroy neither palm-trees nor fields of corn. When you make any covenant, stand to it, and be as good as your word." The hero of the Syrian conquest was Khaled, the *sword of God,* whose personal prowess and adventurous valour was the theme of friend and foe. "Work to-day and rest to-morrow," was his favourite maxim. When proposals of peace were made to him in the name of Heraclius, the Byzantine emperor, he scornfully replied—"Ye Christian dogs, you know your option; the koran, the tribute, or the sword. We are a people whose delight is in war rather than in peace." The army of Heraclius was destroyed, and Damascus was taken on the very day of Abu Beker's death.

Omar, the second caliph, not only completed the conquest of Syria, but reduced Persia and Egypt to submission. Jerusalem fell after a siege of four months (A.D. 637). The caliph went to Palestine to receive the keys of the city with his own hand. More like a pilgrim than a conqueror, he journeyed by slow stages, mounted on a rusty-brown camel, his only baggage a bag of corn, a bag of dates, a wooden dish, and a leathern bottle filled with water. On entering the holy city, the caliph commanded the site of Solomon's temple to be prepared for a mosque, and on this sacred spot arose the celebrated mosque of Omar.

Before the conquest of Syria was completed, that of Persia was begun. The battle of Cadesia (A.D. 636) lasted several days; it ended in the total overthrow of the Persians, and the capture of the royal standard—a leathern apron of a blacksmith, who in ancient times had delivered his country. Three months after this victory, Said, the lieutenant of Omar, walked triumphant in the white palace of the Persian kings, at Ctesiphon, his capital. The sack of Ctesiphon was followed by its desertion and gradual decay. To secure his conquests, Omar founded two new cities: *Bassora,* on the united streams of the Tigris and Euphrates, afterwards a great emporium of commerce; and *Cufa,* on the western bank of the Euphrates, for a time the capital of the caliphs. The whole of Persia gradually succumbed to the Saracen arms. After a noble defence, Harmozan, the prince or satrap of Susa, was compelled to surrender his person and province to the discretion of the caliph. In the presence of Omar, who was clothed in a tattered garment of camel's hair, the satrap was despoiled of his silken robes embroidered with gold, and of his tiara adorned with rubies and emeralds. During the interview the Persian asked for some water, but while drinking betrayed some fear of being killed. "Be of good courage," said the caliph, "your life is safe till you have drunk this water." The ready-witted Persian instantly dashed the vase against the ground, and the caliph, true to the promise that had unintentionally escaped from him, spared the satrap's life. Indeed, the strict fidelity of the Saracens in keeping their promises, was one of the secrets of their successful career as conquerors.

From Palestine the Saracens, under Amru, proceeded to the conquest of Egypt, whilst their brethren, under Saïd, were extending the Moslem rule over Persia. Their most arduous enterprise was the siege of Alexandria, at that time the first trading city in the world. At length, after a siege of fourteen months, and the loss of 23,000 men, the Saracens prevailed (A.D. 641). It is uncertain whether the splendid library of Alexandria, consisting of thousands of invaluable manuscripts, was burnt by the Moslems, or before their invasion; but it is said, that when Omar was consulted as to the fate of this library, he replied: "If these writings agree with the Word of God (Koran), they are useless and need not be preserved; if they disagree, they are pernicious and ought to be destroyed."

In the ten years of Omar's reign "the Saracens reduced to his obedience 36,000 cities or castles, destroyed 4000 churches or temples, and erected 1400 mosques." The conqueror of Syria, Persia, and Egypt was stabbed in the mosque at Medina by a Persian fire-worshipper, and died a few days later (A.D. 644).

Under **Othman**, the third caliph, the Saracens entered upon the conquest of Africa. They also built a fleet, and swept the Levant with their victorious galleys, capturing Cyprus, Rhodes, and the Cyclades. They carried off from Rhodes the brazen fragments of the celebrated Colossus, a gigantic statue of Apollo, erected at the entrance of the harbour three centuries before the Christian era, but thrown down by an earthquake after standing 56 years. The aged caliph, after a reign of eleven years, was murdered in his palace at Medina; calmly seated, with the Koran in his lap, he awaited the death-blow of his assassins.

Ali, the illustrious cousin and son-in-law of Mohammed, was then elected caliph (A.D. 655); but he could never command the universal obedience of his subjects. Ayesha, the widow of the prophet, was his implacable enemy, and joined the malcontents. She took her post, amid the dangers of the field, in the first battle that Moslems fought with men of their own creed. Seventy men who guarded her camel fell during the action; and the cage or litter in which she sat was stuck with javelins and darts like the quills of a porcupine. Ali's most formidable adversary was Moawiyah, the *emir* or Saracen governor of Syria; and when Ali was assassinated in the mosque of Cufa (A.D. 661), he became the first caliph of the house of Ommiyah. The aspiring wishes of the new caliph were finally crowned by the important change of an elective to an hereditary monarchy.

SARACEN EMPIRE UNDER THE OMMIADES.

Fourteen caliphs of the house of Ommiyah ruled in succession by hereditary right (A.D. 661-750). Under the reign of Moawiyah, the first of this line, the victorious career of the Saracens met its first great check. After laying siege to Constantinople for seven years, they were compelled to retire. A second siege, forty-two years later, proved equally fruitless. The success of the Greeks, or Romans of the East, may be chiefly ascribed to the terrible *Greek fire*, which had been recently invented. It was a mixture composed mainly of naphtha, and was rightly termed by the Greeks *maritime* fire, for the flame instead of being extinguished was nourished by water. It was either poured from the ramparts in large boilers, or discharged in red-hot balls of stone or iron, or deposited in fireships sent before the wind among the enemy's ships. The caliph Soliman, who undertook the second siege of Constantinople, sent a huge fleet of 1800 small vessels into the harbour of that city; but the fireships of the Greeks were launched, and in a short time the Saracen fleet was wrapped in unquenchable flames.

Meanwhile the Saracens were extending their dominion along the northern coast of Africa. After expelling the Greeks from Carthage and the other African cities, the Saracens had to contend with the Moors or Berbers, the native barbarians of the old Roman province of Africa. They were at length completely subdued by Musa (A.D. 709). Thirty thousand of the barbarian youth were enlisted in the Saracen army, and trained to obey the precepts of the Koran. The Moors, as a nation, embraced the religion of their conquerors, and adopted their language, manners, and even name; the two races gradually intermingled and became one.

The Saracens were not long in finding congenial employment for their new allies. They had advanced to the verge of the Atlantic, but looking across the strait, between the pillars of Hercules, they could descry a new land to conquer. Spain was at that time a kingdom of the Visigoths. Five thousand Saracens, under the command of Tarik, landed (A.D. 711) at the foot of the rock since called Gibraltar *(Gebel al Tarik)*, the hill of Tarik. A battle was fought at Xeres, near Cadiz, and the Saracens were victorious. Roderic, the Gothic king, mounted one of his fleetest horses and escaped from the battlefield, but in attempting to cross the Guadalquivir he perished in the waters. His diadem, his robes, and his courser were found on the bank. The battle of Xeres was followed by the rapid conquest of Spain. Tarik marched at once to the royal city of Toledo, which capitulated on fair terms. In a few months the conqueror had passed through the length and breadth of the land. When the news of this rapid success reached the ears of Musa, he began to fear that Tarik, his lieutenant, would leave him nothing to subdue. The Saracens treated the conquered with remarkable lenity, and left both Jews and Christians in the enjoyment of religious freedom, on receiving the punctual payment of a moderate tribute. Arabs settled in Spain in great numbers, and in a few generations their language and manners prevailed in that country. Under their sway Spain became one of the most prosperous countries in Europe, with Cordova, on the Guadalquivir, as the centre of their power.

At the end of the first century of the Hegira, the caliphs were the most potent and absolute monarchs of the globe; but they had almost reached the summit of their power, and the furthest limits of their empire. On crossing the Pyrenees to conquer France, the Saracens discovered to their dismay that their arms were not invincible. After their first reverse, however, the Saracens under the famous Abderame, bore the flag of victory as far as the Loire. Eudes, duke of Aquitaine, in attempting to stem the torrent of the invaders, sustained a defeat so fatal to his soldiers that, according to the sad confession of the survivors, God alone could reckon the number of the slain. The conquered provinces of the south of France were despoiled of their wealth; the churches and monasteries, in particular, were stripped of their ornaments and delivered to the flames. It seemed as if all Christendom would soon lie at the mercy of the Mohammedan monarch, and as if the name of Christ was in danger of extinction. From such calamities Christendom was saved by the genius and fortune of one man. Charles, surnamed *Martel* (the Hammer) from his vigorous blows in the battle-field, was at this time, under the title of Mayor, the real ruler of the Franks; for the unworthy successors of Clovis had for some time possessed the regal title without the regal power. All Christian eyes now turned to Charles; his army of Franks and Germans was the hope of Christendom. The battle of Tours (A.D. 732) decided whether the Bible or the Koran, Christ or Mohammed, should command the obedience of Europe. In the first six days of desultory combat, the horsemen and archers of the East proved their superiority; but in the closer onset of the seventh day, the Orientals were vanquished. The first onslaught of the Saracens was tremendous; but the stalwart forms of the Frank warriors, on their powerful German horses, sustained the shock without flinching, and the assailants, recoiling repeatedly as from a wall of iron, encumbered the field with thousands of their dead. After a bloody contest, in which Abderame was slain, the Saracens on the approach of night fled to their camp; and after a series of disasters, their broken host was driven beyond the Pyrenees.

The Moslem empire was now on the eve of partition. A revolution in the East ended in almost the total destruction of the royal house of Ommiyah (A.D. 750), and the foundation of four kingdoms within the limits of the Saracen empire. Abdalrahman, the only prince of the Ommiades that escaped the sword, was received with the acclamations of the Spaniards. He set up his throne at Cordova, and became the father of a line of princes that reigned over Spain above 250 years. Two independent kingdoms were also established in Africa. Egypt and the Moslem countries of Asia remained united, and constituted a powerful state under the government of the Abbassides, the descendants of Abbas, Mohammed's uncle.

SARACEN EMPIRE UNDER THE ABBASSIDES.

The Abbassides retained the sceptre of the caliphs for more than five centuries (A.D. 750-1258). Damascus had been the seat of empire under the Ommiades; it was removed by the succeeding family to their new city of Bagdad, founded in 765 on the west bank of the Tigris. The most renowned of the sovereigns who reigned in this capital were Almansor, Haroun al Raschid (Aaron the

Just), and Almamon. Their splendid palaces, their numerous guards, their treasures of gold and silver, the populousness and wealth of their cities, all formed a striking contrast to the rudeness and poverty of the western nations in the same age. In their court, learning, which the earlier caliphs had despised, was held in honour. The spirit of learning was first encouraged by Almansor, who had applied himself with success to the study of astronomy. Under the patronage of his grandson, Almamon, the philosophical writings of Greece were eagerly sought and translated, the stars were numbered, and the course of the planets was measured. The age of Arabian learning continued nearly 500 years. The world owes much to the Arabs for their skill and industry in the study of medicine and chemistry, also for their numerical system of notation, and the comprehensive language of algebra.

The most illustrious prince of the new dynasty was **Haroun al Raschid** (A.D. 786-808), familiar to every child as the hero of the Arabian tales. Haroun, five years before he ascended the throne, advanced with an army of 95,000 men into Asia Minor, and imposed an annual tribute on Irene, the Byzantine empress. But when Nicephorus became emperor at Constantinople, he resolved to pay no more tribute. He accordingly wrote a letter to the caliph couched in the language of the chess-board: "The queen (Irene) considered you as a rook and herself as a pawn, and so submitted to pay tribute. Restore therefore the fruits of your injustice, or abide the determination of the sword." The imperial envoy at the same time cast a bundle of swords at the caliph's feet. Haroun, smiling, drew his scimitar and hacked the edges of the ill-tempered weapons before him without turning the edge of his own blade. He then bade his secretary write this brief reply: "In the name of the most merciful God, Haroun al Raschid, commander of the faithful, to Nicephorus, the Roman dog. I have read thy letter, O thou son of an unbelieving mother. Thou shalt not hear, thou shalt behold my reply." That reply was written in characters of blood and fire on the plains of Phrygia and Bithynia. Heraclea, in the latter province, was laid in ruins, and it was stipulated that it should so remain as a monument of Saracen power.

The court of this great caliph was adorned with luxury and magnificence; but at the same time it was the centre of genius and learning. Haroun earned his title of the *Just* by repeated visits to all the provinces of his empire, that he might see with his own eyes the real state of his subjects and redress their grievances. Haroun in the East rivalled the policy of Charlemagne, his illustrious ally in the West. His reign ended A.D. 808.

CHAPTER IX.

CHARLEMAGNE AND THE FRANKS.

THE French are descended mainly from the Gauls, a people of Celtic origin, but they derive their name from a tribe of Germans called Franks. Towards the end of the fifth century, the Franks, under their famous leader Clovis, obtained a footing in France, and in a few years became the ruling race in that country. Clovis, the founder of the French monarchy, belonged to the Merovingian line of kings. The Merovingians continued to wear the crown of France until the middle of the eighth century; but during the last hundred years of their sovereignty they were mere *rois fainéants* or do-nothing kings, the real power being in the hands of their mayors of the palace. The mayors were in the first instance masters of the royal household, but as the kings sunk into nothingness, these officers rose to the supreme power. The most noted of the mayors were Pepin of Heristal, his son Charles Martel, and his grandson Pepin the Short. The elder Pepin made the office of mayor hereditary in his own family; Charles Martel, by his success in war, especially by his defeat of the Saracens at Tours, deserved and gained the homage of his countrymen, with the title of Duke of the French; Pepin the Short (King Pippin of our nursery tales) put an end to the nominal rule of the Merovingian kings, and founded a new dynasty called the Carlovingian, from Charles his celebrated father.

Pepin, the first of the Carlovingian kings, obtained his royal title through the influence of the pope. Pepin sent ambassadors to Rome to propound to Pope Zachary this plain question: "Who ought to wear the crown; the man with the royal power, or the man of royal birth?" The pope replied that the crown ought to rest on the head that ruled. Pepin was accordingly proclaimed king (A.D. 752), and anointed by the illustrious Anglo-Saxon Winifrid, better known as St. Boniface, the apostle of Germany. The imbecile Childeric, the nominal king, was shorn of his royal locks, and shut up for the rest of his days in a convent.

Pepin had scarcely reigned ten years when Pope Stephen fled across the Alps, and threw himself upon his protection. Astolph, the Lombard king, was thundering at the gates of Rome, and the sole remaining hope of the Romans was in France and her king. The pope was willing, in return for the services he claimed, to renew Pepin's coronation with his own hands. In the ensuing spring an army of Franks scaled the Alps, and defeated the Lombards. Pepin not only delivered Rome out of their hands, but transferred from them to the pope the Exarchate of Ravenna and the March of Ancona, thus laying the foundation of the temporal sovereignty of the popes. As soon as Pepin returned to France, the Lombards broke the treaty, and laid waste the country up to the walls of Rome. Pepin again crossed the Alps, and his second expedition was not less rapid and fortunate than the first: Rome was again saved, and Astolph was taught the lessons of justice and sincerity by the scourge of a foreign prince, who ruled, as he said, *Dei gratia,* by the grace of God. Besides his conquests in Italy, Pepin drove the Saracens finally beyond the Alps, and annexed Aquitaine to his monarchy. On the eastern border of his kingdom he inflicted several defeats on the Saxons, and reduced Bavaria to vassalage.

There is a story told of Pepin the Short which serves to illustrate his character. Having one day overheard some of his courtiers speak scornfully of him on account of his diminutive stature, he caused a lion and a bull to be turned into an arena, and asked which of his courtiers would dare to attack them. When all had declined to risk their lives in the dangerous combat, Pepin leaped into the arena, and slew them both. His courtiers never afterwards ridiculed him because he was short. Pepin died in 768, leaving his dominions to his two sons—the southern part to Carloman, and the northern to Charles, the famous Charlemagne, or Charles the Great.

CHARLEMAGNE'S CAREER OF CONQUEST.

By the death of Carloman, three years after his accession, Charlemagne became king of the entire Frankish monarchy (A.D. 771). His long reign of forty-six years marks an important epoch in European history. The various Germanic tribes were united by this monarch under one sceptre, and brought under the influence of civilisation and Christianity. To achieve this result, he found it necessary to undertake four great wars—against the Lombards, the Saxons, the Saracens, and the Avars.

Charlemagne had no sooner become sole king than he drew the sword against Didier, king of the Lombards, who had invaded the papal territory, and threatened Rome itself. Charlemagne crossed the Alps, swept the Lombards before him, and after a long siege took Pavia, their capital, and destroyed the monarchy of the Lombards (A.D. 774). Didier, the last of their kings, died in a monastery. Charlemagne assumed the iron crown of Lombardy, and the title of *King of the Franks and the Lombards,* but he allowed his new subjects to retain their old laws and customs. During the seige of Pavia Charlemagne had paid a visit to Rome. "He went to Rome," says his biographer, "to pray there;" but there were political as well as devotional reasons for the pilgrimage. He was received by Pope Adrian and the whole body of the clergy with great pomp in the church of St. Peter's, all the people singing, "Blessed be he that cometh in the name of the Lord." During his stay at Rome an alliance was cemented between himself and the pope, which afterwards greatly aided him in building up the mighty fabric of his empire. The king confirmed to the pope the splendid donation of his father Pepin, and even added to it.

Charlemagne's reign was spent to a great extent in war, but, owing to the marked superiority of his forces, there was no memorable battle fought by this monarch. His chief contest was with the Saxons, who at that time occupied the greater part of Northern Germany, between the Rhine and the Elbe. Both Franks and Saxons were originally of the same stock; but, while the former had adopted Christianity and the habits of civilised life, the latter had clung obstinately to the idolatry and savage customs of their ancestors. The struggle between the two nations lasted, with intervals of peace, for thirty-three years. War in those days was carried on without a settled plan or connected operations. There were neither regular troops, nor funds for their subsistence. After a campaign the troops were generally disbanded, and a new army, if necessary, collected in the following spring. Hence it was that the war against the Saxons, though invariably successful, was protracted so long. In his first campaign (A.D. 772), Charlemagne destroyed their great national idol Irminsul, captured Ehresburg their strongest fortress, and reduced them to submission. But as soon as the conqueror withdrew from their land, the brave Saxons attempted to recover what they had lost. Witikind became the hero of the Saxons in their prolonged resistance; no reverse could cool his ardour, or shake his resolution; after each defeat he retreated into the forests and wilds of Scandinavia, from which he reappeared, after a few months, at the head of new bands of warriors, to renew the hopeless conflict.

Charlemagne regarded his contest with the Saxons as a holy war. One condition of peace always imposed was submission to the rite of baptism, as a pledge of their acceptance of the Christian religion. After every successful campaign thousands of Saxons were baptized by the army of priests that followed in the wake of war. Thus Charlemagne treated his conquered foe in the same way as Mohammed, who gave his pagan enemies the choice between death and conversion. In the prosecution of his holy war, this missionary monarch displayed a spirit directly opposed to that of the Gospel. On one occasion, at Verdun, on the Aller, he massacred 4500 brave warriors, who had surrendered, in cold blood. The Saxons were now driven to desperation; the whole nation flew to arms, and for three years the land was deluged with blood. Wearied out at length with the carnage, Charlemagne made conciliatory proposals to the heroic Witikind. The king assured him of his royal clemency if he would lay down his arms, forsake his idols, and become a Christian. Witikind accepted the conditions, and was baptized in the presence of the king and his whole court (A.D. 785). His example was followed by numbers of his companions in arms; and the Saxons did not renew the contest for the next eight years. At last, after a war of thirty-three years, they were completely subdued; many thousand families were transplanted into Flanders and Brabant, and the most resolute retired into Scandinavia, to reappear somewhat later as the enemies of France in the ranks of the Normans.

Charlemagne had in the meantime extended his dominions beyond the Pyrenees as far as the Ebro, and formed a barrier to the extension of the Saracen Empire in Spain. On his return to France, while his victorious troops were crossing the Pyrenees, his rear-guard was assailed in the pass of Roncesvalles by an avalanche of broken rocks, uprooted trees, and missiles of all kinds from the wooded heights above. In the midst of the panic that ensued the Gascons rushed from their place of concealment, attacked the devoted band in front and rear at once, and completely routed them. Among the dead was the famous Count Roland, whose name is embalmed in many a Norman romance. Charlemagne never returned to Spain, but the district he had conquered remained, under the name of the Spanish March, a part of his growing empire.

Charlemagne next turned his arms against Southern

Germany. Tassilo, duke of Bavaria, having rebelled against his authority, was stripped of his dominions, and sent to mourn over his fall in a monastery to the end of his life. The Sclavonians of Bohemia, and the Avars or Huns of Pannonia (the country of the Drave and Save), next owned the sway of the great king. In all his wars the newly-conquered nations were employed to subjugate their neighbours, and thus the circle of conquest continually expanded, till it embraced all central and western Europe within the circumference of a circle passing through the mouths of the Elbe, the Tiber, and the Ebro, and thus including nearly all the provinces of the old Roman Empire of the West. Nothing was wanting but the title of emperor to crown his career of conquest, and that consummation of his glory was achieved before the end of the century.

Pope Leo III. had been attacked in the streets of Rome, and then thrown half dead into the prison of a monastery. Charlemagne befriended the fallen pope, and proceeded to Rome to mediate between him and the angry citizens. On Christmas-day, in the year 800, Charlemagne attended mass in St. Peter's Church, and while he was kneeling before the altar, the pope suddenly turned round and placed the imperial crown on his head amid the acclamations of the people, who shouted from every quarter, "Life and victory to Charles Augustus, Emperor of the Romans." There was now once more a Western Empire, embracing within its range all the Christian countries of the west except the British Isles.

CHARLEMAGNE AS A CIVIL RULER.

After being elevated to the imperial throne, Charlemagne's military activity ceased, but he exercised to the end of his days a sleepless vigilance in the government of his empire. His fame rests mainly upon his consummate ability as a civil ruler. He permitted the nations subdued by him to retain their ancient laws and customs so far as they were consistent with the "capitularies" which he made, with the sanction of his nobles, for the empire at large. All new laws proposed by the king were brought before an annual diet or assembly of the great men of the realm, both clerical and secular. The empire was divided into counties, each under the authority of a count, whose chief duty was to administer justice. But over these were the counts of the palace, who formed the highest tribunal in the realm for deciding all knotty cases of appeal.

Charlemagne's reign is marked by the revival of letters in Western Europe. The emperor was a munificent patron of learning, and of all the arts of peace calculated to civilise his subjects. Aix-la-Chapelle, his capital, was the favourite resort of the learned men of the west; Alcuin, an Anglo-Saxon monk, held the foremost place among them. The palace became a college for the study and advancement of learning; and the royal scholar, knowing that "there is no royal road to learning," tried in his hours of study to make his learned companions forget that he was their sovereign. To put them at their ease he assumed the name of David, Alcuin he named Horace, another well versed in Greek was called Homer, and a third who wrote poetry was known as Virgil. On returning from the hunting-field or the council-chamber, the great man would throw aside the pomp of royalty, and sit as a learner at the feet of Alcuin or some other scholar of the day. He could speak Latin fluently, and understood Greek. He delighted also in the study of astronomy. The art of writing, however, he never could master, although he took the greatest pains to learn. He always carried writing materials about with him, that he might practise at every leisure moment; and he even kept writing models near his pillow, that he might, when sleepless, beguile the time by copying them: but he began too late in life to learn the art properly. The emperor, who prized learning himself, was anxious to communicate its blessings to others. By a circular letter he directed the bishops to found schools in their cathedral cities, and the chief abbots to open schools in connection with their monasteries. He also founded the university of Paris, which claims to be the most ancient in Europe.

The renown of Charlemagne extended into Asia. The famous Haroun al Raschid was his friend and ally. Among the curious presents sent to the western monarch by the great caliph were the keys of the Holy Sepulchre and a water-clock that struck the hours, the first ever seen in the west. The fame of the great emperor is somewhat tarnished by his domestic life. He had no less than nine wives, most of whom he divorced with little ceremony. In his personal habits, however, he was exemplary in two respects: he was abstemious in diet, and frugal of time. Three or four dishes formed his royal repast; he was very fond of roast venison, newly killed, and served up on the spit. While at table he listened to books of theology or history, particularly the works of St. Augustine and the history of Jerusalem.

Charlemagne died in the seventy-second year of his age (A.D. 814), and was buried at Aix-la-Chapelle. His secretary, Eginhard, tells us that he was buried in his imperial robes, with his sword by his side, his crown on his head, and a golden shield and sceptre at his feet. His Bible and pilgrim's purse were also placed in his tomb. The single inscription "Carlo Magno" on the pavement is all that now marks the spot where his remains were deposited. Considering the age in which he lived, it must be owned that he was an extraordinary man. "Perhaps his greatest eulogy," says Hallam, "is written in the disgraces of succeeding times, and the miseries of Europe. He stands like a beacon upon a waste, or a rock in the broad ocean. His sceptre was as the bow of Ulysses, which could not be drawn by any weaker hand. In the dark ages of European history, the reign of Charlemagne affords a solitary resting place between two long periods of turbulence and ignominy."

CHARLEMAGNE'S SUCCESSORS.

Louis, surnamed Debonair or Good-natured, was unable to prevent the disintegration of the mighty structure of his father's empire. He was the model of a Christian prince for a peaceful and loyal state, but totally unfitted to wield the sceptre over a turbulent and war-loving people. After a reign of three years, he associated his sons in the government. They abused his kindness by constant rebellions, and on his death in 840, fought between themselves for the supreme power. The treaty of Verdun (A.D. 843) terminated their contention by assigning France to Charles the Bald, Germany to Louis, and Italy to Lothaire. Henceforward France and Germany were separate states.

These three divisions of Charlemagne's empire experienced different fortunes, arising in great measure from the different characters of their respective kings. France and her superstitious monarchs fell under the sway of ecclesiastics. Italy became a prey to the ambition of her nobles, who, taking advantage of the weak character of their sovereigns, rendered themselves independent princes. Louis, surnamed the German, proved a just and able ruler; and under his government the Germans became industrious, prosperous, and contented. The Carlovingians ceased to rule in Germany in A.D. 911. And in France they ceased to wear the crown in the latter part of the same century. These French kings were unworthy of their great ancestors. The dregs of this dynasty are branded with the nicknames "of the stammerer," "the fat," "the simple," and "the lazy." The last of these died without issue, and then the crown passed from the phantoms of royalty to men who could really rule. The Archbishop of Rheims, on the death of the last Carlovingian king, urged the election of Hugh Capet, Count of Paris, as a personage "illustrious alike by his deeds and by his power, in whom the nation would find a valiant defender." Hugh Capet was accordingly crowned at Rheims (A.D. 987); and thus was inaugurated a dynasty destined to reign over France for a period of eight centuries, until overthrown by the "Great Revolution." With the accession of Hugh Capet the history of the Franks ends, and that of the French begins.

CHAPTER X.

EUROPE IN THE TENTH CENTURY.

THERE is no great personage in this century to form the central figure of European history. Important changes, however, took place in the map of Europe, which deserve our attention, as they were for the most part of a permanent character. The men who played the most prominent part in effecting these changes were the bold pirates of Scandinavia, whose hardy children were still in quest of their fortunes.

THE NORTHMEN OR NORMANS.

As early as the reign of Charlemagne daring pirates from the northern shores of Europe, calling themselves vikings or sea-kings, infested the coasts of England and France. They were known by the name of Danes in England, and Normans in France. The Danes wrested from King Alfred a half of his fair kingdom, renewed their invasions in the reign of Ethelred the Unready, and, having driven him from the throne, seated their king Canute in his place. When peaceably settled on English soil, they became Christians and adopted the language and civilization of their Anglo-Saxon neighbours, who were originally from the same stock as themselves. In the early part of the tenth century the Normans gained a home in France. But a whole century was passed in piratical incursions before this settlement was effected.

From the shores of the Baltic and the islands of Scandinavia, the fleets of the Northmen sailed on, wherever the tide or the tempest might drive them. "They seemed to be able to defy, in their ill-formed barks, the wildest weather; to be able to land on the most inaccessible shores, to find their way up the narrowest creeks and the shallowest rivers; nothing was secure, not even in the heart of the country, from the sudden appearance of these relentless ravagers." These northmen adopted a uniform plan of warfare both in France and England: they sailed up the rivers in their small vessels, and having fortified the islands, which they occasionally found, they made these strongholds an asylum for their women and children, a repository for their plunder, and a place of retreat for themselves. Ethelred the Unready, in attempting to purchase the goodwill of these plunderers in England, was making use of the same foolish expedient, which had been tried a century earlier by the Carlovingians in France. Of course, the silver paid by these weak princes only whetted the thirst of the invaders for more.

At length, in 911, Charles the Simple was prevailed upon to do a wise thing—to offer to **Rollo**, the Norman chief, a dukedom in the north of France, since called Normandy, on condition that he would become a Christian and live in peace with France. Rollo agreed and took the oath of fealty to the king. On being told that to complete the ceremony he must kneel and kiss the monarch's foot, the haughty chief appointed one of his officers to act as his deputy. The soldier lifted the king's foot so awkwardly, that Charles fell backwards from his seat. The duke and most of his companions were soon afterwards baptized, and the ruined churches in Normandy were rebuilt and occupied by the recent converts. The barbarian Northmen adopted with marvellous facility the language and manners of the nation among whom they had settled; and before the end of the century Normandy had become celebrated for its advancement in the arts of industry, commerce, and civilization.

These northern corsairs did not confine their depredations to England and France. Their dark sails were seen by Charlemagne on the blue waters of the Mediterranean, and it is said that the great monarch, foreseeing the ruin they would bring upon his empire, wept at the sight. They gradually extended their voyages in search of plunder, until even the Adriatic was not free from their ravages. One adventurous band had heard some vague rumours of Rome and her vast wealth. They sailed for the Tiber, but entered the Magra by mistake, and landed near Luna. The bishop and his clergy were celebrating mass on Christmas-day when they heard of these unknown strangers, whom they received with courteous hospitality. **Hasting,** their famous leader, was baptized. Ere long the Norman camp resounded with shrieks of sorrow—Hasting was dead. Some nights after the great captain was borne amid his weeping followers to the grave. As they were about to lower the bier, up sprang the supposed corpse, and cut the bishop, who was reading the burial service, to the earth. The priests were massacred, the city plundered, and all the youths and maidens swept on board the fleet. This is mentioned as a specimen of the Northmen's ferocious barbarity, and of the horrors to which the towns on the coasts and on the banks of the great rivers were exposed in the ninth and tenth centuries throughout Western Europe. No settlement was made by the Normans in Italy until the eleventh century. In 1060 Robert Guiscard, a Norman chief, was created by the pope Duke of Apulia and Calabria. No sooner had the Northmen from wandering pirates become occupiers of the soil they had conquered, whether in England, France, or Italy, than they threw off their old pagan customs, and embraced with warmth the Christian religion; forgot the language of their ancestors, and learned that of the natives with whom they lived.

Meanwhile their kinsmen in their old northern home were not left in the darkness of paganism. Intrepid missionaries sought the Northmen among their own dark pine forests, their blue fiords, and their icy lakes. The first and greatest of these pioneers of the gospel was Anschar, a monk of noble French descent. It is related that his thoughts were turned to missionary life by a remarkable vision. Once he thought he had died suddenly, and that he was taken to the gate of heaven, whose inhabitants and their glory he was permitted to behold; and a voice of the most exquisite sweetness, but so clear that it seemed to fill the world, spoke to him out of the unapproachable light, "Go, and return hither crowned with martyrdom." Anschar began his missionary labours in Denmark in the first half of the ninth century; but it was not till the reign of Canute that the final conversion of the Northmen was accomplished.

RISE OF THE ROMANO-GERMAN EMPIRE.

The German branch of the Carlovingian line became extinct in A.D. 911. The Germans thereupon wisely determined to choose a sovereign from among themselves. They were at this time divided into five nations—Saxons, Thuringians, Franconians, Suabians, and Bavarians; the choice of these nations fell upon Conrad, duke of Franconia. Conrad dying without issue (A.D. 919), the great German dukes elected Henry the Fowler, so called because he was catching birds when the ambassadors came to offer him the crown. Under the wise government of Henry and the three Othos, his successors, Germany rose to the rank of the first power in the west.

Henry the Fowler had to defend Germany against a new and terrible foe, called Magyars, or Hungarians, who had come from Ugria, in the northern part of the Ural Mountains. They were a nomadic race; their tents of leather, their garments of fur; they shaved their hair, and scarified their faces; they rarely asked for mercy, and never bestowed it. These savage warriors became the terror of Europe. In many Christian churches resounded the fearful litany—"Oh! save and deliver us from the arrows of the Hungarians." They invaded Italy, and recrossed the Alps with ten bushels of silver, which had been poured out in their tents as a peace-offering. The Byzantine emperor beheld the merciless savages at the gates of Constantinople. One of their boldest warriors presumed to strike a battle-axe into the golden gate; the city, however, was saved from assault by a heavy ransom. The deliverance of Germany and Christendom was achieved by the German princes, Henry the Fowler and his son, Otho the Great, in two memorable battles (A.D. 934 and 955). The Hungarians, after their last defeat, at Lechfeld, near Augsburg, settled down peaceably within the limits of modern Hungary, and by the year 1000 became Christians. After his great victory over the Hungarians at Lechfeld, Otho formed a military province on the frontier exposed to their inroads, which was called the *Oster* or East March, a name since changed into Austria.

Otho was now justly regarded as the most illustrious sovereign of the west, and as entitled to wear the imperial crown. With this end in view, Otho in 961 appeared in Italy at the head of an army. At Milan he received the iron crown of Lombardy, and a month or two later he was crowned emperor at Rome by Pope John XII. From this time it was generally understood that the prince who was elected in the German diet acquired from that moment the subject kingdom of Italy, and a right to the imperial title. And thus was founded by **Otho the Great** the Romano-German empire. The German emperor, however, could not legally assume the imperial title until he had been crowned by the pope; so on the other hand, the pope could not legally be consecrated until the emperor had given his consent. In the papal schisms which not unfrequently rent the church, when two or more rival popes were set up by their partisans, the German emperor by his decision generally put an end to the contest; and in a synod of bishops he also presumed to judge and condemn a guilty pontiff.

Otho had soon occasion to exercise his great authority. The political troubles of Italy during the last hundred years had produced a fearful demoralization, which pervaded all classes of the people, but more especially the nobility and higher clergy. In this iron age, as it has been called, the popes were sometimes pre-eminent by their vices. John XII., who placed the imperial crown on Otho's head, has earned the title of the *Infamous*. Being detected in some plots against the emperor, he was deposed, and Leo VIII. elected in his stead. About this time Otho began to give large domains to the Italian bishops, who thus succeeded the lawless nobles in the government of many of the towns. Under their milder and juster rule liberty began to revive, and the foundations were laid of those Italian republics which became famous at a later period of the middle ages. Rome itself continued throughout this century a prey to anarchy, and an object of ambition. In 997 we find Otho III., grandson of Otho the Great, taking a terrible revenge for the disorders in that city. An Italian nobleman named Crescentius had set up a rival pope, John XVI., and bid defiance to the emperor. Otho entered Rome with a large army, bent on vengeance; the usurper of the Papal See lost his eyes and his ears, and was then paraded through the streets of Rome on an ass with his face to the tail, and with a wine-bladder on his head. Crescentius was captured with the Castle of Angelo, and beheaded with twelve of his leading partisans; their headless bodies were then hung round the battlements of the castle. Such was the fearful state of society at the close of the tenth century in the metropolis of Western Christendom.

RUSSIA AND THE BYZANTINE EMPIRE.

The Byzantine or Greek Emperor could truthfully assert, that of all the monarchs in Christendom he possessed the greatest city, the most ample revenue, the most flourishing and populous state. Constantinople in the tenth century was at the summit of her magnificence; her stately palaces and churches were the objects of wonder and admiration to every traveller from the west. "It is here," says a Jewish traveller, "in the Queen of Cities, that the tributes of the Greek empire are annually deposited, and the lofty towers are filled with magazines of silk, purple, and gold." The trade and manufactures of the empire were the source of their wealth and prosperity. At this time the Greeks were the only Europeans that understood the art of producing and manufacturing silk. Their fabrics of silk, wool, and linen were prized all over the Continent.

The government of the Byzantine monarch was an absolute despotism. The lives and fortunes of millions hung on his arbitrary will; and hence he was treated as a god among men. When Liutprand, ambassador of Otho the Great, approached the throne of the Eastern sovereign, he was compelled to fall prostrate and touch the ground thrice with his forehead. Overshadowing the throne was a golden tree, which sheltered in its artificial leaves and branches a multitude of birds warbling their imitative notes, whilst at the foot of the throne two lions of massy gold looked and roared like their brethren of the forest. Before the amazed ambassador could recover the use of his tongue, the imperial throne was hoisted by an engine from the floor to the ceiling. Whenever the great man designed to pay a visit to some church, or to some distinguished personage in the city, a herald proclaimed his devout or gracious intention. The streets were cleared and cleaned, flowers were strewn on the pavement, the tumult of the populace was hushed. The applause of the monarch was not left to the rude and spontaneous voices of the crowd, but rendered in melodious accents by well-trained bands stationed at intervals along the royal route.

The most renowned of the Greek emperors in the tenth century was John Zimisces, who, during his reign of six years (A.D. 969-975), achieved some military exploits in Asia against the Saracens, and in Europe against the Russians. The Russians had only lately come before the world. The origin of their name is uncertain, but the bulk of the nation consisted of Sclavonic tribes, that had been reduced to order and obedience by the valour of bands of adventurers from Scandinavia. These Northmen formed the aristocracy of the new Russian nation; and one of their chiefs, named Ruric, became the father of a dynasty which reigned in Russia above 700 years. The two chief Russian towns, at this early period of their history, were Novogorod on lake Ilmen, and Kiev on the river Dnieper, both of them forming the centres of a thriving trade. From the neighbourhood of Novogorod the Russians descended the streams that fall into the Dnieper; their canoes, scooped out of the long stem of a beach, or willow, were laden with slaves and furs, with the spoil of their bee-hives, and the hides of their cattle; these cargoes were deposited in the warehouses at Kiev. From this town the merchants departed in June, in more capacious boats, and followed the windings of the river to the Black Sea. Sailing along near the coast they entered the harbour of Constantinople, from whence they returned with rich cargoes of corn, wine, and oil, the manufactures of Greece, and the spices of India. The merchants, on reaching their northern homes, inflamed their barbarian countrymen with the desire of possessing the wealth of the golden city. Before the end of the tenth century the Russians made three attempts by sea, and one by land, to rifle the treasures of Constantinople. The Russian fleet on the third occasion, was almost annihilated by the terrible Greek fire. By land the Russians were less formidable than by sea. The emperor, John Zimisces, defeated them in several battles, and compelled their great duke Swatoslaus to evacuate his empire. The conversion of the Russians to Christianity dates from the baptism of Olga, the mother of Swatoslaus (A.D. 955). Poland was now a flourishing country held by a powerful Sclavonic tribe, with Cracow as the capital. It was raised to the dignity of a kingdom in A.D. 1025.

Iceland also appears in history about this time. Its first inhabitants are said to have been fugitives from Norway, who arrived there in 874. Notwithstanding the barrenness of the soil, and the severity of the climate, the people prospered, and, about the year 1000, professed themselves Christians. In the north of Spain were now formed the Christian kingdoms which gradually pressed the Mohammedans southward, and ultimately expelled them. In the tenth century there were three of these kingdoms—Leon, Castile, and Navarre.

CHAPTER XI.

RISE AND PROGRESS OF THE TURKS.

In every age the immense plains of Central Asia have been inhabited by nomadic tribes of hunters and shepherds, who were anciently called Scythians, and in modern times Tartars. They are divided into four races, of which the most widely extended is the Turkish race. The Turks first appeared west of the Jaxartes, in the beginning of the seventh century, and settled in the country situated between that river and the Oxus. A century later we find them zealous Mussulmans, and the flower of their race enrolled as guards to the caliph in his palace at Bagdad. Motassem, a son of the celebrated Haroun al Raschid, had as many as 50,000 of these troops in his capital. By the year 1000 we find a Turkish prince on the throne of Eastern Persia.

MAHMOUD.

Mahmoud, the first to assume the title of *sultan*, was one of the greatest of the Turkish princes. He ascended the throne of Eastern Persia in 997, and before his death in 1028 extended his kingdom from the shores of the Caspian to the mouth of the Indus. Never was this conquering prince dismayed by the inclemency of the seasons, the height of the mountains, the breadth of the rivers, the barrenness of the desert, the multitudes of the enemy, or the formidable array of their elephants of war. This heroic Mussulman waged "a holy war" against the heathens of Hindostan; many hundred temples, or pagodas, were levelled to the ground, and many thousand idols were demolished. The spoils of the temples and idols rewarded the zeal of his soldiers. His richest prize was the great temple of Sunnat, on the promontory of Guzerat. In the centre of the temple stood the idol, made of stone, and five feet high. The conqueror raised his mace, and struck off the idol's nose. The trembling Brahmins are said to have offered ten millions sterling for its ransom. The Sultan's officers counselled him to accept the offer; but he replied, "Never in the eyes of posterity shall Mahmoud appear as a merchant of idols." He then repeated his blows, until the image fell in pieces and disclosed a treasure of pearls, rubies, and diamonds, which had been concealed within it.

Mahmoud's name is still revered in the East for his virtue and magnanimity. On one occasion, when he suspected that one of his sons was guilty of a capital crime, he took steps to keep himself in ignorance of the name and quality of the guilty person brought before him, until he had sentenced him to death. "I had reason," he says, "to suspect that none except one of my own sons could dare to perpetrate such an outrage; and I ordered the lights to be extinguished, that my justice might be blind and inexorable." When the lights were rekindled, the sultan fell postrate in thankful prayer, on discovering that the criminal whom he had condemned was not his son. Such was the reputation he had gained as a magnanimous sovereign, that, when he contemplated a war with Western Persia, he received a letter from the mother of the reigning prince in these terms: "The late king's sceptre has passed to a woman and a child, and you *dare not* attack their infancy and weakness." She had rightly estimated his character, and the dominions of her son remained safe from attack until he became a man. His behaviour in the last days of his life evinces the vanity of worldly wealth and human greatness. Two days before his death, he feasted his eyes upon his dazzling hoard, and burst into tears. The next day he reviewed his army of 100,000 foot, of 55,000 horse, and 1300 elephants of war; and again he wept at the thought of his transient power. He was succeeded by his son

Massoud, whose throne and dynasty were overthrown by the Turkmans, a Turkish tribe that dwelt on the eastern side of the Caspian Sea (A.D. 1038).

TOGRUL BEG.

The victorious Turkmans elected a sultan by lot. A number of arrows were inscribed with the names of the candidates, and a child was appointed to draw one of them from the bundle. The prize fell to Togrul Beg, grandson of Seljuk, whose name was applied to the new dynasty. The Turks under the Seljukian princes came for the first time into hostile contact with Christendom, and in the reign of Togrul began that terrible war against the Cross, which lasted 500 years. There were three great sultans of the race of Seljuk, by whom the conquest of Western Asia was begun and completed; their names are Togrul Beg, Alp Arslan, and Malek Shah. They were all zealous Mussulmans, and used their power to propagate their religion. Each day they repeated the five prayers prescribed for the disciples of Islam; each week they gave two days to fasting; in every city they made their own it was their first care to build a mosque.

Togrul Beg proved equal to his splendid fortune, and by his valour and abilities greatly extended his dominions. Having made himself master of Persia and Media, he offered his services to the Caliph of Bagdad, and was accepted as his champion. During the past century the Caliph of Bagdad had been only a venerable phantom, the real sovereignty had been exercised by one of his most powerful nobles under the title of *Emir-al-Omra*, that is, commander of commanders. Togrul soon reduced the caliph's rebellious subjects to obedience, and became Emir-al-Omra. He then turned his arms against Armenia and Asia Minor, and 130,000 Christians fell beneath the sabres, or pierced with the arrows, of his terrible squadrons. The real conquest of these provinces was not, however, achieved by Togrul Beg.

On the sultan's victorious return, he was formally recognised by the caliph as his temporal vicegerent.

The conqueror entered Bagdad on horseback, but at the palace gate he dismounted, and entered the caliph's presence as his humble subject. The caliph was seated behind his black veil with the staff of Mohammed in his hands. Togrul kissed the floor, and waited modestly till requested to seat himself. Two crowns were then set upon his head, and two scimitars girded on his side, in token of his double reign over east and west, whilst a herald proclaimed him vicegerent of the prophet's successor. The Caliph of Bagdad, a sort of Mohammedan pope, was still regarded by the Moslems of Asia as their spiritual head, whilst the sultan was generally accepted as their temporal sovereign. On Togrul's death, without children, his power passed to his nephew, Alp Arslan (A.D. 1063).

ALP ARSLAN.

The name of this second sultan of the line of Seljuk signifies in Turkish "the valiant lion," and it must be admitted that he displayed the fierceness and generosity of the royal animal. He marched against Armenia and Georgia, and annexed these provinces to his dominions. Romanus Diogenes, the Greek or Byzantine emperor, attempted to recover these provinces, but he was defeated and captured. After the battle the captive Emperor of New Rome was brought before the victor in a peasant's dress; he made him kiss the ground beneath his feet, and put his foot upon his neck. Then, raising him up, he struck or patted him three times with his hand, and gave him his life, and, on the promise of a large ransom, his liberty.

Alp Arslan now resolved on the conquest of Turkestan, on the further side of the Oxus, the original seat of the house of Seljuk, and now occupied by new Turkish tribes, that refused to acknowledge the great sultan as their sovereign. The invader had not advanced far into the country when he met his death from the hand of a captive. A Carismian chief had withstood his progress, and being taken, was condemned to a lingering death.

On hearing that he was to be fastened to four stakes and left to perish, the desperate victim, drawing a dagger, rushed headlong towards the throne; and the sultan, disdaining to let his guards interfere, bent his bow, but his foot slipped, the arrow glanced aside, and he received in his breast the dagger of his prisoner, who was immediately cut to pieces. The monarch, mortally wounded, had time to bequeath this dying admonition: "In my youth," he said, "I was advised by a sage to humble myself before God; to distrust my own strength; and never to despise the most contemptible foe. I have neglected these lessons, and my neglect has been deservedly punished. Yesterday, as from an eminence, I beheld the numbers, the discipline, and the spirit of my armies; the earth seemed to tremble under my feet; and I said in my heart surely thou art the king of the world, the greatest and most invincible of warriors. These armies are no longer mine, and in the confidence of my personal strength I now fall by the hand of an assassin." On his tomb was engraven an inscription conceived in a similar spirit: "O! ye who have seen the glory of Alp Arslan exalted to the heavens, repair to Maru, and you will behold it buried in the dust!"

MALEK SHAH.

Malek Shah, the eldest son of Alp Arslan, was, by his personal merit and the extent of his dominions, the greatest prince of his age (A.D. 1072-1092). He had first to contend against his younger brother, who claimed an equal share in the government. On the eve of the battle, whilst Malek, like a good Mussulman, was engaged in his devotions, he besought "the Lord of Hosts to take from him his life and crown if his brother was more worthy than himself to reign over the Moslems." Having seated himself firmly on the throne, he completed the conquest of Turkestan, which his father had entered upon, and then proceeded to annex Asia Minor and Palestine to his dominions.

The conquest of Asia Minor was undertaken at the

instance of the caliph. A prince of the royal line of Seljuk had fallen in battle against Alp Arslan, and his five sons were now eager for revenge. They accordingly made war against the young sultan; but when the two armies expected the signal for battle, the caliph interposed with these words, "Instead of shedding the blood of your brethren, both in descent and faith, unite your forces in a holy war against the Greeks, the enemies of God and his apostle." The sultan and his kinsmen were reconciled, and Soliman, the eldest of the five brothers, was promised the hereditary command of the Greek provinces he should succeed in conquering. The valiant Soliman crossed the Euphrates, and his flying cavalry soon scoured the open country of Asia Minor. Two Greek competitors for the Byzantine throne sought the assistance of their common foe. Soliman formed an alliance with one of them, helped to set him on the throne of Constantinople, and then rewarded himself by taking possession of the Greek provinces of Asia. By the choice of the sultan, Nice, in Bithynia, was prepared for his palace and fortress. On the hard conditions of tribute and servitude, the Greek Christians might retain the exercise of their religion; but their churches were profaned, their priests insulted, and every means adopted to stamp the profession of Christianity with the marks of ignominy. Soliman, by his Mohammedan zeal, earned the name of *Gazi*, the holy champion.

After the annexation of Asia Minor, the Turks directed their arms against the Holy Land, at that time in the hands of Saracen emirs, appointed by the Caliph of Egypt. The fierce Turks proved irresistible, and in 1076 Jerusalem fell into their savage hands. Under the caliphs, the Christians of Jerusalem had been permitted to meet for religious worship. Crowds of pilgrims, even from remote parts of Europe, had been accustomed to visit the holy sepulchre and other places sacred to Christians. But now they were abandoned to the cruel treatment of a host of barbarian Turkmans. The Patriarch, or Archbishop of Jerusalem, was dragged by the hair along the pavement, and cast into a dungeon, to extort a ransom from his Christian flock. Outrages such as these were of frequent occurrence, and provoked that spirt of religious fervour which burst forth into the flame of those holy wars known as the Crusades.

As long as Malek lived, the greatness and unity of the Turkish empire were preserved, but on his death (A.D. 1092), after a series of civil wars, it was divided into four states—*Persia, Syria, Roum,* or Lesser Asia, and *Kerman,* an extensive dominion on the shores of the Indian Ocean. Three years before the Crusaders reached Jerusalem, the Turks in that city were overthrown by the Saracens of Egypt (A.D. 1096), and then the Caliph of Cairo resumed the sovereignty of the Holy Land.

CHAPTER XII.

THE CRUSADES.

TOWARDS the close of the eleventh century many of the noblest hearts in Europe began to burn with the desire of taking up arms for the deliverance of the Holy Land from the Turks and Saracens. The fire of Christian enthusiasm for this holy war was first kindled by **Peter the Hermit**, a native of Amiens, who had been on a pilgrimage to Jerusalem, and had there witnessed the insults and cruelties heaped upon the Christian pilgrims by the Turkish infidels that had possession of the city. On his return, the hermit traversed Italy and France, riding on an ass, with his feet bare, his head uncovered, clothed in a coarse garment bound with a cord, and bearing a crucifix in his hand. He preached to innumerable crowds in the churches, the streets, and the highways: the hermit entered with equal confidence the palace and the cottage; and the people were impetuously moved to repentance and arms.

Peter's eloquent appeal was well supported by the pope, Urban II., who summoned two great councils to promote his great design. The first council, assembled at Placentia (A.D. 1095), was attended by ambassadors of the Greek emperor, Alexius Comnenus, who pleaded the distress of their sovereign, and the danger of Constantinople, which was divided by only a narrow strait from the victorious Turks. The council was easily persuaded that Europe was in danger of invasion from these enemies of the Cross, and that the proposed war might be the means of hurling them back upon the East. The second council was held in the autumn of the same year at

Clermont in France. Meanwhile, the clergy had preached in every diocese the merit and glory of the deliverance of the Holy Land. When the pope ascended a lofty scaffold in the market-place of Clermont, he addressed an audience already inflamed with the desire of taking up arms against the infidels. Only a few burning words had fallen from his lips, when thousands with one voice exclaimed aloud, "God wills it, God wills it!" "It is indeed the will of God," replied the pope. He then bade them wear a red cross on their left shoulder, as a token of their engagement to serve as champions of Christ. The proposal was joyfully accepted. Those who enrolled themselves in the army of the Crusaders were taught to believe that their sins would all be pardoned, and that if they perished in the Holy War they would receive the crown of martyrdom.

The hostilities thus undertaken against the Turks and Saracens extended over two centuries, and include seven distinct wars, known as the Seven Crusades. Though the Crusaders failed in their object—the permanent deliverance of the Holy Land from the Moslem power; yet, by crippling the might of the Seljuk Turks on the plains of Palestine, they saved Europe for three centuries from Turkish invasion.

THE FIRST CRUSADE (A.D. 1095-1099).

An unruly rabble of at least 300,000 men, women, and children, set out under Peter the Hermit and his lieutenant, Walter the Penniless, before the real warriors under competent leaders were ready to march. This disorderly crowd never reached the Holy Land: they were overwhelmed by the Turkish arrows in the plain of Nice, and a pyramid of bones informed their better diciplined companions who followed them, of the place of their defeat.

None of the sovereigns of Europe took a part in the first crusade. The chief leaders were **Godfrey of Bouillon** or Boulogne; Hugh, count of Vermandois, a brother of the King of France; Robert, duke of Normandy, the eldest son of William the Conqueror; Raymond, count of Toulouse; and Bohemond, brother of Robert Guiscard, who was accompanied by his cousin Tancred. These leaders conducted the troops by different routes to Constantinople, from whence they were shipped by the Greek emperor across the Bosphorus. The principal force of the Crusaders consisted in their cavalry; and when that force was mustered on the plains of Bithynia, the knights and their martial attendants on horseback amounted to 100,000 fighting men, completely armed with lance, helmet, and coat of mail. On the rear of the cavalry hung a promiscuous crowd on foot, including priests and monks, women and children; few of whom ever returned with a branch of palm from the Holy Land. As France supplied the largest number of fighting men, the name of Franks is sometimes applied to the whole army of Crusaders, and sometimes they are spoken of under the more general appellation of Latins.

The Crusaders commenced their war against the infidels by laying siege to Nice, the Turkish capital of Roum. The Sultan of Roum at this time was Kilidge-Arslan, the son of the great Soliman. Nice being situated on lake Ascanius, it could not be taken until invested by water as well as land. Alexius, the Greek emperor, having caused a vast number of boats to be transported on sledges from the sea to the lake, Nice was encompassed, and the Turks compelled to surrender. The Crusaders then resumed their march towards Palestine, but a few miles before they reached Dorylæum in Phrygia, they were attacked by Kilidge-Arslan. The cavalry on either side performed prodigies of valour: on this side the couched lance and the weighty broadsword, on that side the brandished javelin and the curved sabre; on this side the cumbrous armour and the deadly cross-bow, on that side the thin flowing robes and the long Tartar bow. As long as the horses were fresh and the quivers full the Sultan had the advantage, but in the evening swiftness yielded to strength and the Turks were defeated. Kilidge-Arslan evacuated his kingdom of Roum, and hastened to implore the aid of his Moslem brethren in Persia and the East.

Whilst the main body marched on to Syria, Baldwin,

brother of Godfrey, crossed the Euphrates with a small force, and founded a Latin kingdom, with Edessa as its capital.

Meanwhile, the Crusaders laid siege to Antioch; and here they drained to the lees the cup of misery. At the end of seven months they were still encamped outside the walls; 300,000 commenced the siege in the autumn of 1097, and in the following spring only one-sixth part remained to take the city. In the conduct of the siege whatever strength and valour could perform was achieved by the soldiers of the Cross. Among other feats we are told that the sword of Godfrey cleft a Turk in two halves so deftly, that while one fell to the ground, the other was carried on by his horse to the city gate. Antioch was at length taken by a night attack; but the Crusaders were in turn besieged by an army of Turks and Saracens under Kerboga, prince of Mosul. Five and twenty days the Christians spent on the verge of destruction; in their extremity they collected the fragments of their forces, sallied from the town, and in a single memorable day (June 28, 1098) annihilated or dispersed the Moslem host.

The next ten months were spent in discord and disorder. It was not until June, 1099, that the relics of the Crusaders appeared before Jerusalem. After a siege of forty days, Godfrey of Bouillon stood victorious on the walls of the holy city. A frightful massacre of 70,000 Moslems sullied the glory of the conquerors; but in the mistaken view of the Christian warriors, the holy city by this sacrifice was purged from defilement. The victors now prepared to visit the holy sepulchre: bareheaded and barefoot they ascended the hill of Calvary, along the way our Saviour carried His cross, and with tears of joy and penitence kissed the stone that had concealed the world's Redeemer.

The Crusaders now took steps to secure their dear-bought prize. By the unanimous voice of the army, Godfrey, the worthiest of the Christian champions, was chosen to reign as King of Jerusalem. But in a city where his

Saviour had been crowned with thorns, the devout soldier refused to wear a royal diadem. Within a fortnight the new king sealed his right to reign by the battle of Ascalon, in which he utterly defeated the Sultan of Egypt. After this victory, which is the closing act of the first crusade, most of the Crusaders returned home.

The permanent defence of the holy city devolved chiefly on two orders of knights, who combined the double character of a monk and a soldier. These military monks were called Hospitallers and Templars, because the former were originally attached to the hospital of St. John at Jerusalem, and the latter resided at first near the site of Solomon's temple. The flower of the nobility of Europe aspired to wear the badge, and to profess the vows, of these famous orders. To these was afterwards added a third society of knights, known as the Teutonic order.

By the arms of Godfrey and the two Baldwins, his brother and cousin, who succeeded him, the kingdom of Jerusalem gradually embraced the whole of Palestine. The emperor Alexius may be compared to the jackal, that is said to follow the steps, and to devour the leavings of the lion. He took possession of Nice, the Crusaders' first conquest; and, while the Turks were fully occupied with their strange enemy from the West, he made himself master of the entire circuit of the coast of Asia Minor, and the whole of that country west of the Meander. The Seljuk Turks still retained their hold on the rest of Asia Minor, with Iconium as their capital; whilst Syria was partly in the hands of their Moslem brethren, and partly in the power of the Latins. As the enemies of the Cross had been stunned, not destroyed, by the vigorous blows of the Crusaders, they were soon on the alert, both in Egypt and Syria, to regain the ground they had lost.

THE SECOND CRUSADE (A.D. 1147-1149).

The dangers of the Latins in Asia and the loss of Edessa, the most advanced outpost of Christendom, led to the second crusade. The smouldering fires of enthusiasm in Western Europe blazed out anew at the preaching of St. Bernard.

This remarkable man was abbot of Clairvaux in Champagne. He had become famous by the austerity and sanctity of his life, by his genius and eloquence, and by his genuine contempt for all worldly honour and distinction. The more he withdrew from the gaze of the world, the more was he courted by the great ones of the earth, who esteemed his wisdom and implored his blessing. So frequently, indeed, was St. Bernard consulted by prince and peasant, that he might be called the oracle of Western Europe. At the command of Pope Eugenius III., this great abbot became the apostle of the second crusade.

At Vezelai in Burgundy, in the presence of Louis VII. and his queen Eleanora, St. Bernard addressed an immense concourse of people, assembled on the hill-side outside the town; and before he had concluded his impassioned speech, his voice was drowned in resounding cries of "the Cross! the Cross!" The king and queen, deeply moved, knelt at the abbot's feet and received the cross from his hand; and such was the eager rush for the sacred emblem that, after distributing a vast number of crosses prepared beforehand, St. Bernard and his assistant monks were obliged to tear up their garments to supply the demand.

The abbot of Clairvaux then proceeded to preach the crusade in Germany, and to enlist the emperor, Conrad III., in the holy war. The Germans, though ignorant of his language, were won over by the pathetic vehemence of his tone and gestures. The emperor was not so easily affected; but at length he also fell a captive to his extraordinary eloquence and personal influence. At the conclusion of his address, the emperor, moved even to tears, exclaimed, "I acknowledge the gifts of the divine mercy, and I will no longer remain ungrateful for them; I am ready for the service to which God hath called me." At these words a universal shout of joy burst from the assembly. Bernard then took from the altar the consecrated banner, and delivered it to the emperor, by whom it was to be carried at the head of the Crusaders.

It appears, from contemporary records, that one great difficulty which Bernard had to encounter in preaching the crusade, originated in the religious societies for the building of churches and cathedrals, then the great object of popular devotion. These sacred building societies were formed of persons of both sexes, and of all ranks. No one was admitted to the honour of labouring in them, until he had given clear evidence of the sincerity of his faith, and had taken a vow of obedience to the superior of the association. It is said that lords and ladies might be seen in those days, attached to heavy burdens, like beasts of draught, to assist in the building of some sacred edifice. Bernard found it difficult to persuade men, who had thus consecrated their lives to God's glory in their native land, to desert the sacred work in which they were engaged, for a perilous object of dubious attainment; yet even this obstacle was surmounted by his fervid eloquence.

The armies of the second crusade were equal in dimensions to those of the first; it is affirmed that nearly a million persons of both sexes and all ages responded to the summons of the great preacher. This crusade, however, proved a gigantic failure. The Greek emperor, under the mask of friendship, laboured in every way to ruin the enterprise. Every promise of assistance was readily made, and then treacherously violated. In every step of their march they were stopped or misled; the governors had private orders to fortify the passes and break down the bridges against them; the stragglers were pillaged and murdered; the soldiers and horses were pierced in the woods by arrows from invisible hands; the sick were burned in their beds; and the dead bodies were hung in gibbets along the highways. The emperor Conrad, and Louis of France, with a few thousand troops, entered Jerusalem, but the main body perished before reaching Palestine. A fruitless siege of Damascus was the final effort of the second crusade.

THE THIRD CRUSADE (A.D. 1189-1192).

Notwithstanding the failure of the second crusade, the kingdom of Jerusalem contrived to exist forty years longer, in consequence of the discord of the Turks and

Saracens. At length all the Moslem forces of Egypt, Syria, and Arabia, were united under the heroic **Saladin.** This famous prince, after becoming Sultan of Egypt, began a career of conquest that extended his empire from the African Tripoli to the Tigris, and from the Indian Ocean to the mountians of Armenia. Saladin was brave and generous, temperate and chaste, just and charitable. Though a rigid Mussulman, his virtues commanded the esteem of his Christian enemies. Having united Saracen and Turk under his standard, he invaded Palestine at the head of 80,000 horse and foot (A.D. 1187). A great victory at Tiberias opened up the way to Jerusalem, which, after a siege of fourteen days, fell into his hands. The lives of the Christians were spared, but it was stipulated that the Latins should evacuate the Holy Land and return to Europe. The fall of Jerusalem was followed by the capitulation of nearly all the other towns held by the Christians; Tyre alone successfully resisted the conqueror, and became the rendezvous of the Christians in the early part of the third crusade.

When the news spread throughout Europe that Jerusalem was again in the hands of the infidels, it needed neither hermit nor abbot to awaken a fiery zeal against the enemies of our faith. The Italians were the first to embark in the ships of Genoa, Pisa, and Venice. Upon their arrival, the Latins were numerous enough to leave the walls of Tyre and encamp before Acre. Meanwhile, the sovereigns of the West—Frederick Barbarossa of Germany, Philip Augustus of France, and **Richard Cœur de Lion** of England, were marshalling their forces.

The siege of Acre lasted two years, and cost the lives of a countless host. Never did the flame of enthusiasm burn with fiercer and more destructive rage. Saladin, in the beginning of the siege, had assembled his troops, and pitched his camp a few miles from Acre, so that the besiegers had to cope with an enemy outside the city as well as one within the walls. Nine battles were fought in the neighbourhood of Mount Carmel, with such vicissitude of fortune, that in one attack the sultan forced his way into the city, and in another the Christians penetrated into the sultan's tent.

Meanwhile, a small remnant of the emperor's forces had reached Acre, but Frederick himself had been drowned one summer day while bathing in the river Selef in Cilicia. It was not until the spring of the second year of the siege that the fleets of France and England sailed into the bay of Acre (A.D. 1191). The arrival of Philip and Richard inspired the besiegers with new life and hope. The king of England soon distinguished himself as the first warrior of the day. In a short time the town was taken, and the road to Jerusalem was unbarred. But now the hopes of the Crusaders were foiled by disunion between their leaders. Philip, being jealous of Richard's fame, returned to France.

The Crusaders, now under Richard's sole command, marched along the sea-coast to Ascalon. This march of 100 miles was a great and perpetual battle of eleven days. In every fight the king was foremost, cutting down his opponents with his terrible battle-axe. Such was the terror of his name that a pilgrim, who visited the Holy Land sixty years later, informs us that his name was used by the women to silence their children, and that when a horse started, his rider was wont to exclaim, "Dost thou think that King Richard is in that bush?" But with all his exertions Richard could only get within sight of Jerusalem. The retreat of the Crusaders, just when the prize was within their grasp, is quite inexplicable, and in the eyes of the trembling Moslems it was miraculous. Cœur de Lion, ascending a hill to catch a glimpse of the city, veiled his face, and with an indignant voice exclaimed, "Those who are unwilling to rescue, are unworthy to view the sepulchre of Christ!" The third crusade was terminated by a truce of three years and three months; and it was agreed that the Christian pilgrims should visit Jerusalem and the holy sepulchre without tribute or hindrance, and that the towns on the sea-coast, from Jaffa to Tyre, should remain in Christian hands. Richard embarked for Europe to find a long captivity in Germany, and a premature grave in France. A short time after this the renowned Saladin died at Damascus, and by his death his empire was dissolved. It is memorable that, before he expired, he ordered his winding-sheet to be carried as a standard through every street of the city; while a herald went before and loudly exclaimed, "This is all that remains to the mighty Saladin, the conqueror of the East."

THE FOURTH AND FIFTH CRUSADES.

Palestine was never the scene of another crusade, although four others were undertaken with Palestine as the ultimate object in view. No sooner did Innocent III. become pope than he proclaimed the obligation of a new crusade. His appeal was responded to by the Count of Flanders and many of the most powerful barons of France (A.D. 1203). But their forces were diverted to the siege of Constantinople, and their vows were forgotten in the capture of the city.

Another armament in 1218, conducted by the King of Hungary, was wasted in fruitless attempts upon Egypt. A host of men were landed at the eastern mouth of the Nile in the hope of breaking the Moslem power in Palestine by the conquest of Egypt, at that time the chief seat of their power; but the enterprise completely failed. Ten years later, however, Frederick II. of Germany, profiting by the discord of the Mohammedans, made an advantageous treaty without bloodshed. He obtained from the sultan the restitution of Jerusalem, Nazareth, and other towns, almost the only stipulation being that the Mosque of Omar should remain open to Moslem worshippers.

THE SIXTH AND SEVENTH CRUSADES.

The two last crusades were undertaken by **Louis IX.**, one of the few sovereigns who have been justly honoured with the title of saint. In 1244, Jerusalem had been taken and sacked with savage cruelty by the Carismians, a barbarous horde from the shores of the Caspian. Not long afterwards the Carismians were expelled from Syria by the Saracens of Egypt, and the Holy Land fell once more under the rule of the Egyptian sultan. Little now remained to the Latins in the East but the fortresses of Acre and Tyre, together with Tripoli and Antioch.

Louis embarked in June, 1248, while his mariners sung in chorus the *Veni Creator*, and set sail for Egypt, which he regarded as the key of the Holy Land. Damietta fell an easy prey to his arms, but this was his first and last conquest. An epidemic spread among his troops at Damietta, and when he advanced inland his progress was stopped by an impassable canal. He took possession of the strongest position he could find and encamped. The Turks surrounded him, and with their Greek fire destroyed his machines of war. Too late the king began a retreat. Such calamities now fell upon his devoted army, from famine, pestilence, and the sword, as have scarce ever been surpassed. Louis himself might have escaped if he would have deserted his soldiers: he was made prisoner with the greatest part of his nobles; all who could not redeem their lives were inhumanly massacred, and the walls of Cairo were decorated with a circle of Christian heads. The king was at first loaded with chains, but the sultan sent him a robe of honour, and permitted him to embark with the relics of his army on the restitution of Damietta, and the promised payment of 400,000 pieces of gold.

The memory of his early vow excited Louis, after twenty years spent in the wise and peaceful government of his country, to undertake the seventh and last crusade (A.D. 1270). The Cross was also assumed by Prince Edward, son of Henry III. of England, and by a great number of English knights. Instead of sailing direct to Palestine, the French fleet made for Tunis, in the wild hope of planting Christianity in that Moslem stronghold. The French landed near ancient Carthage, and began the siege of Tunis. The plague broke out in the camp of the besiegers, and the soldiers died by thousands on the burning sands. Louis himself was seized with it, and finding himself on the brink of death, he desired to be laid upon a bed of ashes, and there he soon expired, with the words of the Psalmist on his lips: "I will enter into Thy house, O Lord: I will worship in Thy holy temple." His son and successor soon afterwards returned to France.

Prince Edward, however, would not abandon the enterprise. At the head of 1000 soldiers he delivered Acre from a siege, and by his personal valour emulated the fame of Cœur de Lion; but he effected no substantial good.

The conquests of the Crusaders were finally extinguished by the Mameluke sultans of Egypt. The Mamelukes were of Tartar origin, and had been introduced into Egypt as slaves. Being employed as mercenary troops, they gained great distinction by their valour, and at length raised their chief captain to the supreme power, after assassinating the sultan. Antioch had been taken by these terrible Mamelukes two years before the death of St. Louis: they had massacred 17,000 of the inhabitants, and sold 100,000 into slavery. The other Latin towns successively fell before their arms; and in A.D. 1291 Acre, the last stronghold of the Christians, and the most dissolute city in the world, passed into the hands of the Mamelukes. Death or slavery was the lot of 60,000 captives, and most of the fugitives were drowned before they could reach the friendly shores of Cyprus.

CHAPTER XIII.

EUROPE IN THE FOURTEENTH CENTURY.

BEFORE the age of the crusades had wholly passed away, Europe was beginning to emerge from the darkness of the Middle Ages. The period thus designated embraced a thousand years, reckoning from the extinction of the Western Empire in the fifth century; it was characterised by gross ignorance and superstition, by the tyranny of the strong, and the servitude of the weak. The century which followed the last crusade saw the dawn of a brighter day; it was marked by the decline of the excessive power of the pope, by the growth of liberty and patriotism, and by the progress of civilization and commerce.

DECLINE OF THE PAPAL POWER.

The marked change in the position and power of the pope, wrought by the silent change of public opinion during the period of the crusades, cannot be more forcibly apprehended than by contrasting the struggle between Pope Gregory VII. and Henry IV. of Germany in the *eleventh* century, with the contest between Pope Boniface VIII. and Philip of France in the *fourteenth* century.

Gregory VII., commonly known as *Hildebrand*, raised the papal power to a dizzy height, and made crowned heads bow submissively before his throne. In those superstitious days the clergy exercised a marvellous sway over the minds of the laity; for men feared that a curse pronounced on them by a priest would consign their souls to eternal perdition. By a sentence of excommunication, as this curse was termed, a person was declared to belong no more to Christ but to the devil, and every one who befriended him was supposed to incur his guilt and punishment. If sentence of excommunication was pronounced against a king without bringing him on his knees before the pope for absolution, there were still two other thunderbolts which could be hurled against the impenitent monarch; his country could be laid under an interdict (as was England in the reign of King John), and his subjects could be released from their oath of allegiance, by which he was virtually deposed.

Without entering into the causes of dispute between Hildebrand and Henry, it will suffice for our purpose to show the marvellous ascendency of the pope over the emperor, in consequence of the prevailing spirit of the age in which they lived.

When Hildebrand threatened to excommunicate the emperor, if he failed to appear before his tribunal to answer the charges brought against him, he was resolved to set the pope at defiance. Having held a synod of German bishops at Mentz, Henry wrote a letter to Pope Gregory concluding in these terms—"I, Henry, by the grace of God king, with all the bishops of my realm, say unto thee, DOWN! DOWN!" But the emperor's bold words recoiled on his own head. The pope replied by excommunicating him. Henry's defiant words were as the harmless thunder, but Hildebrand's sentence was as the destructive thunderbolt. Henry's friends deserted him, and in a few months he was under the necessity of seeking absolution from the pope to save his tottering throne from falling. Not a day was to be lost. It was midwinter; but the Alps, white with snow and slippery with ice, must be crossed without delay. The emperor, on his descent from the Alps, repaired to Canosa, in the strong fortress of which the pope was at that time residing. "On a dreary winter morning," says Dean Milman, "with the ground deep in snow, the king, the heir of a long line of emperors, was permitted to enter within the two outer of the three walls which girded the castle of Canosa. He had laid aside every mark of royalty; he was clad only in the thin white linen dress of the penitent, and there, fasting, he awaited in humble patience the pleasure of the pope. But the gates did not unclose. A second day he stood, cold, hungry, and mocked by vain hope. And yet a third day dragged on from morning to evening over the unsheltered head of the humbled monarch. Gregory at length yielded an ungracious permission for the king to approach his presence. With bare feet, still in the garb of penitence, stood the king, a man of singularly tall and noble person, accustomed to flash command and terror upon his adversaries, before the pope, a grey-haired man, bowed with years, of small unimposing stature."

Thus was successfully asserted in the face of Europe, the right of the pope to be the judge of kings. Such was the power of the pope just before the first crusade; and we know, from English history, how well the extraordinary claims of the papacy were enforced by Innocent III., in the reign of King John, at the beginning of the thirteenth century. But before the end of that century the power of the papacy had passed its zenith.

In 1294, when Edward I. was king of England, and Philip the Fair reigned in France, the papal throne was occupied by Boniface VIII., who, by overstraining his assumed authority over these monarchs, brought ruin upon his own head, and humiliation on his successors.

The quarrel between **Boniface VIII.** and Philip the Fair, is one of the great epochs in the papal history, the turning point after which, for a time at least, the papacy sank with a swift and precipitate descent, never to rise again to the same commanding height as before. To the pope's claim to superiority over the secular power, the king's ambassador, Peter Flotte, replied—"Your power in temporal affairs is a power in word, that of the king, my master, in deed." The claims of the pope were thus summarised in all their nakedness in a document, called *the little bull*, which was circulated in France (A.D. 1302) with the pope's forged signature appended to it. "Boniface, bishop, servant of the servants of God, to Philip, king of the Franks. Fear God and keep his commandments. We desire you to know that you are subject to us in temporal as well as spiritual affairs; and that, if you have bestowed any benefice, the appointment is null. All who believe not this are guilty of heresy." Though this document was not genuine, it not unfairly summed up the claims which the pope had advanced in a recent bull. The king drew up a reply to "the little bull," couched in corresponding terms, which he sent around his dominions: "Philip, by the grace of God, king of the French, to Boniface, who assumes to be the chief pontiff, little or no greeting. Be it known to your stupidity that in temporals we are subject to none; and that we will support with all our might those on whom we have bestowed or shall bestow benefices. All who believe not this we hold for fools and idiots." This strange address was received with satisfaction by the majority of the nation. And when the king, still further, caused the pope's bull to be burned in Paris in his presence, the astonished citizens, instead of trembling at the consequences, viewed the king's defiance of the pope with approbation.

Boniface, in great wrath, declares that he could depose the king as easily as he could discharge a groom. And in another bull he says, "We pronounce that it is necessary to salvation to believe that every human being is subject to the pontiff of Rome." The pope was, at length, determined to launch a terrible curse upon the head of the contumacious king. But the day before that appointed for shooting this last shaft from the papal quiver, Boniface was a prisoner in the hands of Philip's emissaries. He was treated with cruel indignity by his captors, who set him on a vicious horse, with his face to the tail, and so led him through the street to his place of imprisonment. In his hour of adversity he played a noble part. "If I am betrayed like Christ," he said, "I am ready to die like Christ." He was rescued from his persecutors, but in a few days died of a fever, brought on by fatigue, vexation, and anxiety (A.D. 1303).

The papacy was still further humbled by the same unscrupulous monarch. Philip contrived to secure the election of Clement V., and to induce him to fix his residence at Avignon, in Provence. Here for seventy years the popes resided under the influence of the French king. This period, which has been aptly called the Babylonish captivity of the popedom, was terminated by the death of Gregory XI. in 1378. The papacy, however, was still further weakened by the great schism which followed. Two rival popes were set up, who hurled anathemas against each other, and divided all western Christendom into two hostile sects. The patience of the Christian world was at length exhausted by the adverse claims of the rival pontiffs; and when a third competitor was added, it was generally agreed that the schism should be healed by a general council. The council met at Constance (A.D. 1414-18), and the three popes were compelled to resign, or were deposed. The elevation of Martin V. to the papal chair restored peace and unity to the Western Church.

THE GROWTH OF LIBERTY.

When the crusades were first preached, the feudal system prevailed throughout the West. There were but two classes of society, the nobles and their dependants, many of whom were in a state of slavery or serfdom. The inhabitants of the town were as much serfs and vassals to their feudal superiors as the peasantry; they were composed for the most part of poor mechanics, who worked for the profit of the feudal lord, within whose domain they lived. Some fiefs contained many towns; all of them were in the hands of some great baron, who had absolute power over the lives and property of the inhabitants. The barons often used their power cruelly, and drove the citizens at length to form associations for mutual defence.

The maritime cities of Italy, and the towns of Lombardy, were the first to throw off the yoke of their tyrants. In 1167, the League of Lombardy was formed, when twenty-three Italian cities united to claim the right of electing their own magistrates and making their own laws. By the decisive victory of Legnano (A.D. 1176) over Frederick Barbarossa of Germany, the chief cities of Italy established the right of forming themselves into Republics.

In France, Louis the Fat (A.D. 1108-37) became the patron of the busy artisan and the thriving tradesman. He granted charters, on the condition of receiving some fixed payment, to many of the towns on the royal domains, by which they acquired the right of electing their own magistrates, and of forming a militia for their own defence. His example was followed by most of the French nobles, and in a very short time there were but few French cities that did not enjoy municipal freedom. Meanwhile, similar changes were taking place in England and Germany.

Thus, throughout the West, in the twelfth and thirteenth centuries, there arose a middle class of society of such importance, that in England, as early as 1266, deputies from the boroughs were invited by Simon de Montfort to share in the national councils, and in France the same policy was adopted by Philip the Fair. Indeed, this monarch, throughout his reign (A.D. 1285-1314), systematically repressed the power of the nobility, and promoted the elevation of the bourgoisie or middle class. The emancipation of the serfs soon followed the rise of this new class of free citizens. The chartered cities granted protection to all who sought shelter within their walls; the clergy exercised their great influence in favour of manumission; and in the reign of Louis X. of France (A.D. 1314-16), we find the serfs not only permitted, but compelled, by that monarch, to purchase their freedom.

The enjoyment of liberty, and the possession of property, created a new spirit in the breasts of the humbler classes. Men learned to love their country, to rejoice in their freedom, and to value their privileges; and hence the virtue of patriotism began to play an important part in human affairs.

THE SPIRIT OF PATRIOTISM.

The patriotic spirit that glowed in the breasts of the citizens and free peasantry, on their escape from the tyranny of their feudal lords, is very apparent, in the valorous deeds of the English yeoman at Crecy and Poitiers, in the glorious victory of the Scots under Bruce at Bannockburn, in the stout resistance made by the burghers of Flanders to their French masters, and still more in the successful stand made by the Swiss mountaineers against the encroachments of the Imperial House of Hapsburg. Omitting the two former instances as already familiar to the reader, we will confine our attention to the patriotic endeavours of the Flemish artisans and the Swiss shepherds.

At Courtrai, 1302, the Flemish burghers humbled the pride of the haughty French knights in the dust, and taught them, for the first time, that "a nation of shopkeepers" could fight bravely for their country. "Contempt for smiths and weavers," says the author of the *Eighteen Christian Centuries*, "blinded the fiery nobles. They rushed forward with loose bridles, and as they had disdained to reconnoitre the scene of the display, they fell headlong, one after another, horse and plume, sword and spur, into one enormous ditch which lay between them and their enemies. On they came an avalanche of steel and horseflesh, and floundered into the muddy hole. Hundreds, thousands, unable to check their steeds, or afraid to appear irresolute, or goggling in vain through the deep holes left for their eyes, fell, struggled, writhed, and choked, till the ditch was filled with trampled knights and tumbling horses, and the burghers on the opposite bank beat in the helmets of those who tried to climb up with jagged clubs, or hacked their naked heads. And when the whole army was annihilated, and the spoils were gathered, it was found there were princes and lords in incredible numbers, and four thousand golden spurs to mark the extent of the knightly slaughter."

The spirit of patriotism, displayed at this period by the

free-born sons of industry, is still more conspicuous in the splendid story of the *Swiss War of Independence.*

It must be at once confessed that the story of the Swiss hero, **William Tell**, is fabulous; but it is instructive as setting forth, with great vividness, the tyranny of the bailiffs appointed by Albert, Duke of Austria, and the brave patriotic spirit that kindled the hearts of the Swiss mountaineers.

The romantic story is thus told: Gessler, an Austrian bailiff, ordered the Swiss to make obeisance as they came within sight of the ducal hat of Austria, which he had set upon a pole in the market-place of Altorf. Tell, chancing to arrive the next morning at this town, was surprised to see the people of Altorf bowing in respectful silence, as they passed near the pole. The governor's spies, having observed a stranger standing erect before the symbol of authority, brought him before Gessler, who doomed him to die unless he could shoot an arrow so as to pierce an apple placed on his son's head. The son, encouraging his father to try his skill, stood motionless with an apple on his head. The father, in an agony of fear, drew his bow, and the arrow cleft the apple to the core. Before the shouts of applause had died away in that old market-place, the voice of the governor was heard demanding, in tones of anger, "Why hast thou that second arrow in thy girdle?" "That second shaft," replied Tell, "was to pierce thy heart, tyrant, if I had chanced to harm my son." Leaving the pleasant fields of fiction, we will resume our march along the highway of historic truth.

Albert of Austria having threatened the liberty of the Swiss, there stood forth as the deliverers of their country, Stauffacher of Schwitz, Furst of Uri, and Melchthal of Underwald, under whose leadership their respective cantons unanimously took up arms and expelled their oppressors (A.D. 1308).

In 1315 Leopold of Austria determined to punish the confederate cantons that had rebelled against his father. The Swiss posted their small army at Morgarten, in the Canton of Schwitz. The duke is said to have ostentatiously displayed, on his march to the field of battle, an extensive supply of rope wherewith to hang the chiefs of the rebels. Early on a November morning, some thousands of iron-clad Austrian knights slowly ascended the hill on which the Swiss were stationed. Wrapt in a thick mist, and sheltered by huge rocks, a band of desperate Schwitzers posted themselves just above the road by which the Austrians must pass; and, at the right moment, precipitated vast fragments of rocks from the overhanging cliffs, and threw the close-packed ranks into wild disorder. Down from the neighbouring heights rushed the mountaineers, and with halbert and iron-headed club, spread dismay and death through the crowded ranks of their foes, who, jammed in between the rocks, could neither fight nor flee. Leopold himself contrived to escape, but the flower of his chivalry perished on the rugged heights of Morgarten. The men of Schwitz, from the conspicuous part they played in this action, had the honour of giving the name of their canton to the whole country, known in ancient times as Helvetia. By the victory of Morgarten was laid the foundation of Swiss independence.

But many a victory had to be gained before their task was done, and right nobly it was achieved at last. The steadiness of the Swiss in the field of battle is almost without a parallel. It was even established as a law, that whoever returned from battle after a defeat should forfeit his life by the hands of the executioner. At the famous battle of Sempach (A.D. 1385), the Swiss sealed their right to independence as a nation. On that day 1400 mountain shepherds went out to meet 9000 Austrian men-at-arms, who stood in close array with levelled spears. The Swiss were falling fast before the bristling wall of steel, when **Arnold of Winkelried,** commending his wife and children to his countrymen, threw himself with open arms upon the Austrian spears, and, collecting as many as he could grasp, buried them in his prostrate body. Through the breach thus made his companions leaped, and ere long the victory was theirs, and Switzerland was free.

PROGRESS OF CIVILIZATION.

Crossing the Alps from Switzerland, the home of liberty, we come into Italy, renowned at this period as the birthplace of modern learning. In 1300, Dante began his famous poem, *the Divine Comedy*, a vision of the invisible world; and by its publication, a few years later, gave a fresh impulse to literature. As Dante is the father of Italian poetry, so is Chaucer, who flourished half a century later, the father of English poetry. Meanwhile, a revival of classical learning was taking place in Italy, which gradually extended to the countries of the West. The merit of this revival is due principally to two Italians, named Boccaccio and Petrarch. Their chief care was devoted to the preservation and collection of ancient manuscripts; for as printing had not yet been invented, the stores of classical learning were in danger of perishing from neglect and the ravages of time. Their next care was to multiply these manuscripts so as to bring them within reach of the student. Under their fostering hand the copying of manuscripts grew into a flourishing branch of trade.

Several inventions, or perhaps importations from the remote East, accelerated the progress of Europeans in learning and the arts about this time. The art of making *paper* from linen rags was introduced into Europe about the middle of the fourteenth century; the first great factory of linen-paper of which we have any certain account was established at Nuremberg (A.D. 1390). Before the manufacture of paper, manuscripts had to be copied on parchment, a material incomparably scarcer and dearer.

This invention was but the prelude to one still more important, that of *printing* from movable types. Solid blocks of wood, graven with pictures and legends, were used in China from a remote period. They were first used in Europe for the manufacture of playing cards. The card manufacturers in the fourteenth century began to publish woodcuts of remarkable persons, accompanied with brief descriptions graven on the block. The great improvement of having movable types is probably due to John Gutenberg of Mentz (A.D. 1436), who is said to have established at Strasburg the first printing press known in Europe.

Scarcely less powerful in its influence upon the destinies of the human race was the invention of *gunpowder*. Roger Bacon, in the thirteenth century, described the composition of gunpowder; but it was not employed in warfare until the next century, being first used by the Moors at the siege of Baza, in Spain (A.D. 1312). Gunpowder was at first used for heavy cannons; it was not until late in the fifteenth century that portable guns began to be used by soldiers.

Another great invention, *the mariner's compass*, became generally known to Europeans in the fourteenth century, but there is no distinct proof of its employment in navigation till A.D. 1403. The polarity of the magnet was, indeed, known to the Chinese many centuries before the Christian era, but it is uncertain when they first used the magnetic needle as a guide to sailors.

PROGRESS OF COMMERCE.

The crusades gave a great impulse to commerce, which the maritime cities of Italy were the first to profit by. The ships of Venice, Genoa, and Pisa transported the Crusaders to Palestine, and supplied them with provisions and munitions of war. The vessels returned home laden with spices and other articles of Oriental luxury, and thus a profitable trade sprung up between the nations of the East and West. At the conclusion of the crusades, Genoa was left in sole command of the trade of the Black Sea, whilst Venice, by her alliance with the Sultan of Egypt, enjoyed the monopoly of the trade with India and other Asiatic countries, and thus Venice became the great emporium of silks, spices, and jewels. Italian merchants, commonly called Lombards, carried these goods to the northern and western kingdoms of Europe; and the wealth they thus acquired enabled them to become the chief bankers and money-lenders in Europe, and to this day the pawnbrokers exhibit the arms of Lombardy, consisting of three balls, as their sign.

In the fourteenth century the Flemish cities and the Hanse towns of Germany became the seats of commercial activity. The free cities of Germany formed a confederacy, called *the Hanseatic league*, for the protection of their trade from pirates and robbers, and to guard the privileges to which they were entitled by their charters. The chief centre of the confederacy was Lubeck. The league had four principal factories or trading-stations in foreign parts, at Bruges, London, Bergen, and Novogorod. Through the Flemings the Hanse towns were brought into connection with the commercial cities of Italy; the merchants met in the markets and fairs of Bruges, and there the homely but useful produce of the Baltic was exchanged for the costly merchandise of India. This opening of a northern market powerfully accelerated the growth of our own commercial activity, especially after the woollen manufacture had begun to thrive under the wise policy of Edward III., who encouraged the Flemish weavers to settle in England, and teach his subjects their art. The merchants of London and Bristol were soon able to vie in luxury and wealth with the richest nobles of the land, and to lend large sums of money to the king when the national treasury was exhausted.

CHAPTER XIV.

MONGOLS, TURKS, AND MOORS.

In this chapter we propose to pass in review the victorious career of the Mongols in Asia; the success of the Turkish arms in Europe, culminating in the capture of Constantinople; and the expulsion of the Moors from Spain. The history of the Mongols centres round two conquerors of renown, named Zingis Khan and Tamerlane.

ZINGIS KHAN.

The Mongols, who still occupy the territory northward of the great wall of China, are, like the Turks, a race of Tartars. Early in the 13th century a Mongol, who acquired the title of **Zingis**, *the most great*, united all the Tartar tribes of Central Asia under his sceptre. This result was only achieved by a series of great victories and still greater cruelties. After his first victory, over the hordes who had owned his father's sway but refused obedience to himself, he ordered seventy caldrons to be placed on the fire, and seventy of the foremost rebels to be cast headlong into the boiling water. Having become the despot of all the Tartar hordes that pitched their tents between the Caspian Sea and the wall of China, he led his forces against the civilised countries of Asia. His victorious army entered the royal city of Pekin, and five Chinese provinces were annexed to his empire. The rich and populous countries between the Caspian and the Indus were next overrun by his destructive hordes. It is thought that they committed more ravages in four years than were repaired in the next four centuries. If Attila the Hun was *the scourge of God* in Europe, Zingis the Mongol is equally deserving of the same title in Asia. Zingis died in 1227, with his last breath exhorting his sons to complete the conquest of China.

After another half century has elapsed, we find his grandson, Cublai, has accomplished the dread conqueror's dying injunction. Meanwhile, another grandson, named Holagou, extinguished the rule of the caliphs of Bagdad. That city was stormed and sacked by the Mongols; and their savage commander pronounced the death of Mostasem, the last of the temporal successors of Mohammed (A.D. 1258). He also so shook the throne of the Sultan of Iconium that the Seljukian dynasty did not long survive his violent treatment. Under another grandson of Zingis, named Batou, the Mongols overran Russia, and established their dominion in that country. They even advanced as far as the Baltic, and, in the battle of Lignitz, defeated the dukes of Silesia and the princes of Poland, filling nine sacks with the right ears of the slain.

The decline of the Mongol empire was as rapid as its rise; 140 years after the death of Zingis his degenerate race was expelled by the native Chinese, and the Mongol emperors were lost in the oblivion of the desert. This rapid decadence of the Mongol power gave free scope to the growth of the Ottoman empire.

THE OTTOMAN TURKS.

The Ottomans, who still reign at Constantinople, derive their name from Othman, whose father was a soldier and subject of Aladin, one of the Seljuk sultans of Iconium. In the year 1299, Othman invaded the Greek territory of Asia Minor, but the progress of his arms was slow. His son Orchan, however, profiting by the civil wars of the Greek claimants to the throne of Constantinople, achieved, almost without resistance, the conquest of Bithynia as far as the shores of the Bosphorus and the Hellespont (A.D. 1339). Soon afterwards his aid was implored by Cantacuzene, regent of the Greek empire. Orchan married a daughter of the regent, placed his father-in-law on the throne of Constantinople, and transported into Europe

10,000 horse, under his son Soliman, for the service of the new emperor. The Turks having obtained a footing in Europe never again withdrew; but a century had yet to elapse before they could enter Constantinople as conquerors.

The chief instrument in the hands of the Turks for their conquests in Europe was derived from the Europeans themselves. The Turks, respecting at first the territory of their ally, the Greek emperor, made war on all the Sclavonian nations between the Danube and the Adriatic, and selected the stoutest and handsomest of the captive youth for service in their own army. Many thousand were educated in the religion and arms of their Turkish masters; and the new militia was consecrated by a venerable dervish (a kind of Mohammedan monk). Standing in front of their ranks, he stretched the sleeve of his gown over the head of the foremost soldier, and his blessing was delivered in these words: "Let them be called *Janizaries* (or new soldiers); may their countenance be ever bright! their hand victorious! their sword keen! may their spear always hang over the head of their enemies; and wheresoever they go may they return with a *white face*," *i.e.*, with honour unsullied. Such was the origin of those haughty troops, the terror of Europe, and sometimes of the sultans themselves. Their ranks were replenished year after year by the capture of Christian youths. At the time of their institution they possessed a decisive superiority in war, since a standing body of infantry, in constant exercise and regular pay, was not maintained by any of the princes of Christendom.

The Turks did not long regard the Greek territory as exempt from their arms; by the end of the fourteenth century little remained to the Greek emperor but his capital. The first prince of the Ottoman dynasty to assume the title of sultan was **Bajazet**, and his reign (A.D. 1389–1403) brought the Greek empire to the verge of ruin. The character of Bajazet is strongly expressed in his surname of *Ilderim*, or the lightning. He had to contend against a combination of European princes. In the battle of Nicopolis (A.D. 1396), Bajazet defeated a confederate army of 100,000 Christians, under the standard of Sigismund, king of Hungary. In the confidence of their strength and the justice of their cause, they had declared that if the sky should fall they could uphold it with their lances. They suffered, however, a total defeat, the far greater part being slain or driven into the Danube.

The victorious sultan now set his heart on Constantinople, the queen of the East, and he would certainly have crowned his conquests by its capture had he not been overthrown by an Asiatic conqueror stronger than himself. By the victory of Timour, or Tamerlane, over Bajazet, the fall of Constantinople was delayed about fifty years.

TIMOUR OR TAMERLANE.

The glory of the Mongol name was revived by the great **Timour**, who, although a Turk by birth, claimed to be the representative of the Mongol Khans. Timour was born forty miles to the south of Samarcand, in Transoxiana (*i.e.*, the country across the Oxus). When Transoxiana was invaded by the Khan of Cashgar with an army of Calmucks, Timour stood forth as the deliverer of his country; and at length was invested with imperial command (A.D. 1370). Timour now aspired to the sovereignty of the world, and before his death he extended his dominion over the greater part of Asia. His most important conquest was that of Hindostan, undertaken in A.D. 1398. Timour crossed the Indus and successively traversed, in the footsteps of Alexander the Great, the *Punjab*, or five rivers that fall into the master stream; and stood in arms before the gates of the great city of Delhi, which had flourished for three centuries under Mohammedan rule. The sultan Mahmoud, despising the apparently meagre forces of his enemy, left the protection of the walls of Delhi, and drew out his army for battle. Timour gained an easy victory, and made his triumphal entry into the city. He then carried his victorious arms as far as the Ganges; but left the conquest of the entire peninsula to his successors. Baber and the "Great Moguls," who succeeded him, established their throne at Delhi, which became under them the capital of all India.

Recrossing the Indus and returning to Samarcand, his capital, Timour organised an army for the conquest of Western Asia, and for the humiliation of his rival, Bajazet. Timour defeated the Mamelukes in Syria, took Aleppo and Damascus, which he reduced to ashes, and on the ruins of Bagdad erected a pyramid of 90,000 human heads; for this sanguinary monster was accustomed to have the bleeding heads of his victims curiously piled in columns and pyramids, as monuments of his power. Then with a prodigious army he marched against the Ottoman sultan, who was advancing to meet his antagonist with 400,000 men. Timour, intent on encountering the sultan in the heart of the Ottoman kingdom, avoided his camp, traversed the salt desert and the river Halys, and invested Angora; whilst *Ilderim*, ignorant of the movements of his enemy, compared the Tartar swiftness to the crawling of a snail. On hearing of the siege of Angora, Bajazet returned on the wings of indignation to the relief of that town. A memorable battle was fought (A.D. 1402) in the plains of Angora, which has immortalised the fame of Timour and the misfortunes of Bajazet. Bajazet, on the irretrievable defeat of his troops, fled from the field on the fleetest of his horses. But he afterwards fell into the hands of his conqueror, who is said to have confined him in an iron cage, and to have exposed him in his passage from city to city to the mockery of the inhabitants.

This great victory gave Timour possession of Western Asia. Europe was saved from his arms by the narrow sea that rolls between it and Asia. The two passages of this sea, the one at Constantinople, the other at Gallipoli, were in the hands of the Greeks and Turks respectively. In the presence of their common foe, they forgot their own enmity, and neither the threats nor the promises of the great conqueror could prevail upon either of them to lend him a single vessel.

Foiled in his design upon Europe, Timour resolved on the conquest of China, and he returned to Samarcand to make preparations for that great enterprise. Neither age nor the severity of the winter could retard the impatience of Timour; he mounted on horseback, passed the Sihoon or Jaxartes on the ice, marched 300 miles from his capital, and was then overtaken by the messenger of death. Fatigue, and the indiscreet use of iced water, accelerated the progress of his fever, and the conqueror of Asia expired in the seventieth year of his age. On his death his armies were disbanded, and his empire dissolved.

CAPTURE OF CONSTANTINOPLE.

The fall of Constantinople was only deferred by the defeat of Bajazet. After the death of Timour the Ottoman monarchy began to flourish with fresh vigour, whilst the Byzantine empire continued to decline, from the folly and religious discord of the Greeks. The only hope of escaping destruction lay in the union of the Greeks and Latins; but every attempt made to bind in one communion the Christians of the East and West ended in failure. Meanwhile, the Turks were being welded into one compact nation by the virtues and wisdom of their sultans. To Amurath II., who reigned for thirty years (A.D. 1421-51) just previous to the taking of Constantinople, the Turks are especially indebted for their ultimate success.

The Greeks, however, in their distress were not wholly abandoned by the Christian nations. In 1444, the Pope Eugenius IV. called upon the Latins to take up arms in defence of their brethren in the East. The Hungarians and Poles readily responded to the call of the pontiff, but his appeal was coldly received by the great nations of the West. The crowns of Hungary and Poland were at that time united on the head of Ladislaus, a young and ambitious soldier, who acted under the guidance of a celebrated warrior named Huniades. Many brave knights of France and Germany enlisted under the banner of Ladislaus. The cause of the Greeks was also espoused by Philip of Burgundy, who sent a gallant fleet from the coast of Flanders to the Hellespont, where it was joined by the fleets of Venice and Genoa.

It was hoped that Ladislaus would successfully attack the Turks on land, whilst the allied fleets cut off all intercourse with their friends in Asia. The Turks were defeated in two great battles by the valour and conduct of Huniades. But when the victorious army advanced along the shores of the Black Sea, in the expectation of finding a confederate fleet to second their operations, they were alarmed by the approach of Amurath himself, who had contrived to transport his forces from Asia through the mercenary treachery of the Genoese. A disastrous battle ensued, near Varna, which is memorable for the defeat and death of the brave Ladislaus. The king, having resolved to conquer or die, rushed forward till his career was stopped by the impenetrable phalanx of the Janizaries. His horse was pierced by the javelin of Amurath; he fell among the spears of the infantry; and a Turkish soldier proclaimed with a loud voice, "Hungarians, behold the head of your king!" One half of the army fell around him; and the Turkish ranks were so thinned, that Amurath confessed that a second and similar victory would be his ruin.

Before the Hungarian invasion, Amurath had resigned his sceptre to his young son; but the public danger drew him from his retirement, and placed him again on the throne. After the victory of Varna he again resigned the crown, but the rebellious spirit of the Janizaries again drew the reluctant sultan from his place of repose. Several princes have voluntarily descended the steps of the throne, but Amurath alone has repeated the choice of a private life. After twice divesting himself of the royal robes, he was constrained from a patriotic motive to wear them till his death (A.D. 1451); and by that time his son, Mohammed II., was old enough to wield his sceptre. The last emperor of Constantinople was now on the throne, bearing the name of the founder of the city.

On the succession of Mohammed, Constantine's ambassadors were assured of the sultan's goodwill towards their master; but while peace was on his lips, war was in his heart, and he had secretly sworn to obtain possession of Constantinople. In the spring of 1453, the siege began. The Turks assembled a large army for the work; Constantinople in her decay numbered only 100,000 inhabitants, and could only muster 7000 soldiers for her defence. Yet such was the strength of the fortifications and the natural situation of the place, that the reduction of the city appeared to be hopeless, unless a double attack could be made upon it—from the harbour as well as from the land. As the mouth of the harbour was inaccessible, Mohammed transported by land a large fleet of small vessels, and launched them in the higher part of the harbour, where the water was too shallow for the larger vessels of the Greeks to sail.

After a siege of forty days the fate of Constantinople could no longer be averted. The diminutive garrison was exhausted by the double attack. The fortifications which had so often resisted an enemy with success, were dismantled on all sides by the cannons, which had now become formidable engines of war. Mohammed, after consulting his astrologers, fixed on the 29th of May as the fortunate and fatal day for the assault. For two hours the Greeks kept the Turks at bay, and then the Janizaries arose fresh, vigorous, and invincible. Constantine cast away the purple, and amid the tumult that followed, he fell by an unknown hand, and his body was buried under a mountain of the slain.

On the same day the conqueror entered the city in triumph. At the principal door of St. Sophia he alighted from his horse and entered the dome. By his command this magnificent cathedral was turned into a mosque, and on the ensuing Friday the *muezin*, or crier, ascended the most lofty turret and invited "the faithful" to prayer. The other churches were shared between the two religions; and for the next sixty years the Greeks enjoyed the benefit of this equal partition.

THE MOORS IN SPAIN.

Whilst the Turks and their religion were taking root in the *east* of Europe, a very different fortune awaited the Mohammedans in the *west*. Whilst the Turks were founding a Moslem kingdom on the ruins of the Greek empire, the Moors (as the Mohammedans of Spain were termed) were fast losing every acre of ground they held in Europe. The triumph of the Crescent in the East was succeeded by that of the Cross in the West. The loss of Constantinople was in a great measure counterbalanced by the capture of Granada, the Moorish capital, by the Spaniards about forty years later.

When the Moors conquered Spain, in the eighth century, there was one little district in the north-west among the mountains of Asturias that remained free. In that remote corner of Spain a little Christian kingdom was founded, which was destined to grow and multiply, and gradually to elbow the Moors into a confined territory around Granada, and finally to expel them altogether from the peninsula. In the eleventh century we find four Christian kingdoms in Spain—Leon, Castile, Navarre, and Aragon. These kingdoms, originally small and weak, gradually extended themselves, till, in the middle of the eleventh century, a line drawn from the mouth of the Ebro to that of the Douro, would divide Christian Spain in the north from Moslem Spain in the south. In the twelfth century another Christian kingdom was established in the peninsula. Originally Portugal was a province of Castile; it dates as an independent state from the year 1139, when Alfonso, the governor of Portugal, gained a glorious victory over the Moors, and thereby much extended his territory. His soldiers proclaimed him king on the battle-field.

In 1236, the Moorish king was obliged to surrender Cordova, the ancient capital, and to retire within much narrower limits, with Granada as the seat of government. Twelve years later he was obliged to acknowledge himself a vassal of the king of Castile. A long series of battles and sieges, extending over the next two centuries, left Moors and Christians in the same relative position. At length, by the union of the crowns of Castile and Aragon, the Spaniards became strong enough to overthrow the Moorish kingdom. The two crowns were united in 1479, when Ferdinand, who had previously married Isabella, Queen of Castile, ascended the throne of Aragon. Nearly all Spain was now under the united sway of these two able sovereigns. Their first great design was to annex the kingdom of Granada to their dominions.

"The city of Granada," says Washington Irving, "lay in the centre of the (Moorish) kingdom, sheltered, as it were, in the lap of Sierra Nevada, or chain of snowy mountains. It covered two lofty hills, and a deep valley that divides them. One of these hills was crowned by the royal palace and fortress of the Alhambra, capable of containing 40,000 men within its walls and towers. Never was there an edifice accomplished in a superior style of barbaric magnificence; and the stranger who, even at the present day, wanders among its silent and deserted courts and ruined halls, gazes with astonishment at its gilded and fretted domes and luxurious decorations, still retaining their brilliancy and beauty in defiance of the ravages of time." The glory of the city, however, was its vega or plain, forming a vast garden of delight, refreshed by the silver windings of the Xenil and its thousand rills. "In a word, so beautiful was the earth, so pure the air, and so serene the sky of this delicious region, that the Moors imagined the Paradise of their prophet to be situate in that part of the heaven which overhung the kingdom of Granada."

When Ferdinand and Isabel came to the throne, they sent to demand the arrears of tribute due by Muley Hassan, King of Granada, to the Castilian crown. "Tell your sovereigns," was the haughty reply, "that the kings of Granada who used to pay tribute in money to the Castilian monarch are dead. Our mint at present coins nothing but blades of scimitars and heads of lances."

"I will pick out," said Ferdinand, "the seeds of their pomegranate one by one" (*Granada* being the Spanish for *pomegranate*). The strong and wealthy town of Alhama, situated within a few leagues of the capital, was the first seed picked out. Town after town was taken, and victory after victory was won by the Spaniards. The old Moorish towers and castles, that for ages had frowned defiance to the battering-rams and catapults of the ancients, were toppled down by the modern artillery of the Spanish engineers.

At length, the time had come for picking out the last seed of the pomegranate. Abdallah, the last Moorish King of Spain, was obliged to surrender his capital on honourable terms after sustaining a siege of eight months (A.D. 1491). On the same day that the Spanish sovereigns entered Granada, the fallen monarch quitted it. On reaching the crest of the hill from which the last glimpse of the city could be obtained, the heart of Abdallah melted into tears. "Allah Achbar!" (God is great!) he could say no more for grief. His mother reproached him for his weakness: "You do well," said she, "to weep like a woman for what you failed to defend like a man." The unhappy monarch could only reply, "Allah Achbar!" The rocky height from which the Moorish king took his sad farewell of the princely abodes of his youth, is commemorated by the poetic title of *El ultimo sospiro del Moro*, "The last sigh of the Moor." Abdallah soon afterwards passed over into Africa, and fell in battle in the service of an African prince, his kinsman.

CHAPTER XV.

DISCOVERY AND CONQUEST OF AMERICA.

To the Portuguese belongs the glory of leading the way in the discovery of new lands. It was their success on the coast of Africa that kindled the spirit of curiosity and enterprise, which led to the discovery of the New World.

John I., who became King of Portugal in 1411, sent out a fleet which proceeded 160 miles beyond Cape Non, so called from the idea that it was the utmost limit of navigation. The Portuguese sailors in successive voyages gradually grew bolder, and ventured farther and farther from the coast. The Madeira islands were their first important acquisition; in a short time the sugar and wine of Madeira were a source of wealth to the merchants of Portugal. Before the middle of the fifteenth century the Portuguese had reached Cape Verde, and seen men with skins as black as ebony. Some of the sailors began to fear that if they advanced still further south, the heat of the torrid zone would scorch their skin and make it equally black. On venturing at length to sail still nearer the equator, to their astonishment they found a region, not only habitable, but populous and fertile. The coast of Guinea they found rich in ivory, gold, and rich gems. By this discovery commerce was enlarged, and by the prospect of gain an eager spirit of adventure was kindled.

John II., who was now King of Portugal (A.D. 1481), encouraged his subjects to settle on the "Gold Coast," and aided them materially in pursuing still farther the path of discovery. It occurred to his sagacious mind that India could be reached by following the coast of

Africa. He accordingly fitted out a squadron of ships with this design, and intrusted the command to Bartholomew Diaz. Diaz advanced 1000 miles farther south than any former navigator, and at last descried the lofty promontory which forms the southern extremity of Africa (A.D. 1483). But the violence of the winds, and the mutinous spirit of the sailors, compelled him to turn his crazy vessels homeward. Diaz had called the promontory which terminated his voyage the *Stormy Cape;* but the king, who believed that the long-desired route to India was now found, named it the *Cape of Good Hope.* Fifteen years had yet to elapse ere Vasco de Gama, having rounded that cape, reached India, and anchored in the harbour of Calicut (A.D. 1498). In the meantime, the New World had been discovered by

CHRISTOPHER COLUMBUS.

This extraordinary man was born at Genoa, about the year 1436. When at school he acquired some knowledge of the mathematical sciences, in which he afterwards excelled. In the early years of his manhood he was a bold adventurous mariner, spending his leisure hours in drawing charts and maps. He became convinced that, as the world was round, India might be reached by sailing westward across the Atlantic. Many years of anxiety and bitter disappointment passed away, before he could prevail upon any prince to give him the means of making this grand experiment. At length, in the winter of 1491, he was summoned to the court of Ferdinand and Isabella, who were at that time superintending the siege of Granada. Columbus arrived in time to witness the memorable surrender of that city to the king and queen, who now felt themselves at liberty to forward his great design. By their aid, Columbus was enabled to equip three small vessels, named Santa Maria, Pinta, and Nina. Columbus, with the title of admiral, hoisted his flag on board the Santa Maria, and set sail from the little port of Palos, a little before sunrise, in presence of a vast crowd of spectators (Aug. 3, 1492).

Columbus steered direct for the Canary Islands, and there he refitted his crazy and ill-appointed vessels, and thence set sail on his voyage of discovery (Sept. 6). On the second day he lost sight of the Canaries, and then commenced his troubles, chiefly arising from the dismay and terror of his sailors on seeing nothing but the sea around them. By steering steadily westward he came within the sphere of the trade-wind, which blows invariably from east to west within the tropics. He advanced before this steady gale with such rapidity, that it was seldom necessary to shift a sail. But the greater the progress of the ships, the greater the alarm of the sailors. On the 1st of October, after they had been three weeks at sea, they were 770 leagues to the west of the Canaries, and still no land was visible. The terrified sailors began to murmur audibly, and some of the more daring proposed to their comrades to throw the admiral overboard and return to Spain. But still their undaunted chief held on his course. At length, when more than thirty days had passed, and still nothing could be seen but the sea and the sky, Columbus was obliged to promise his men that, if in three days longer land was not discovered, he would tack about and return to Europe. Many signs of approaching land, soon after this, gave even the most despondent fresh hope. On the evening of the 11th of October, after public prayers for success, Columbus, being convinced that land was near, ordered the sails to be furled and strict watch to be kept, lest they should be driven ashore before morning. During that night of expectation all kept on deck with eyes intently gazing westward. A little after midnight, the joyful cry of "land! land!" was heard from the Pinta. Agonising was the suspense, until the morning light revealed an island, with verdant meadows interspersed with trees. The voices of the sailors singing the *Te Deum*, as a hymn of thanksgiving to God, now swept across the still waters to the silent shore. The sailors then threw themselves at the feet of Columbus, imploring his pardon and extolling his greatness.

As soon as the sun rose all the boats were manned and armed. The men soon reached the shore, which they found crowded with wondering spectators. Columbus, dressed in gay scarlet, leapt ashore with the banner of Spain in one hand, and a naked sword in the other. In a few moments a crucifix was erected, and every Spaniard, falling prostrate before it, returned thanks to God for their prosperous voyage. The simple natives gazed with admiration upon the strangers, whom they regarded as a superior order of beings, descended from the sun. Their bodies were naked, and their skin of a dusky copper colour. They were shy at first through fear, but soon became familiar with the Spaniards; and with transports of joy received from them hawk's bells, glass beads, and other baubles. Columbus was not aware that he had found a new continent, but supposed he had come upon the eastern extremity of Asia, and probably upon some islands lying off India. He had really landed upon one of the Bahama Islands. In consequence of this mistake the islands he had discovered were called the Indies, and the natives were spoken of as Indians. Cruising among the islands, which have ever since retained the name of the West Indies, the Spaniards discovered Cuba and Hayti, or Hispaniola. Columbus was in ecstasy on beholding the beautiful scenery of Hayti. "Tongue," he says, "cannot express the whole truth, nor pen describe it; and I have been so overwhelmed with the sight of so much beauty, that I have not known how to describe it."

A great misfortune soon afterwards befell Columbus. Whilst he was asleep, his ship struck a rock and soon became a wreck. He had for some time lost sight of the Pinta, and as the Nina was not large enough to take all back to Spain, he resolved to build a fortress on the island of Hayti, and leave some of his men there. Before setting sail for Spain he contrived to get a considerable quantity of gold from the natives in exchange for hawk's bells and other trinkets, and also took on board some of the natives and specimens of the productions of the islands.

After a perilous voyage, Columbus reached Palos on the 15th of March, 1493, about seven months after his departure from it; and to complete the joy of the inhabitants in the evening of the same day, the missing Pinta entered the harbour. The strange news soon travelled all over Spain, and from every steeple a joyous peal was sent forth in honour of the glorious event. Columbus hastened to Barcelona to present himself before his royal patrons. The king and queen, encircled by a brilliant court, awaited his arrival on the appointed day. On his approach they rose from their seats, and bestowed on him the rare honour of a seat in their presence. When the great discoverer had finished the recital of his adventures, the whole assembly fell on their knees in gratitude to God, whilst the solemn strains of the *Te Deum* from the choir of the Chapel Royal resounded through the hall.

Columbus after this made three voyages to the New World, but his subsequent career was marked by misfortune and disappointment. The Spaniards who accompanied him as colonists to the West Indies, were for the most part mere lawless adventurers in quest of gold; and as their golden dreams were only partially realised, they charged the great navigator with deceiving them, and by their cruelty towards the natives brought on a sanguinary war. Ferdinand, on receiving complaints respecting his viceroy, sent out Bovadilla, as commissioner, to investigate his conduct. This officer, on his arrival, put Columbus in irons and sent him back to Spain. Bovadilla alone seems responsible for this outrage, for when it was known in Spain, the whole nation, including the king and queen, kindled with indignation at this act of injustice and ingratitude. These irons Columbus afterwards preserved as relics, and ordered them to be buried in his grave.

After making a fourth and last voyage of discovery, Columbus sank into obscurity and neglect, and ended his days in poverty at Valladolid (A.D. 1506). The real character of the discovery made by Columbus was not known until years after his death. When at length it was discovered to be a new continent, having no connection with Asia, instead of being called after Columbus, it derived its name from Amerigo Vespuccio, a Florentine gentleman, who visited the southern part, and gave his name to the countries that he depicted on his map.

CONQUEST OF MEXICO.

Columbus had opened the door of a New World to the Spaniards, and left them on the threshold. They continued to make such progress in exploring its unknown regions, that, at the end of twelve years from his death, they had sailed along the eastern coast of America from Florida to the Rio de la Plata. They had also crossed the isthmus of Panama, and stood on the shores of the great Southern Ocean. Meanwhile, the English had sailed along the coast of North America from Labrador to Florida.

The natives of America were for the most part in a state of primeval simplicity; there were only two nations, namely, Mexico and Peru, that had emerged from the rude ignorance of barbarism. These two nations, fortunately for themselves, remained unknown to Europeans twenty-six years from the discovery of America. Mexico was the first to fall a prey to the bold unscrupulous Spaniards, who had crossed the Atlantic in quest of fame and fortune.

In April, 1518, Velasquez, the governor of Cuba, planned an expedition for the conquest of Mexico, and placed it under the command of **Hernando Cortes**, a Spanish hidalgo, or gentleman, residing in the island. The desire of planting the cross in heathen lands, and the lust of gold, seem to have been the two chief motives which prompted the Spaniards to all their enterprises in the New World. Cortes under this double influence succeeded in attracting about 400 adventurers to his standard. "Nothing was now to be seen, or spoken of, but selling lands to purchase arms and horses, quilting coats of mail, making biscuits, and salting pork for sea-store." Cortes, being in danger of losing his command through the jealousy of Velasquez, set sail with all speed, his own ship carrying at the mast-head a standard of gold and velvet, on which were embroidered the royal arms of Spain, and a cross with a Latin motto bearing this meaning, "Brothers, follow this holy cross with true faith, for under it we shall conquer." Nothing is more surprising in the history of the world than the deeds of blood and cruelty, committed under the cloak of religion, and in the name of the Prince of Peace. According to the notions of the age, it seemed right to Cortes and his freebooters to take by any means, fair or foul, the property and lands of the heathen. But, in truth, they were entering upon a most unjust and merciless war of aggression, in which Might was the only measure of Right.

Cortes landed with his troops near the site of the modern Vera Cruz (April 1519), and astonished the natives with the sight of his horses and the sound of his guns, both of which were equally new and terrible to them. Cortes had an interview with the Mexican governor of the district, and required him to inform Montezuma, the king, that the white men who had landed on his coast desired to come and see him in his capital. Though the capital was 180 miles distant, yet in a few days magnificent presents arrived from the king; cotton stuffs of delicate texture, pictures of natural objects formed with feathers of different colours, and two large circular plates, one of massive gold representing the sun, the other of silver, an emblem of the moon. As Cortes could not obtain the royal permission he sought, he determined to advance without it. But before setting out from his camp he laid the foundations of the town of Vera Cruz, where he left a sufficient force as a garrison to secure a place of retreat in case he needed it. And finding that a conspiracy had been formed by some of his soldiers and sailors to sieze a vessel and return to Cuba, he prevailed upon the majority of his men to render such a design for ever afterwards impracticable by the destruction of his fleet. With almost universal consent, the ships were drawn ashore, and, after being stripped of everything that might be of use, broken in pieces. By this resolute and almost unparalleled step, 500 men were shut up in a hostile country, filled with powerful and unknown nations, with no resource but their own valour and power of endurance.

Four months after disembarking, Cortes set out on his march inland. His army consisted of 400 Spaniards on foot, and 15 horse, accompanied by 1300 warriors of a friendly tribe of natives. A few days' march brought the invaders to the small mountain and province of Tlascala, situated about half-way between the sea coast and the capital. The Tlascalans were a warlike race, but after three battles they had not succeeded in killing a single Spaniard. Arrows and spears, headed with flint or fish-bone, stakes hardened in the fire, and wooden swords, though destructive weapons among native Indians, could hardly penetrate the quilted jackets which the Spaniards wore. Before beginning the combat, on their first encounter, the Tlascalans sent to the camp of their enemies a large supply of poultry and maize, desiring them to eat plentifully, "because they scorned to attack an enemy enfeebled by hunger; and it would be an affront to their gods to offer them famished victims, as well as disagreeable to themselves to feed on men in such emaciated condition." On finding their enemies invincible, they agreed to assist them in their war with Montezuma.

Resuming their march towards the capital, and descending from the mountains, they beheld the lovely plain of Mexico spread out like some gay and gorgeous panorama before them. In the centre they saw with rapturous delight a large lake, whose banks were studded with towns and hamlets, and upon an island near the middle the fair city of Mexico, with her white towers and pyramidal temples. As they approached the city their amazement increased. One of the strangest sights that attracted their attention was the *chinampas*, or floating gardens—little islands consisting of mould laid on rafts, planted with flowers, shrubs, and fruit trees, and containing a small cottage in the centre, occupied by the proprietor, who, by means of a long pole, could shift his little domain along the margin of the lake. The islet on which Mexico was built was connected with the mainland by three distinct causeways of stone, intersected at intervals by drawbridges.

As Cortes approached, ambassadors from the king invited him to enter his capital, and on arriving at the gate of the city he was met by the monarch himself, seated on a palanquin, blazing with burnished gold, under a canopy of gaudy feather-work, powdered with jewels, and fringed with silver. The Mexican monarch resembled an Oriental despot, and in the eyes of his subjects was almost a divine being. His nobles entered his apartment barefooted, their eyes fixed on the ground, and making three bows on approaching his seat, they addressed him as, "Lord, my lord, great lord."

The Spaniards were conducted to their quarters, in the middle of the city, adjoining the temple of the great war-god. This temple was afterwards visited by Cortes and his companions: arrived at the summit of the tower, they shuddered at the sight of a block of jasper, on which, they were told, human victims were laid when the priests tore out their hearts, as an offering to the gods. And before the idol of the war-god they saw a pan of incense, with five human hearts burning. "The priests," we are told, "were dressed in long black mantles, like sheets with hoods. Their long hair was matted together with clotted blood; their ears were slit, and they smelt horribly, as it were of sulphur and putrid flesh."

The further fortunes of the Spaniards must be told in few words. Montezuma was seized, and kept as a prisoner in the Spanish quarters. Through him Cortes ruled for some months in the kingdom of Mexico. In June, 1520, the usurper received a strong reinforcement from Cuba, raising his army to 1300 men. The Aztecs, or Mexicans, driven to despair, rose in arms against the stranger in their midst, and fought with increasing energy, day after day, for a whole week. The Spaniards, fearing total destruction, attempted to leave the city under cover of the night, but as the Aztecs had taken the precaution to break down all the drawbridges, only 500 contrived to escape, with the loss of artillery, fire-arms, and ammunition.

Five months after their expulsion from Mexico, the Spaniards were again on the march towards it. In May, 1521, the siege commenced, and by the aid of famine the city was taken at the end of three months. The surviving inhabitants soon disappeared from the city, which was now in ruins, like some vast cemetery with the corpses disinterred, and the tombstones scattered about. The whole country was now lying helpless under the heel of the conqueror.

CONQUEST OF PERU.

Three years after the conquest of Mexico, a single ship, under the command of **Francisco Pizarro**, set sail from Panama, on a voyage of discovery along the west coast of South America. After a long series of disasters, Pizarro had the good fortune to discover the wealthy country of Peru (A.D. 1526). Having collected a band of ruffianly fellows, he invaded the shores of the unwarlike Peruvians, and found everywhere gold and silver in abundance, forming not merely the ornaments of the people, but in the houses of the affluent common utensils for domestic uses.

At the time of the Spanish invasion, the *inca*, or emperor, ruled over a territory extending 1500 miles along the Pacific Ocean. The incas were not only obeyed as monarchs, but almost revered as divinities. Their seat of government was Cuzco, founded, according to tradition, in the eleventh century, by Manco Capac, the first of the incas.

When Pizarro first landed, a civil strife was raging between two brothers for the crown, which enabled him to gain an easy footing in the country. The contest had just been decided in favour of Atahualpa, when Pizarro directed his march to Caxamarca, near which the inca was encamped with his victorious troops. Pizarro's force consisted of 62 horsemen, and 102 foot soldiers. Before he had proceeded far, an ambassador from the inca met him, with valuable presents and assurances of a friendly reception at Caxamarca. On entering the city, Pizarro took possession of a large court, on one side of which was the inca's palace, and on the other a temple of the sun, the whole surrounded with a strong rampart of earth. Pizarro resolved to adopt the policy of Cortes, and to seize the unsuspecting inca, when he came, according to promise, to pay the strangers a visit at Caxamarca.

The next day the monarch arrived in great state to welcome his unbidden guests to his kingdom. First appeared 400 men, as an advanced guard, in a uniform dress. The inca, sitting on a gorgeous throne, was carried on the shoulders of his principal attendants. And the whole plain was covered with troops amounting to 10,000 men. As Atahualpa drew near the Spanish quarters, a monk advanced with a crucifix in one hand, and a breviary in the other, and after explaining to the inca some of the doctrines of Christianity, he proceeded to inform him that the pope had granted all the regions of the New World to the King of Spain. The monk then graciously promised the astonished monarch, that if he would instantly become a Christian, he should rule in the name of the Spanish king. Atahualpa observed, that he did not understand how the pope could give away what did not belong to him, and that he had no intention of changing his religion. On desiring to know where the priest learned things so extraordinary, he was referred to the breviary. The inca opened it eagerly, and turning over the leaves, lifted it to his ear; "This," said he, "is silent; it tells me nothing;" and threw it with disdain to the ground. The enraged monk, turning to his countrymen, cried out, "To arms!" At once the martial music struck up, the cannon and muskets began to fire, the horse sallied out fiercely to the charge, the infantry rushed on sword in hand. The Peruvians, astonished and dismayed, fled on every side, except a small knot of nobles that gathered round their king, and sacrificed their lives in his defence. Pizarro forced his way to the royal seat, and seizing the inca by his arm, dragged him off as a prisoner to his quarters. The fate of the monarch increased the consternation of the fugitives, who were ruthlessly cut down by the pursuing Spaniards.

The royal captive, who was confined in an apartment 22 feet in length and 16 feet in breadth, offered as the price of his liberty to fill it with vessels of gold, as high as he could reach. Pizarro closed eagerly with this marvellous proposal, and a line was drawn upon the walls of the room, to mark the stipulated height to which the treasure was to rise. The king sent messengers throughout his dominions, and golden vessels continued to arrive day after day; but before the entire amount could be obtained the soldiers demanded their share of the booty, and so all, except some pieces of curious workmanship, were melted down and apportioned. The perfidious Spaniards, instead of releasing their captive, thought it more expedient to execute him, and to proclaim one of his sons as his successor.

Pizarro, having been joined by fresh forces, marched on to Cuzco, the capital. After many fierce encounters, the Spaniards forced their way into the city, and found there still greater treasures than they had already received as Atahualpa's ransom. By the capture of the capital the conquest of Peru was virtually achieved (A.D. 1533). Pizarro, not approving of Cuzco as the seat of government, laid the foundations of a new city on the river Rimac, which, under the name of *Lima*, is still the capital of Peru. So great was the discord that now arose between Pizarro and the other Spanish chiefs, that the Peruvians had the satisfaction of seeing them turn their swords against one another. At length (A.D. 1541), Pizarro was slain by conspirators, who burst into his palace during the siesta, at mid-day, crying out, "Long live the king, but let the tyrant die!"

CHAPTER XVI.

AGE OF THE REFORMATION.

THE same age that saw men eagerly bent on the discovery of new lands in America, found them also equally intent on the discovery of lost truth in religion. As the invention of the mariner's compass enabled men to search successfully for new lands, so the Bible by the invention of printing enabled men to seek out old truths, and to effect that great revolution in religious faith and discipline which is universally known as the Reformation. By that great event, as much as by all others combined, the history of European nations in the sixteenth century was shaped and its course determined.

During the Middle Ages the general ignorance that prevailed kept men's minds enslaved to a superstitious creed, and made them the easy victims of a system of spiritual tyranny, whose head and centre was the Pope of Rome. A few noble hearts had already rebelled against that system of domination, and had tried to break the fetters of superstition, long before such efforts were crowned with success.

In the fourteenth century Wickliffe appears in England, and appeals from the pope to the written Word, which he translated into his mother tongue, and thereby laid the first stone of the Reformation in England. In the time of Wickliffe a Bohemian princess became the wife of the English king, Richard II., and a considerable intercourse arose between the two countries. In this way, perhaps, the doctrines of Wickliffe appeared shortly after his death in Bohemia, where John Huss held up the lamp of truth. This brave reformer was brought to the council of Constance (A.D. 1415), and sentenced to be burnt as an obstinate heretic. Savonarola, much later in the same century, was an eloquent preacher of evangelic truth at Florence. Torture and the flame silenced also his tongue, that had so often attacked with keen-edged words the abuses of the Church (A.D. 1498).

But of all the men who prepared Christendom for a reformation, the first place, but not the chief merit, is due to **Erasmus** of Rotterdam. As a critic, he caused Scripture to be better known to scholars, by publishing (A.D. 1516) the first printed edition of the Greek Testament; and as a commentator, he caused it to be better understood. He also did good service in the cause of religion by his keen satires, in which he lashed the abuses of the Church, especially as seen in the monks and friars, as with a rod of nettles. But his name as a reformer is not entitled to much respect: "When the tug of war came, he showed that he had only been for a reformation on paper; he would detect abuses, but not correct them; he was desirous of the end, but afraid of the means; he was for the excision of the pound of flesh, but then it must be done without shedding one drop of blood." Erasmus had the light of truth, and knew how to expose error, but he lacked that fire of love, which makes a man willing to risk all for the truth's sake. Erasmus, however, served as a bridge over which many passed, when the true reformer appeared.

MARTIN LUTHER.

Martin Luther, the son of a working miner, was born at Eisleben, in Saxony (A.D. 1483). In his early manhood he took on himself the vows of an Augustan monk, and spent three years within the cloisters of Erfurt. Here he passed through a period of mental agony, bordering on despair. But by the fatherly counsel of Staupitz, the Vicar-general, and the prayerful study of the Bible, he gained peace of mind, and beheld the dayspring arising in his soul. In 1507, Luther was ordained priest, and in the next year was appointed by Frederick of Saxony to a chair in the University of Wittemberg, and here his lectures in divinity attracted pupils from distant parts. He gained still greater celebrity by his fervid eloquence as a preacher. The little wooden chapel in the convent of Wittemberg, with its little old pulpit of rough fir, soon became too small for the crowd of eager listeners. He was then invited by the council of Wittemberg to be the preacher for the city.

In 1512, Luther went to Rome on some monastic business, and while there, was shocked to find that religion was a subject of mockery with many of the priests, and that the "Eternal City" was the scene of folly, vice, and hypocrisy. The scales were gradually falling from his eyes during his abode in Rome. One day, when he was climbing up Pilate's Stair on his bare knees, as an act of penance, he was suddenly arrested by an inward voice, saying, "The just shall live by faith." When Luther left Rome, his faith in the pope and the papal system had received a rude shock, five years later it was ready to perish, and in three years more it had ceased to exist.

Pope Leo X., wishing to raise money for St. Peter's church, then in course of erection at Rome, commissioned Tetzel, a Dominican monk, to open a market in Germany for the sale of indulgences. The pope in his bull declares that those who truly obtain his indulgences are released from the total or partial punishment due to sin, whether in this world or in purgatory. Tetzel and others, charged with the sale of these indulgences, went far beyond the pope's instructions, and magnified their virtue in the most extravagant and blasphemous terms. "At the very instant," said Tetzel to the crowds that came out to buy his wares, "that the money clinks at the bottom of the strong box, the soul of your departed friend comes out of purgatory, and flies upward into heaven." There was no sin, however monstrous, which the shameless monk had not both the will and the power to remit for money. It was in vain for the German pastors to insist on penance; here was the pope's agent at hand ready to absolve from all pains and penalties for gold and silver. When news of these shameful proceedings came to Luther's ears, he exclaimed, "Please God, I'll make a hole in his drum."

Tetzel in due course came with his unholy traffic into the neighbourhood of Wittemberg. Luther from his pulpit denounced the iniquity of the sale, and then proceeded to draw up ninety-five theses, or propositions, against the doctrine of indulgences, which he nailed up on the gates of the church of Wittemberg. In these theses, Luther maintained that, unless there was real contrition on the part of the sinner, the indulgences were utterly worthless except to the seller—"nets which fish for money and delude the simple." Luther at this time had no notion that he was declaring war against the pope, but thought that he was fighting the pope's battle against the flagrant excesses of his emissaries. Scarcely had the sound of the hammer, that nailed the theses to the church door, died away, than a sound as of many waters passed over the whole of Germany, and ere a month had elapsed the muttering of the storm was heard in the papal palace. But its significance at first was not understood by the pope. "Brother Martin," quoth he, "is a man of fine genius;" and he was inclined to regard the whole matter as a battle of kites and crows. He was soon undeceived, and became alarmed on hearing of the marvellous effect produced in Germany by the bold words of truth pronounced by the courageous monk.

Luther had the good fortune to win the support of Frederick the Wise, Elector of Saxony, who had long been vexed at the vast sums drained from his subjects for the papal treasury. Frederick wrote to His Holiness, to palliate Luther's conduct, and to induce him to deal leniently with the offender. Leo was willing to try persuasion before having recourse to violent measures, and accordingly appointed Cardinal Cajetan to prevail upon Luther to retract. But in this he was unsuccessful. Luther's position was now critical. He was in the position of Huss and other reformers, who had been burnt as heretics. He had none to protect him but the elector of Saxony, who was wise and powerful indeed, but not earnest enough in the cause of truth to draw the sword to maintain it. Leo, unwilling to offend the elector, allowed nearly three years to pass without hurling against the daring reformer the papal thunderbolt.

Meanwhile, the tide of thought in Luther's mind was carrying him farther from Rome. All discussions and debates only widened the breach. The most noted of these debates took place at Leipsic, between Luther and the learned Dr. Eck. Ranke thus describes Luther's person and character at this time:—"He was of the middle size, and so thin as to be mere skin and bone. He possessed neither the thundering voice, nor the ready memory, nor the skill and dexterity of his distinguished antagonist. But he stood in the prime of manhood and in the fulness of his strength. His voice was melodious and clear, he was perfectly versed in the Bible, and its aptest sentences presented themselves unbidden to his mind; above all, he inspired an irresistible conviction that he sought the truth. He was always cheerful at home, and a joyous, jocose companion at table; even on this grave occasion, he ascended the platform with a nosegay in his hand; but, when there, he displayed intrepid and self-forgetting earnestness, arising from the depth of a conviction until now unfathomed, even by himself." The chief fruit of this disputation in the Reformer's mind was the clear perception of this important principle — that the Scriptures are the only ultimate grounds of authority in religion.

The patience of the pope was, at length, exhausted. On the 15th June, 1520, he issued his damnatory bull excommunicating Luther, delivering him over to Satan, requiring the secular princes to apprehend him, and condemning his books to be burned. Luther, nothing dismayed, on the 11th December of the same year, returns measure for measure, and raising a huge pile of wood without the walls of Wittemberg commits the bull to the flames. Time was when this would have been frenzy, it was still perilous; but public opinion was with the Reformer. The anathema was torn in pieces at Erfurt, and was ill received everywhere.

Charles V., the young Emperor of Germany, a few months later summoned Luther to a great diet of the empire, convened at Worms (A.D. 1521). Luther did not hesitate one moment about yielding obedience, and set out for Worms, attended by the herald who had brought the emperor's letter and safe conduct. While on his journey many of his friends, remembering the fate of Huss under similar circumstances, entreated him not to rush into the midst of danger. But Luther, superior to such terrors, silenced them with this reply, "I am lawfully called to appear in that city, and thither will I go in the name of the Lord, though as many devils as there are tiles on the houses were there combined against me." The reception he met with at Worms proved to the world that he was the idol of the people. Such crowds collected to see him, that it was impossible for him to reach the city hall, except by going across the gardens and back ways. Before the diet he behaved with modesty and firmness. He refused, however, to retract, unless his opinions were proved to be false by the rule of God's Word; "otherwise," said he, "I neither can nor will retract anything, for it is unsafe for a Christian to say anything against his conscience." Then steadily contemplating the assembly, which held his life in their hands, he added: "Here I stand, I can do no otherwise. God help me. Amen." He was allowed to depart unharmed, but a severe edict against him was soon issued in the emperor's name.

As Luther was returning home, a band of horsemen in masks rushed suddenly out of a wood, and, acting under the instructions of his friend the elector, carried him to the strong castle of Wartburg, to be out of harm's way. In this Patmos, as he called it, he remained nine months, until the fury of the storm had abated. He availed himself of his forced leisure and retirement for the manufacture of his weapons. He translated the New

Testament into German, and published several treatises in defence of his doctrines.

Luther's success in his German translation of the Greek Testament was in great measure due to **Philip Melancthon,** who in 1518 had been appointed Greek Professor in the University of Wittemberg. Between these two men an undying friendship grew up; and by their united efforts the Reformation was mainly effected. They were naturally fitted to be a mutual help in fighting the great battle of their day; Luther, by his intrepidity and ardour for doing battle against falsehood and its patrons; Melancthon by his gentleness, suavity, and tranquil earnestness for allaying men's passions, and inspiring them with a love of truth.

While Luther was carrying on his peaceful labours in his retreat, Carlstadt and other extreme reformers were at Wittemberg, smashing images, tearing down pictures, and by their extravagant conduct bringing Luther's work into discredit. At the risk of his life, the great Reformer appeared at Wittemberg, and soon obliged Carlstadt to withdraw to Strasburg, where he renewed his excesses.

While the Reformation in Germany, under the directing hand of Luther, was advancing gradually, it was proceeding at a ruinous pace in Switzerland. The chief of the Swiss reformers was **Ulric Zwingle.** In the Whitsuntide of 1524, the Council of Zurich, in concert with him, destroyed all the images, burned all the crosses, and silenced every organ in the churches of their canton. An attempt was made in 1529 to compose the differences between the German and Swiss reformers. The two chiefs met at Marburg, but their opinions respecting the Lord's Supper proved irreconcilable. Moreover, while the Swiss reformer rejected all rites and ceremonies not expressly enjoined in the Bible, the Saxon reformer insisted on retaining all that was not forbidden. Two years later, in a war between the Roman Catholic and the Protestant cantons of Switzerland, Zwingle, who had taken the sword, perished with the sword. His fate was followed for a time by the triumph of the unreformed religion in Switzerland.

Zwingle's work was taken up by **John Calvin**, who settled in Geneva in the summer of 1536, a year after he had published the first outline of his chief work—*The Institutes of the Christian Religion.* Calvin was so greatly esteemed as a reformer, that Geneva became a great centre of the Reformation, and the name of Calvinists supplanted that of Zwinglians, as the designation of the Swiss Protestants.

Meanwhile, the Reformed Faith, by the joint labours of Luther and Melancthon made steady progress in Germany; and before the death of the great Reformer (A.D. 1546), the Lutheran doctrines were generally received in one half of the German States, and in the northern countries of Europe; whilst in Switzerland, Holland, and Scotland, the tenets of Calvin were gaining ground, and taking root in the hearts and minds of the people. The doctrines of the Reformation were not allowed to spread and find a home in these countries without strong opposition from the Pope, the Emperor of Germany, and other Roman Catholic princes. As the progress of the Reformation was so intimately blended with the political fortunes of the German empire, it may be traced out most conveniently by following the course of events in

THE REIGN OF CHARLES V.

Charles V. was the most powerful monarch of Christendom in the age of the Reformation. The magnitude of his dominions was due to his birth, but his commanding influence in great measure to his genius. His grandfather, Maximilian (Duke of Austria and Emperor of Germany), had married Mary of Burgundy, daughter and heiress of Charles the Bold, and in her right obtained possession of the fertile and wealthy provinces of the Netherlands. Their son, Philip the Handsome, was united to Joanna, daughter of Ferdinand and Isabella of Spain. She became the mother of two sons, Charles and Ferdinand. The elder of these sons, afterwards Charles V. of Germany, was born in 1500. At the age of fifteen, on the death of his grandmother, Mary of Burgundy, he assumed the government of Flanders. A year later, on the demise of Ferdinand of Spain, he inherited the crown of Spain with its golden dependencies in the New World. By the death of Maximilian, in 1519, he came into possession of the Austrian dominions; and the electors of Germany shortly afterwards chose him as their emperor.

The Empire of Germany, it should be explained, was a confederation of various States, each under the immediate sovereignty of its own ruler, whilst the whole was combined under the supreme direction of the emperor, who presided over the imperial diet (composed of all the princes of the States), with the right of vetoing any law that assembly might pass. The privilege of decreeing who should wear the imperial crown, belonged to the seven most powerful princes, bearing the title of electors.

Charles V., though the greatest monarch of his day, had a formidable rival in Francis I. of France. Many years of his reign were spent in severe contests with this powerful prince. Henry VIII. of England used to boast that he held the balance of power between these rivals, and that his sword was sufficient to carry victory to the side he espoused. It would be tedious to relate in detail the varying fortune which attended the arms of the two rivals. Italy was the grand theatre of war. Francis I., at the battle of Pavia (A.D. 1525), was taken prisoner after his horse had been killed under him. Ten thousand of his troops, including many of his nobles, lay dead before the walls of Pavia, and in two weeks not a Frenchman remained in Italy. Thus as he wrote to his mother, "All is lost save honour." After he had been in prison a year, Charles agreed to release him, on receiving certain promises which were never kept. The contest was soon renewed, and is memorable for the capture of Pope Clement, who had joined the "Holy League," formed by Francis against the emperor. Rome was sacked by the imperial troops, and the pope, who had shut himself up in the castle of Angelo, was compelled, by famine, to yield himself a prisoner (A.D. 1527). The treaty of Cambray, signed the same year, restored liberty to the pope, and peace to Western Europe.

The dissensions between the pope and the emperor proved extremely favourable to the progress of the Reformation. Charles had little inclination, and still less leisure, to take any measures for suppressing the new opinion in Germany, until they had struck their roots too deep to be eradicated. The emperor's own example, during the heat of his resentment against Clement, emboldened the Germans to treat the papal authority with little reverence. In a diet of the empire held at Spires (A.D. 1529), after he had settled his disputes with the pope, a decree was passed prohibiting any further innovations in religion before the meeting of a general council. The elector of Saxony and a few other princes entered a solemn protest against this decree as unjust. This protest acquired for them the name of *Protestants*, a name since applied to all who favour the doctrines of the Reformation.

Next year the emperor himself presided at a diet at Augsburg (A.D. 1530). His presence seems to have communicated to all parties an unusual spirit of moderation and a desire for peace. The articles of the Protestant faith, known as the *Confession of Augsburg*, were drawn up by Melancthon, and read publicly in the diet. The Romanist party had the ascendency in the diet, and the confession was condemned, all persons being forbidden to hold or teach the doctrines therein set forth. Charles, however, contented himself with barking without actually biting. Nevertheless the Protestant princes assembled, first at Smalcalde, and afterwards at Frankfort, and entered into an alliance for mutual defence.

The Turks now appear on the scene as the political enemy of Germany, and the unintentional friend of Protestantism. Their sultan, Solyman the Magnificent, invaded Hungary at the head of 300,000 men (A.D. 1532). To meet this formidable force at the head of a loyal army, Charles annulled the decree against the Protestants, and succeeded in raising an effectual barrier against any further aggression of the Turks. His wars against the Moslem invader, and his old enemy, the French monarch, gave him full employment for several years to come.

The most remarkable event in these wars was the emperor's successful expedition against the celebrated corsair, Barbarossa, to whom Solyman had given the command of the Ottoman fleet, and who had made himself King of Tunis. The Mediterranean had for a long time been infested by Turkish and Moorish pirates, who not only plundered the vessels of Christian nations, but sold their crews as slaves. In 1535, Charles's fleet, consisting of 500 vessels, and having on board 30,000 men, entered the harbour of Goletta, near Tunis, and captured the royal pirate's fleet. The great fort of the town, bristling with 500 cannon, was taken by storm. The victorious troops then marched upon the capital, and utterly routed an army drawn up to protect it. Meanwhile, 10,000 Christian slaves, in the horrid dungeons of Tunis, knocked off each other's irons, and having seized the citadel, turned the guns upon their captors. As Charles approached the city, they went out to meet him, and falling on their knees, as he entered the gate of the city, thanked and blessed him as their deliverer.

Whilst Charles was thus engaged, great excesses were committed in Germany by a new sect of enthusiasts, called Anabaptists—a name derived from their practice of baptizing anew all that joined their community. Their chief prophets were Matthias, a baker, and Boccold, a tailor. Acting under the direction of these fanatics, the Anabaptists assembled at Munster, which they called Mount Zion, and there prepared for making war upon "the ungodly nations" round about. After the death of Matthias, Boccold was elected "King of Zion." He wore a crown of gold, carried a Bible in one hand, and a naked sword in the other. He declared that "whatever was highest should be made low, and whatever was lowest should be exalted." Accordingly, the churches of Munster, as the most lofty buildings, were levelled with the ground; and one of the chief men of the city was degraded to the office of common hangman. For fifteen months this fanatic ruled in Munster, and set an example of polygamy, which the Mormons have since followed. The city being taken after a long blockade, the tailor king was captured, carried in chains throughout the cities of Germany, and finally put to death with lingering tortures at Munster, the scene of his royalty and his crimes (A.D. 1535).

The war between Charles and Francis was brought to an end by the treaty of Crespy (A.D. 1544); and shortly afterwards the emperor concluded a truce with Solyman.

Charles, being now free to turn his attention to the internal state of his empire, resolved to root out the Reformed Faith by force of arms. The Elector of Saxony, the head of the Protestant League, was made prisoner at the battle of Muhlberg, in 1547. Luther and Francis had died some months previously. Thus the triumph of the emperor seemed complete. The sword of his great rival was rusting in the grave, the voice of the great reformer was hushed in death, and the chief Protestant prince was now a prisoner in his hands. But a new enemy arose from a most unexpected quarter.

Charles had made Prince Maurice Elector of Saxony, as a reward for his distinguished services in the late war with the Protestant princes. Maurice, at heart a Protestant, had betrayed the Protestant cause to gain the crown of Saxony; he was now resolved to betray the emperor to secure religious liberty. Having entered into a secret alliance with the French king, Henry II., he suddenly took the field against the emperor, who was lying ill of the gout at Innspruck. Castles and cities surrendered as he advanced, and so rapid was his progress, that the emperor barely escaped falling into his hands. Charles was obliged to fly in the middle of a stormy night, and to travel on a litter by torchlight across the Alps. He had scarcely left Innspruck, when Maurice entered it, to find the prize had just escaped him. A vigorous war followed this daring attempt; but the Protestants maintained their advantage; and Charles, in dread of a French war, concluded the peace of Passau (A.D. 1552), which secured freedom of religion to the Protestants of his empire.

Of all the memorable events of this reign, the last is by no means the least interesting. At the age of fifty-six, Charles, grown weary of the cares of government, descended from the throne, and spent the last two years of his life in the monastery of St. Justus, near Placentia, in Spain. His son Philip succeeded him as King of Spain and the Netherlands, and his brother Ferdinand as Emperor of Germany. Charles had previously resigned to his brother the archduchy of Austria, and he by marriage with Anne of Hungary, had also become king of that State. Ferdinand became the founder of a line of German emperors which ended with Charles VI. in 1740; and from Charles descended a line of Spanish kings, which became extinct in 1700. These two branches of the Austrian family, the German and the Spanish, long acted in concert to promote their own aggrandisement, and to check the growing spirit of civil and religious liberty. As devoted Romanists, they were ever bent on the suppression of Protestantism.

Charles spent the first year of his retreat, either in innocent amusements to divert his mind from sad thoughts, or in devout exercises to prepare his soul for another world. Gardening and framing models of machines were his favourite occupations. He was particularly curious with regard to the construction of clocks and watches; and having found, after repeated trials, that he could not bring any two of them to go exactly alike, he reflected, it is said, with a mixture of surprise and regret, on his own folly, in having bestowed so much time and labour on the still more hopeless attempt of bringing mankind to a precise uniformity of opinion on religious truths. About six months before his death the gout returned with great violence, and enfeebled his mind as much as his body. Feeling himself near death, he resolved to celebrate his own funeral service. His domestics marched to the chapel of the monastery with black tapers in their hands. He himself followed in his shroud, and before the service for the dead was chanted, he was laid in his coffin with much solemnity. After all the servants had withdrawn on the conclusion of the service, Charles rose out of his coffin, and the next day he was seized with a fever, which terminated fatally (A.D. 1558).

The age of Charles V. was illumined by a galaxy of painters, who flourished in Italy: Leonardo da Vinci, celebrated for his painting of "The Last Supper;" Raphael, famous for his Madonnas; Corregio, whose "Ecce Homo" is particularly well known; Titian, remarkable for the beauty of his colouring; Paul Veronese, an eminent master of ornamental painting; and surpassing them all, Michael Angelo, the chief architect of St. Peter's at Rome, and equally eminent in sculpture and painting.

IGNATIUS LOYOLA AND THE JESUITS.

Whilst the fabric of the Roman Catholic Church was falling to pieces from the attacks of Luther and other reformers, there arose a firm pillar of that Church in the person of Ignatius Loyola, and the Society of Jesus which he founded. The Jesuits, as the members of this society are called, were the most faithful, intrepid, and successful soldiers that ever enlisted under the banners of papal Rome. The *early* Jesuits were men of earnest piety, of extraordinary zeal in the papal cause, and of entire devotion to the interests of their order; and by their self-denying efforts arrested the fall of the papacy in the countries of Southern and Western Europe.

Ignatius Loyola was a gentleman of Biscay; he entered the army of Ferdinand of Spain, and had his leg broken at the siege of Pampeluna (A.D. 1521). While confined to his bed he read the *Lives of the Saints.* His enthusiastic mind was kindled with the desire of emulating their deeds. He declared himself a knight of the

Virgin Mary, and attached to himself Francis Xavier and four others, who formed the nucleus of his society. On the top of Montmartre these six men, one starry night, devoted themselves by a solemn oath to the cause of the tottering Church. And, in 1540, the order of Jesuits was formally instituted by the pope, after they had taken an oath of implicit obedience to His Holiness, promising to go wherever he might send them, and to execute his bidding whatever it might be, without condition or reward. Loyola was appointed the first general of the order, with absolute power over its members. Under his direction they were to be mere passive instruments, like clay in the hands of the potter, yielding to his commands an unquestioning obedience without regard to their own will or conscience. They undertook, in short, to observe the orders of their general, as if they emanated immediately from Christ himself.

The Jesuits increased with marvellous rapidity. The most zealous and devoted sons of the Romanist Church everywhere joined their ranks. From Portugal, their first headquarters, they spread into all lands. They wormed themselves, as confessors, into the confidence of princes; acquired deserved influence as the educators of youth; earned a reputation as eloquent preachers; and gained great renown by their boldness, activity, and success as missionaries. Mr. Lord, the author of "Modern Europe," thus sums up their extraordinary achievements in the lifetime of the founder: "Before he died (A.D. 1556), his spiritual sons had planted their missionary stations amid Peruvian mines, among the marts of the African slave trade, in the islands of the Indian Ocean, and in the cities of Japan. Nay, his followers had secured the most important chairs in the universities of Europe, had made themselves confessors to the most powerful monarchs, teachers in the best schools of Christendom, and preachers in its principal pulpits. More than all this, the order had become an organization, instinct with life, endued with energy and will, and forming a body which could outwatch Argus with his hundred eyes, and outwork

Briareus with his hundred arms. It had forty thousand eyes open upon every cabinet and private family in Europe, and forty thousand arms extended over the necks of both sovereigns and people. It had become a mighty power in the world, inseparably connected with the education and the religion of the age; it was the prime mover of all political affairs, the grand prop of absolute monarchies, the last hope of the papal hierarchy."

As missionaries, the Jesuits gained great credit. **Francis Xavier**, "the apostle of the Indies," not only planted the Gospel in India, but even in remote Japan. Two fierce persecutions, however, have left no trace of his labours in Japan, except a bitter hatred of the very name of Christianity. A similar result attended the Jesuit missions in China. In America they were more successful, especially in Paraguay, then inhabited by savage hordes of Indians. The Jesuits settled among the natives, and taught them the useful arts of life, as well as the things relating to their eternal interests.

It was as teachers, however, that the Jesuits gained their greatest triumphs. Since the revival of learning, no body of men has played so prominent a part in education as the Jesuits. With characteristic sagacity and energy, they soon seized on education as a stepping-stone to power and influence; and with their talent for organization, they framed a system of schools which drove most competitors from the field, and made Jesuits the instructors of Roman Catholic, and even, to some extent, of Protestant Europe. For more than a century the fore most men in Europe received their learning from the Jesuits, and for life regarded their old masters with reverence and affection. "Gratis receive, gratis give," was the society's rule, so that their schools were accessible to rich and poor alike.

The Jesuits in the early days of their society were undoubtedly the benefactors of humanity, but as time went on their false principles gradually developed. Their unquestioning obedience to the general of their order, removed the sense of personal responsibility, and made them ready to execute any criminal act required of them. They have been notorious for attempting the lives of Protestant princes, to advance, as they believed, the interests of true religion. Their ruling maxim too often was, "Let us do evil that good may come." In the course of the seventeenth and eighteenth centuries, the order was expelled from most European countries, and in 1775 it was suppressed by the pope. Our own age, unhappily, has witnessed its revival.

CHAPTER XVII.

RELIGIOUS WARS AND PERSECUTIONS.

PHILIP II., son of Charles V., became King of Spain and the Netherlands in 1556. Two years previously he had married Mary, Queen of England. He was the gloomiest bigot that ever disgraced a throne; and as Spain, during his reign, was the foremost state in Europe, he possessed considerable power of working misery, ruin, and death on men and nations, whose religious creed differed from his own. For almost a hundred years from his accession, Europe, rent by religious dissensions, was the unhappy theatre of wars and persecutions carried on in the name of religion.

THE INQUISITION.

The tribunal called the Inquisition, one of the most fiendish courts ever established, had for its object the extirpation of heresy. The Inquisition of Spain has gained a most unenviable notoriety for its atrocities. The record of its proceedings reads like an account of the transactions of an infernal court presided over by demons. It may be briefly described as a bench of monks, having its spies in every house, to dive into the secrets of every breast, and to worm out a man's opinions on matters of religion. It arrested its victim on bare suspicion, tortured him till he confessed himself a heretic, and finally burned him for heresy. Two witnesses, and these to separate facts, were sufficient to consign the highest noble in the land to a dismal dungeon; and there he was left to himself till hunger and misery should break his spirit. When that time was supposed to have arrived, he was examined; but no witness was ever confronted with him. That accuser might be his own son or father, wife or daughter; for all were enjoined under penalty of death to inform the inquisitors of every suspicious word which might fall from even their nearest relatives.

The torture took place most frequently at midnight in a gloomy dungeon, dimly lighted by torches. The victim was stripped nearly naked, and stretched upon a machine called a rack. The executioner, enveloped in a black robe from head to foot, with his eyes glaring through slits in the sash-hood that muffled his face, applied successively all the ingenious contrivances that malicious cruelty had devised; water, weights, fires, pulleys, screws, all the apparatus by which the sinews could be strained without snapping, and the bones bruised without breaking. The poor victim was tortured again and again, until he was ready to confess anything; so that the stake or the scaffold was the sole refuge from the rack.

The last scene in this dismal tragedy was the *auto da fé*, "or act of faith," when the condemned prisoners, who had been allowed to accumulate for some time, were publicly handed over to the secular arm to be punished. When the appointed morning arrived, the victim was attired in a yellow robe without sleeves, embroidered with a scarlet cross, and well garnished with figures of devils and flames of fires. On his head was placed a large conical paper mitre, on which was the picture of a human being, in the midst of flames, and environed by imps. His tongue was then painfully gagged, so that he could neither open nor close his mouth. Attired in this horrible and ludicrous manner, each prisoner was led into the public square, and a procession was then formed with great pomp to the place of execution. It was headed by little school children, and they were immediately followed by the band of heretics. Then came the magistrates and other great men of the city, and after them the inquisitors with their officers, all on horseback, with the blood-red flag of their "sacred office" waving above them. An excited rabble came behind. On arriving at the appointed place, a sermon was preached, and the fifty-first psalm chanted. The condemned were now obliged to mount a scaffold, where the executioner stood ready to conduct them to the fire. The inquisitors then delivered them into his hands, with an ironical request that he would deal with them tenderly. Those who remained steadfast to the last were then burned at the stake; any who, in the last extremity, confessed their errors were considerately strangled before being thrown into the flames.

Prior to the Reformation, the fires of the Inquisition in Spain were lighted almost exclusively for the Jews and the Moors, who were suspected of having a secret leaning to the religion of their ancestors. So many victims were sentenced to be burned in the very first year of the Inquisition (A.D. 1481), that the prefect of Seville was forced to construct a stone scaffold for the executions, which may still be seen near that city. On this platform of death were erected four statues of plaster, called the four prophets, to which the condemned were fastened. We find in the records of Seville that, in the course of eight years, 2592 of these unhappy persons were burned in that city alone.

When the doctrines of Luther found their way into Spain, the inquisitors no longer confined their attention to Jews and infidels; "Lutheran heretics" were sought out and led to the stake. With the accession of Philip the fires of persecution burned still more fiercely. In 1559, an *auto da fé* was celebrated at Seville, in which twenty-one Protestants were burned, some of whom were ladies of the highest rank. During the next ten years of Philip's reign at least one *auto da fé* was celebrated annually in Spain.

An attempt made by this monarch to establish an ecclesiastical court in the Netherlands, similar to the Inquisition in Spain, aroused the spirit of his Dutch and Flemish subjects, who shuddered at the thought that this chamber of horrors should ever become one of the institutions of their free land, and threw them into a state of rebellion, ending in the independence of the northern provinces and their union into one state, under the name of Holland, or the Dutch Republic.

RISE OF THE DUTCH REPUBLIC.

The Netherlands, at the time of Philip's accession, comprised seventeen provinces. In the maritime provinces, of which Holland and Zealand were the two chief, the people were mostly Protestants, and in them accordingly was shown the most determined spirit of resistance to the tyrannical measures of their despotic and bigoted sovereign. The inhabitants of the southern provinces were, for the most part, attached to the Roman Catholic religion, and consequently their opposition to Philip's tyranny was less vigorous and enthusiastic. But as the struggle between Philip and his subjects in the Netherlands had for its object civil freedom as well as religious liberty, both Protestants and Romanists regarded their sovereign as their common enemy. All the offices of State were filled by Spaniards, and in all the towns Spanish soldiers held the garrisons, so that they were virtually under the rule of a foreign prince.

In 1566 the crisis came. The king was resolved that the Inquisition should extinguish "heresy" in the Netherlands; "I would rather be no king at all," he said," "than have heretics for my subjects." His Protestant subjects were equally resolved that the authority of the king should be extinguished before their religious principles, which he called heresy. During the last half century they had endured much from persecution; the roll of Protestant martyrs was already a long one. But now the popular fury burst forth in a disastrous flame. Stately cathedrals and churches were defaced or demolished, the painted windows shattered, the images pulled down, the pictures torn in shreds, and the organs broken in pieces.

The Duke of Alva, a man of execrable cruelty, was sent with an army of 15,000 men to take vengeance for these outrages. Blood was shed like water, the prisons were crammed with the accused, the scaffolds crowded with the condemned. The Inquisition, meanwhile, carried on their sanguinary labours. Eighteen thousand persons perished at the scaffold or the stake by Alva's orders; and thousands more fled from their ill-fated country, many of them finding an asylum in England, and enriching that kingdom by their industry and skill in manufactures. Even **William the Silent**, Prince of Orange, the future deliverer of the Dutch, thought it prudent to retire to his family estates of Nassau, in Germany. Here he entered into communication with Elizabeth of England and other Protestant princes, and from most of them received supplies of men or money. The issue of his first attempt was unfortunate. Indeed, it was not until Alva and the Inquisition had carried on the work of blood for four years longer, that the first gleam of good fortune shone upon him.

William had stationed a fleet of cruisers along the coasts of Holland and Zealand, to damage the Spanish shipping, and to occupy any advantageous position along the shore. Great was the havoc which the "water-beggars," as they called themselves, worked among the Spanish merchantmen. Emboldened by famine, a few hundred of these water-beggars made a descent on the island of Voorn, and took the town of *Brille*, which was reckoned one of the keys of the Netherlands. Alva was at Brussels on the point of hanging eighteen of the leading tradesmen of that city, when the news from Brille snatched him away from this congenial employment. It appears that the tyrant had imposed such heavy taxes upon the sale of provisions, that the tradesmen refused to do any business. The brewers refused to brew, and the bakers to bake. To correct this ruinous state of things, he had made up his mind to hang eighteen of the principal tradesmen of the city in front of their own shops. Eighteen gibbets had been erected, a ladder twelve feet in length stood beside each gibbet, and the very nooses had been made on the ends of the ropes, when the news came that the rebels had seized Brille.

By the capture of that quaint old town, the first stone of the Dutch Republic was laid (A.D. 1572).

Alva, fully aware of the importance of the news, did not stay to hang the refractory brewers and bakers of Brussels, but despatched with all speed a body of troops, under Count de Bossut, to retake the place. Bossut laid siege to Brille, and was in a fair way of winning it with his artillery, when a patriotic carpenter, belonging to the city, plunged into the water with his axe in his hand, and swimming to a sluice which the Spaniards had overlooked, hacked it open. A deluge of water poured in, swamped the artillery, drowned a number of the Spaniards, and forced the rest to take to their ships. This victory kindled a bold resolute spirit among the men of Holland and Zealand. In a short time all the towns of these two provinces, except Amsterdam and Middelburg, had expelled their garrisons; and in three other provinces of the north similar risings took place, till sixty or seventy towns in all had thrown off the yoke of the Spaniard.

And now Alva began a series of sieges to recover the lost towns. He proclaimed the extermination of man, woman, and child in every city which should oppose his authority; but the hearts of the Hollanders were rather steeled to resistance than awed to submission by such terrible threats. Many a town maintained a gallant defence; *Haarlem*, in particular, gained an imperishable name by the desperate bravery with which, for seven months, it stood out against a large army under Alva's son. On the first attempt to take the town by storm, the Spaniards were encountered by the whole population. Swords and muskets could not be found for all the willing hands that swarmed to the walls at the first signal of alarm. Heavy stones, boiling oil, molten lead, and live coals were thrown on the heads of the besiegers; hoops smeared with pitch and set on fire were dexterously flung around their necks. "These citizens do as much as the best soldiers in the world could do," wrote Don Frederick to Alva, his father. And before the end of the siege, Alva, in a letter to his sovereign, informs him that "never was a place defended with such skill and bravery as Haarlem." According to some accounts the siege cost the Spaniards 10,000 men. When at last the famished citizens opened their gates, the leading men were butchered in cold blood; and when the executioners were tired of their bloody task, they tied their remaining victims in pairs, back to back, and flung them into the lake of Haarlem.

The brutal Alva was now recalled, and Requesens, a more humane man, was appointed to succeed him (A.D. 1573). Affairs about the same time took a favourable turn for the Hollanders. The Prince of Orange took Middelburg, after his fleet had gained a great victory off Bergen. The contest now centred in *Leyden*, around which Valdez, the Spanish general, drew a circle of sixty forts. The two leading spirits within the walls were Van der Dousa and Van der Werf. After a close siege of two months, gaunt famine began to stalk through the streets; but there was no talk of surrender. "When we have nothing else left," said Dousa, in reply to a message from Valdez, "we will eat our left hands, keeping the right to fight with." But at length danger seemed on the point of prevailing over patriotism. A crowd of famished wretches, assembling with hoarse clamours around Van der Werf, their burgomaster, as his tall haggard figure was passing through the streets, demanded that he should give them food, or else surrender. "I have no food to give you," was his reply, "and I have sworn that I will not surrender to the Spaniards; here is my sword, plunge it into my breast, and let the hungriest of you eat my flesh." There was no more talk of surrender. From the ramparts they hurled renewed defiance at the enemy. "Ye call us rat-eaters and dog-eaters," they cried, "and it is true. So long, then, as ye hear dog bark or cat mew within the walls, ye may know that the city holds out."

Meanwhile, William the Silent had collected a large supply of provisions; but with all his exertions he could not succeed in bringing them to the relief of the destitute city. As a last resource he ordered the dykes to be broken through to admit the ocean and restore to the waves their former territory around Leyden, in the hope of washing the Spaniards out of their forts. "Better a drowned land than a lost land," said the patriots; so hatchets, hammers, spades, and pickaxes were set to work, and by the labour of a single night the labour of ages was undone. The orchards, farms, and cornfields around the besieged city became an expanse of water. Across this inland sea a flotilla of 200 boats, piled up with fish and bread, made their way to the wall of the famished city. The Spaniards retreated before the rising waters, and Leyden was saved (A.D. 1574). The University of Leyden was established in the following year, as a memorial of this gallant defence, and its prosperous issue.

The heroic stand made by the men of Leyden was the death-blow to the tyranny of Spain in the Protestant provinces. William also tried to break the yoke of the foreigner in the southern states; but in this, after alternations of victory and defeat, he was ultimately unsuccessful. The provinces in the north, however, gained their independence, and became a new European state. The foundation of this state was laid by a treaty of union between the northern provinces, signed at Utrecht (A.D. 1579). Two years later Philip was formally deposed as a tyrant, and William, Prince of Orange, was elected, with the title of *Stadtholder*, hereditary chief of "The Seven United Provinces," which subsequently received the name of Holland, or the Dutch Republic.

About this time the Spanish tyrant offered a reward of 25,000 golden crowns, with a patent of nobility, for the murder of the stadtholder. In consequence of this diabolical offer his life was hourly in danger. The first attempt on his life was made at Antwerp (A.D. 1582), where he was shot at by a half-crazed fanatic. Two years afterwards his body was pierced with three balls from a horse-pistol. Mortally wounded he fell, exclaiming, "God have mercy on me, and on this poor people."

Prince Maurice, the next stadtholder, was able to retain what his father had won, though he had to contend against the Duke of Parma, the first general of the age, who at that time held the chief command of the Spanish armies in the Netherlands. Queen Elizabeth, indeed, sent 4000 men under the Earl of Leicester to his aid; but through the incapacity of their commander the English were of little service to their allies. It was in the course of this campaign, in a skirmish near Zutphen, that Sir Philip Sydney was killed. Prince Maurice, though he derived but little material support from the English, contrived to maintain the independence of the Republic; and before his death Holland was virtually recognised by Spain as an independent state.

The young republic flourished with all the vigour of youth. The Dutch not only held their ground at home, but acquired vast possessions abroad. A girdle of Dutch colonies encompassed the globe. The Dutch seamen fought manfully with the English sailors for the supremacy of the seas. Their merchantmen were on every coast, and the merchandise of the whole world in the warehouses of their capital.

THE HUGUENOTS.

The Protestants of France were called Huguenots, a name derived from a German word signifying confederates. They have rightly received this distinctive title; for they were not simply Protestants, but *confederates*, banded together on political grounds, as well as from religious motives. The most earnest Huguenots were doubtless sincere in their attachment to the Reformed Faith, but the majority of them were probably more influenced by political than religious considerations. Hence the history of the Huguenots is the history of a civil and religious war, in which the great principles of the Reformation were overshadowed by state policy, forgotten in the tumult of arms, and dishonoured by the spirit of revenge. The Huguenots were the great enemies of despotism in every form; and so for nearly a century, except during the beneficent reign of Henry IV., they were arrayed against the arbitrary rule of the French Court, till their political power was destroyed by Cardinal Richelieu, the greatest statesman of his day.

About the middle of the sixteenth century, the Reformation began to make considerable progress in some parts of France. In 1558, we are assured there were no less than 2000 places dedicated to the reformed worship, and attended by 400,000 people. At this time also the Protestant leaders were men of high rank; such as Antoine de Bourbon, first prince of the blood royal, and, through his wife, King of Navarre; also Louis, Prince of Condé, his younger brother; and the veteran Admiral Coligny. Through their influence mainly, an edict was published at St. Germains, in 1562, by which permission was granted to the Huguenots to hold meetings for religious worship outside the walls of towns. The zealous Romanists of France bitterly resented this edict, and in less than two months from its proclamation their resentment broke out in a murderous assault upon the Huguenots at Vassy. The Duke of Guise happened to be passing through this little town with a retinue of 200 well-armed men, when the Protestants were assembled for divine worship. On the duke's attendants interrupting the service, they were assailed by stones, and the duke himself was struck in the face. The enraged soldiers now fired upon the unarmed people, killing 60 outright, and wounding 200 more. Such was the first act of the great civil and religious war that desolated France for many long years to come.

The war was carried on with great spirit and varied fortune till 1570, when by a treaty, signed at St. Germains, the Huguenots obtained the free exercise of their religion. Still further, as if to heal the wounds inflicted by the civil war, and to cement the union of the rival parties, the king, Charles IX., offered the hand of his sister, Marguerite, to the young prince, Henry of Navarre, son of Antoine de Bourbon, and at that time head of the Huguenot party. But this proposal, though carried into effect, was only the prelude of a dark plot, which the king's mother (the infamous Catherine de Medici) and the Duke of Guise had invented for the total destruction of the Huguenots.

The marriage of Henry with Marguerite, which was celebrated at Paris on the 18th August, 1572, attracted to the capital Coligny, Condé, and the leading Huguenots. They were only lured there to be murdered. On the festival of *St. Bartholomew*, within a week of the royal wedding, was perpetrated one of the blackest crimes on record Two hours after midnight the bells sounded an alarm from all the steeples of Paris. Assassins armed to the teeth, and distinguished by white crosses in their hats, simultaneously emerged from every dark corner of the city, and broke into the Huguenots' houses, which had been previously marked. Among the first victims was the illustrious Coligny. The Duke of Guise went in person to his house, and remained in the court below, while one of his myrmidons ascended to the old warrior's chamber, burst open the door, and plunged his sword into his heart. The bleeding corpse of the admiral was then flung down from the window at the feet of his exultant enemy. The work of blood went on throughout the night. Thousands of the unhappy Huguenots perished before dawn. Many of them fled half-naked from their houses, but only to be butchered in the streets. The queen-mother and her attendants were spectators of the appalling scene from the windows of the Louvre, and Charles himself is said to have repeatedly fired his arquebus upon the miserable fugitives, as they slunk along the quays of the Seine, or attempted to swim across the river. It is supposed that 5000 persons were slain in Paris before the bloody work was done; nor would Henry of Navarre and the Prince of Condé have been spared, if they had not promised to change their religion.

The massacre was not confined to Paris; orders were also sent into the provinces to put the Huguenots to the sword. In many places these orders were obeyed with alacrity, but not in all. The governor of Bayonne, in answer to the king's mandate, wrote as follows: "Your majesty has many faithful servants in Bayonne, but not one executioner."

At Rome, the news of this great blow for the extermination of heretics was received with extravagant joy; the pope and cardinals went in state to St. Peter's, to return thanks to Heaven for this pious achievement; and even medals, bearing the pope's effigy on one side, were struck in commemoration of this French mode of celebrating an *auto da fé*. It is satisfactory to know that the king's mind was constantly haunted by the recollections of this terrible tragedy, and that on his death-bed he suffered fearfully in looking back on the atrocities which had disgraced his reign. He died in 1574, and was succeeded by his brother, Henry III.

The Huguenots soon raised their heads again. Henry of Navarre, on escaping from the clutches of the queen-mother, again put himself at their head, and within four years from the massacre of their brethren, the full and public exercise of their religion was authorised by King Henry throughout France. Rochelle and seven other towns were placed in their hands as a pledge of his sincerity. This compact was highly displeasing to the more devoted Romanists of France, who formed a confederacy, called the "Holy League," with the Duke of Guise at its head, for depriving the Huguenots of their religious rights. The authority of the duke, especially at Paris, overshadowed that of the crown so completely, that Henry caused him to be assassinated. Then descending to the apartments of his mother, the infamous Catherine de Medici, the royal murderer exclaimed, "Madam, congratulate me; I am once more King of France, for this morning I have put to death the King of Paris." Catherine's death occurred a few days afterwards, and in the same year (A.D. 1589), the king himself fell a victim to the assassin's knife.

The heir to the throne was the leader of the Huguenots, Prince of Navarre. The Romanists refusing to recognise him as their sovereign, a civil war ensued, which lasted five years. To save his country from ruin,

Henry consented to change his religion, and was crowned with the title of **Henry IV.** Though he had turned Romanist himself, yet by the edict of Nantes (A.D. 1598), he secured to the Huguenots religious freedom, and all the rights of free citizens. Before this no Protestants could be magistrates, or hold any office of trust in the state, except in their own towns; but now they were admissible to all places of honour and dignity in the kingdom. The reign of Henry IV. was not only a blessing to the Huguenots, but it brought peace and prosperity to the whole nation. The peasantry, in particular, found a friend in their king, who was often heard to say that he should never feel content till "every peasant in the kingdom should be able to have a fowl in the pot on Sundays." In all his plans for the welfare of his people he was aided by the sagacity and wisdom of his chief minister, the Duke of Sully; under the auspices of the king and his minister, silk and other manufactures began to flourish, and a new spirit of frugality and economy presided over the national treasury. By their combined efforts peace and plenty began to smile over the land. The reign of this illustrious prince was unhappily brought to an end by the dagger of a madman, named Ravaillac, who, mounting upon the wheel of the royal carriage, stabbed the king to the heart (A.D. 1610).

His son, Louis XIII., ascended the throne when only nine years old. The country fell into a state of anarchy, which continued until 1624, when the celebrated **Cardinal Richelieu** came into power as prime minister. For eighteen years, until his death, this haughty minister and clever statesman held his place at the helm of state. Whilst scheming for his own ambitious ends, he freed his country from anarchy; whilst working for his own personal good, he advanced also his country's greatness. It is true, he exalted himself above the king, but he took care that every one else in the realm should humbly submit to the royal authority. "He made his master the second man in France, but the first in Europe."

One of the main objects of Richelieu's domestic policy

was the humiliation of the Huguenots, who were remarkable for their love of freedom, civil as well as religious. As the cardinal was bent on establishing a despotic government in France, he regarded the Huguenots as a barrier across the path that he had marked out for himself, and he resolved to break that barrier down. He therefore laid siege to Rochelle, their great stronghold (A.D. 1627). It was so strongly fortified, both by sea and land, that it could only be taken by cutting off from it all supplies of provisions. As England, the mistress of the seas, was a friend of the Huguenots, it seemed at first beyond the power of the cardinal to starve them into surrender. Besides, there were 30,000 resolute men within the city, under the command of Guiton, a man of iron will and courage, who threatened to poniard the first citizen that should venture to speak of opening the gates. The cardinal undertook the direction of the siege himself. Finding that all his efforts to take the city by land were useless, whilst the sea was open to the besieged, he resolved on cutting off their communication with the sea by constructing a mole at the mouth of the harbour, at a sufficient distance from the town to be beyond the range of its cannon. At first the besieged laughed as the stones were tumbled into the sea, and seemed lost in its deep waters. But the work went steadily on, and to the dismay of the famine-threatened Huguenots a line of stone, half a mile long, appeared above the waves. And when, at length, ships laden with provisions arrived from England, their commanders were baffled, and obliged to retreat without relieving the famished city. The fate of Rochelle was now sealed, but the defence was protracted until half the population had perished from hunger. By the capture of Rochelle (A.D. 1628), the political power of the Huguenots was broken beyond recovery; and in less than a twelvemonth the final ruin of their cause was achieved.

THE THIRTY YEARS' WAR.

The famous Thirty Years' War, which began in 1618, and was carried on in Central Europe, may be regarded as the sequel of the Reformation in Germany. It was waged by the Emperor of Germany against the Protestant princes of the empire and the Protestant kings of Northern Europe. The dimensions of the war varied considerably at different times, sometimes a few states being involved, and sometimes many. The war had its political as well as its religious aspect. As both the Emperor of Germany and the King of Spain belonged to the House of Austria, and as they generally acted in concert for their mutual advantage, it was the aim of Richelieu and other astute statesmen of the day to reduce the power of that house.

By the treaty of Passau (A.D. 1552), Charles V. had granted religious toleration to his Protestant subjects, and had recognised their claim to all the civil rights enjoyed by the Romanists. Charles's immediate successors respected the terms of this treaty, and for fifty years Germany was tolerably tranquil. But early in the seventeenth century the old hostile spirit between the two great religious parties again broke out. In 1608, the Protestant princes of the empire entered into a confederacy, called the *Evangelical Union*, and this association was opposed by another, called the *Catholic League*.

Open war, however, did not break out till ten years later. It began on a small scale in Bohemia (A.D. 1618), when Matthias was emperor. He had, by his harsh treatment of the Bohemian Protestants, provoked them to throw off his authority. Before he could punish his rebellious subjects, death intervened. He was succeeded in the empire by his cousin, Ferdinand II., who was an inveterate enemy to the Protestant cause. The Bohemians would not acknowledge him as their sovereign, and chose for their king Frederick, Elector Palatine of the Rhine. This prince had married Elizabeth, daughter of James I. of England; but he derived nothing from his pedantic and unwarlike father-in-law, "save a liberal supply of peaceable advice and scholastic quotations instead of money and legions." The fate of Bohemia and of the king of their choice was decided in a single battle, fought at the White Mountain, about two miles from Prague

(A.D. 1620). Maximilian, Duke of Bavaria, fighting on the side of the emperor, at the head of 50,000 troops, gained a complete victory. The Bohemian nobles who had rebelled lost their estates, the Protestant clergy were banished, and all the Protestant laity forfeited their religious freedom. The unfortunate Frederick, instead of gaining a kingdom, in the end lost his palatinate, a part of which, with the title of elector, was bestowed by Ferdinand upon the Duke of Bavaria.

Frederick, however, was not allowed to fall without a struggle. For nine years the strife raged before Frederick and his Protestant allies laid down .their hopeless arms. A remarkable feature of this war was the conspicuous part played in it by two Bohemian solders of fortune. Count Mansfeldt fighting on Frederick's side, and Count Wallenstein on the other. Each of these famous men raised a large army, and, by pillaging the cities and states in which they encamped, made the war support itself. Neither of them was much better than the licensed chief of an army of freebooters. As their troops subsisted by plunder, they soon became as obnoxious to their friends as their foes; and, consequently, when Wallenstein had crushed every head that dared to lift itself against the emperor, all Germany demanded the dismissal of the brigand chief (A.D. 1530). Ferdinand reluctantly cancelled his commission; and though at the head of 100,000 victorious troops, devoted to their leader, he promptly obeyed the imperial mandate, and retired to his estates in Bohemia, confidently expecting the time when his services would again be indispensable to the emperor.

It is interesting to catch a glimpse of this remarkable man in the silent recesses of his palace at this epoch of his life. He is described as a tall, thin man, of a sallow complexion, with short red hair, and small sparkling eyes. He had a peculiar dislike to noise; when residing at Prague, chains were drawn across the streets leading to his palace, that the sound of wheels might not reach his ear. All within the palace was wrapped in gloomy silence; six barons and as many knights were in constant attendance on his person, sixty pages were at hand to do his bidding, and fifty guards occupied his antechamber, and yet the silence of death reigned over all. Within sat the silent, smileless chief, like some dark bird of prey, croaking out at intervals his imperious orders, or writing his despatches with lightning speed, or trying to read his future destiny by the aid of astrology.

The emperor at the time of Wallenstein's retirement was the undisputed master of Germany. Having the Protestants of Germany at his feet, he was determined to use his power for their ruin. But just when their cause seemed hopeless a new champion arose in the person of **Gustavus Adolphus**, king of Sweden. Gustavus could bring but a small army into the field, but that army was devoted to their leader, and that leader was the greatest general of the age. He maintained a rigorous discipline in his army, punishing with severity all theft and disorders. He was as careful of the religion and morals of his soldiers as of their military efficiency; whether on a campaign or in barracks every regiment was ordered to form round its chaplain for morning and evening prayers. The hardships of war he shared with the meanest soldier, and its perils with the bravest captain. Such was the martial king that now stood forward as the champion of the Protestants of Germany.

In a diet held at Stockholm (20th May, 1630), the king, taking in his arms his daughter Christina, then only four years old, presented her to the States of the realm as the future sovereign, in case he should never more return. The whole assembly was dissolved in tears, whilst the king delivered his farewell address. "Not lightly or wantonly," said he, "am I about to involve myself and you in this dangerous war. God is my witness that I do not fight to gratify my own ambition. But the emperor has supported my enemies, persecuted my friends and brethren, trampled my religion in the dust, and even stretched his revengeful arm against my crown. The oppressed states of Germany call loudly for aid, and, by God's help, we will give it to them. I commend you to the protection of heaven. Be just, be conscientious, and act uprightly, and we shall meet again in heaven. I bid you all a sincere—it may be—an eternal farewell."

A month later Gustavus landed on the island of Rugen, in Pomerania, with 15,000 men; and kneeling on the shore, returned thanks to God for the safe arrival of his fleet and army (24th June, 1630).

Ferdinand at first made merry at the thought of such a handful of men coming to invade his mighty empire. The wits of his court called Gustavus the Snow King, who would melt as he advanced into the warm regions of the south. The emperor, however, took care to send an able general, Count Tilly, to oppose the invaders. Tilly had long commanded the Bavarian armies without ever losing a decisive battle. A strange and terrific aspect bespoke the character of this man: of diminutive size, with hollow cheeks, a long nose, a broad and wrinkled forehead, large whiskers, and a pointed chin; he was generally attired in a doublet of green satin, with slashed sleeves, and on his head he wore a small high peaked hat, surmounted by a long red feather which hung down his back. He was the first to point out to the emperor the formidable character of Gustavus as an antagonist. "This is a player," said the old marshal, "from whom we gain much, if we lose nothing." Ferdinand found that his enemy was indeed a Snow King, that could carry on a campaign amid the snows of winter, and keep the field through the year.

Steadily did the Snow King work his way southward, and instead of melting away, his army increased in bulk like a rolled snow-ball. But before he could reach Magdeburg, that Protestant stronghold had been stormed, sacked, and burnt by Tilly's brutal soldiery (10th May, 1631.) "For four days," says Schiller, "the scene of carnage here was such as history has no language, art no pencil, to portray. Neither the innocence of childhood, nor the helplessness of old age—neither youth, sex, rank, nor beauty—could disarm the fury of the conquerors." Nothing remained of the town but the cathedral, a church, and a few houses round about them; nothing remained of the inhabitants beyond a thousand who had taken refuge in the cathedral.

Gustavus, being now joined by the Elector of Saxony, marched upon Leipsic, which had opened its gates to the imperial troops under Tilly. On the event of the battle now to be fought hung the fate of the Protestants of Germany. The two armies were about equal; and the two generals were among the greatest of the day. The king chose for his battle-cry, "God with us;" whilst that of the imperialists was "Jesu, Marie." Tilly's usual clearness and calmness forsook him on this eventful day; the dark shade of Magdeburg seemed to hover over him. With his right wing, however, he soon routed the Saxons opposed to him; but meanwhile, his left wing was utterly defeated by the Swedes. The victorious Swedes then attacked the troops of Tilly that had broken the Saxon line, and, gaining the heights on which the enemy's artillery was planted, turned upon them the full fire of their own cannon. The imperial army was soon a complete wreck, and their general a wounded fugitive. Amid the dead and wounded the grateful king threw himself upon his knees, and thanked God for his victory (7th September, 1631).

Gustavus Adolphus now carried the war into the territory of Maximilian, the Elector of Bavaria, the emperor's most powerful ally. As the king marched southward towards Bavaria, the keys of towns and fortresses were delivered to him by the inhabitants as to their native sovereign. Tilly, burning to avenge his defeat at Leipsic, posted his forces along the river Lech, the western frontier of Bavaria, and defied his antagonist to cross. Gustavus not only passed the river in spite of all Tilly's endeavours to prevent him, but gave the old marshal a most signal defeat (3rd April, 1632). Here ended the career of the beaten general. Struck in one of his legs by a cannon shot, he was carried off the field shortly before the rout of his army, and died a few days afterwards.

All Europe was astonished at the career of the Snow King, and some of the nations began to fear that he would come down upon them like an avalanche, when he had overrun Germany. Soon after the victory of the Lech, the Swedes entered Munich in triumph; whilst the Saxons made themselves masters of Prague, Ferdinand was not only humbled, but threatened with absolute ruin.

The hour had now come for which Wallenstein had panted. No sooner did he raise his standard at the emperor's command, than it was resorted to by the needy and rapacious adventurers from all quarters of the empire. His army soon outnumbered that of Gustavus. After a good deal of manœuvring, the two generals met on the plain of Lutzen, twelve miles from Leipsic (6th Nov., 1632). At dawn the two armies were ready for action, but a thick fog delayed the attack till noon. Three times was the battle lost and won that day. Night put an end to the fight before the fury of the combatants was exhausted. Each party on withdrawing from the field claimed the victory; but as the Swedes, on the following morning, were permitted to take possession of all the Austrian cannon and baggage, the victory was really theirs. But it was a victory without joy, for it was bought with the life of their beloved king.

After the battle of Lutzen we almost lose sight of Wallenstein, who two years later was assassinated. When the helm of war dropped from the hands of Gustavus, it was taken up by his prime minister, Oxenstiern, who was perfectly acquainted with his deceased master's designs, and abler than any one else to carry them out with success. Within three years from the death of their great champion, the Protestants of Germany made peace with the emperor on satisfactory terms.

Thirteen years of this desolating war still remained. It was now solely political in character. Richelieu, who had long secretly favoured the Swedes, formed an open alliance with them. After an endless series of skirmishes, sieges, and battles, the famous Thirty Years' War was terminated by the treaty of Westphalia (A.D. 1648). The chief terms of this important treaty were these: (1) That Sweden should obtain the larger part of the duchy of Pomerania, and be paid five millions of thalers; (2), that Alsace should be annexed to France, together with the bishoprics of Metz, Toul, and Verdun; (3), that Holland and Switzerland should be recognised as independent states; (4), that Charles Louis, son of the unfortunate Elector Palatine, should share with the Elector of Bavaria the dominions of his father; (5), that the city and district of Magdeburg and Minden should be given to Prussia; (6), that the Protestants should enjoy the free exercise of their religious worship. The authority of the emperor was, from this time, much diminished; and he became little more than the nominal head of a confederacy of sovereign states.

The horrors of this terrible war can hardly be realised in our day. The thousands slain in actual battle form but a small proportion of the entire number that died from famine, pestilence, and the sword. It is thought that at least one half of the whole population perished. "After thirty years of battles, burnings, murders, and diseases, Germany no longer looked like itself. The proud nation was changed into a miserable mob of beggars and thieves. Famishing peasants, cowardly citizens, lewd soldiers, rancorous priests, and effeminate nobles, were the miserable remains of the great race which had perished." The prosperity of the country was for a long period destroyed. The fields were allowed to run to waste, and the workshops to lie in ashes. The spirit of industry had fled, and vice, with her twin-sister ignorance, long threw their baleful shadow over the wretched land.

CHAPTER XVIII.

LOUIS XIV. OF FRANCE.

Louis XIV. was for about half a century the central figure, not merely of France, but of Europe. In the eyes of his vain-glorious people, who were dazzled by the splen dour of his court and the magnitude of his ambitious projects, he was for many years *Le Grand Monarque.* But if a *great* prince is one who by his wisdom and virtue promotes, in an unusual degree, the power and prosperity of his country, Louis has no claim to that title; by the lavish expenditure of his country's wealth, and by sacrificing the best blood of her sons in needless wars, he brought his kingdom to the verge of ruin.

LE GRAND MONARQUE AND HIS COURT.

The reign of Louis XIV. is remarkable among other things for its extraordinary duration. He became king in 1643, when only four years of age, and wore the crown until he was an old man of seventy-six. Thus he began his reign when Charles I. was king of England, and ended it after the accession of George I. During his minority, France was governed by his mother and Cardinal Mazarin, who was appointed chief minister on the death, and by the recommendation, of Richelieu. This crafty and subtle Italian completed the work of establishing a thorough despotism that Richelieu had begun; and at his death (AD. 1661) left his royal master the most absolute monarch that ever reigned in France. "There was now in France but one master." Louis, who was at that time twenty-three years of age, resolved to be his own prime minister. Having mastered the intricate duties of that high office, he dismissed the ministers whom Mazarin had recommended, and made Colbert his financial minister and chief adviser.

The key to his whole policy is found in his well-known reply to some one who spoke to him of the state: "L'état! c'est moi." He wished to be considered the author of every great enterprise in his kingdom, and his own glory to be kept in view as the one great universal object. He regarded the people as existing for the king rather than the king for the people. He was a perfect egotist; vanity, selfishness, and ambition were the ruling motives of his life. But he was by no means a worthless king. Throughout his long reign he applied himself to the business of his high office with marvellous punctuality and assiduity. Everything at his Court and in his Cabinet was done with the regularity of clock-work.

The pomp and splendour of his Court, and the punctilious etiquette that the king practised and exacted were the theme of admiration throughout Europe. "The Court," says his great panegyrist, "became the centre of pleasure and the model of all other courts. It seems as if nature at that time took a pleasure in producing in France the greatest men in all the arts, and in assembling at the Court whatever was beautiful in women and noble in men. The king surpassed all his courtiers in the elegance of his person and the majestic beauty of his countenance. The sound of his voice gained the hearts which his presence intimidated. He had a gait which became him and his rank, but which would have been ridiculous in any other."

There was no palace in the kingdom deemed worthy to receive this great monarch, until he built the palace of Versailles on a scale of grandeur before unknown in France. The chief feature is its monotonous and formal magnificence. The extensive gardens planted around it are distinguished by the same formal beauty. Everything in them is stamped with mathematical precision; even the very trees stand like ranks of well-drilled soldiers, and grow exactly in the same shape, bough for bough.

In this magnificent abode, *Le Grand Monarque* lived as a god, the object of constant adulation, the inimitable model of grace and dignity, the fountain of all favours and honours. The goddess of this Court was not the Queen of France, Maria Theresa, the discreet and virtuous daughter of Philip IV. of Spain, but a haughty and imperious beauty, the Marchioness de Montespan. Whoever would gain a favour from the king paid court to his mistress. When her power over the royal egotist at length declined with her beauty, Madame de Maintenon became the favourite at Court. By her fascinating conversation and ready wit, she gained such ascendency over the king, that on the death of the queen she became his wife, being married to him in private (A.D. 1685.) But it was a dear-bought honour. Her duty was to keep the king amused, and this she found no easy task. In a letter to a friend, she complains of "the torment of having to amuse an unamusable king."

Louis seems never to have enjoyed the immunities of private life. He appears to have been in public from morning to night. Being regarded as a model by the fashionable world, his mode of life is worth our knowing, as we shall thereby gain an insight into the manners and customs of the age. At eight o'clock precisely every morning his valet called him, and then his old nurse ushered into his apartment the first physician and surgeon of the Court to feel his pulse and inspect his tongue. The grand chamberlain, with a crowd of courtiers at his heels, was then admitted to attend his *levée*. The first ceremony was to hand the king his powdered peruke; and this was always presented before his curtains were undrawn at the end of a long cane, for his majesty thought it undignified to be seen in his own natural locks. Truly an artificial age, void of one touch of nature. The attendant nobles coveted the honour of assisting the king at his toilette; one handed him his shirt with cambric sleeves and ruffles, another put on his silk stockings, a third stood ready with his knee-breeches of satin; this one held his looking-glass, that one was privileged to offer him his embroidered waistcoat, whilst another claimed the honour of putting on his red-heeled shoes with silver buckles. When the ceremonies of the levée were at length over, the king occupied himself in transacting business with his ministers till dinner-time. He dined in public, with nobles posted behind his chair to anticipate his every wish; whilst a throng of admiring courtiers, standing in groups, enjoyed the high privilege of seeing their monarch eat. His vast palace was crowded with titled servants and their suites of attendants. They prepared and took part in the constant fêtes, balls, and carousals, which were the unfailing amusements of the Court, even in times of the direst distress. Thus the king lived in the midst of pomp and splendour. But as time went on, the spirit which had found satisfaction in them fled. The pomp and ceremonies of the Court in the king's old age have been compared to "wedding-dresses upon corpses"—all was weariness and disgust, icy splendour and frigid formality.

FOREIGN AFFAIRS.

Louis's ambition led him into many wars, by which his territory was somewhat enlarged, but at an enormous expenditure of blood and treasure. "War," says a French historian, "at the end of a few years, renders the conqueror almost as wretched as the conquered. It is a gulf in which all the streams of wealth are lost."

In 1665, Louis laid claim to the Spanish Netherlands, on the pretence that they belonged to him in right of his wife, Maria Theresa of Spain. Flanders was overrun with ease and rapidity; but so formidable a league was formed against the aggressor, embracing England, Sweden, and Holland, that, in 1668, he agreed to make peace.

Louis had signed the treaty only to gain time. He soon afterwards entered into a secret treaty with Charles II. of England, who, for a pension of £200,000 a-year, promised to assist the French king in subjugating Holland. Having also secured the neutrality of Sweden and Germany, Louis marched an army of 120,000 soldiers—many of whom were armed with that new and terrible weapon, the bayonet — into the Dutch territory (A.D. 1672). William, Prince of Orange, afterwards William III. of England, by his military ability and patriotism, saved his country from the tyranny of the French, as his ancestor, William the Silent, had rescued it from the Spaniards. Now, as then, the sluices were opened, and the country around Amsterdam ceded to the waves. Notwithstanding the splendid efforts of the great French generals, Turenne and Prince Condé, the Dutch, though defeated, would not be conquered. They resolved "to die," if necessary, "in disputing the last ditch." After six years spent in unavailing attempts to break the spirit of the Dutch, Louis made peace with Holland at Nimeguen (A.D. 1678). Spain, having fought on the side of the Dutch, had to pay to France, as the price of peace, eleven towns on the frontiers of Flanders, and the whole of Franche-Comté, which formed a part of the old province of Burgundy, on the confines of Switzerland.

During the late war, the French fleet had won almost its first laurels. Three times in a single year the French admiral, Duquesne, defeated the Dutch fleet. In the second fight the celebrated De Ruyter, who commanded the Dutch, was slain. These successes were the more remarkable, because when Louis assumed the government, the navy of France was miserably small and in wretched condition. Even her commerce was carried on mainly by means of Dutch and English vessels. In a few years, however, Louis, aided by Colbert, contrived to throw new life and vigour into the French marine. Dockyards and arsensals were established at Brest, Rochefort, Toulon, Dunkerque, and Havre; and strenuous efforts were made to construct a navy that should be worthy of France. The creation of a powerful navy was certainly one of the true glories of this reign.

The treaty of Nimeguen was followed by eleven years of comparative peace. In 1689, Louis, in the face of a stronger combination than ever, renewed the war. William, Prince of Orange, had in the meantime become

King of England, so that his power was now very formidable. Louis sent troops to Ireland to support the cause of James II., but the hopes of that monarch vanished with his defeat on the banks of the Boyne (A.D. 1690). In every other quarter the French were at first successful, especially at sea. On the day before the battle of the Boyne, the French admiral, Tourville, beat the combined fleets of England and Holland off Beachy Head. Tourville sustained, however, a complete defeat from Admiral Russel, in 1692, off Cape La Hougue; and thus England was freed from all dangers of invasion from the French army that had been assembled for that purpose at Cherbourg, under King James. For nine years the provinces on the Rhine were deluged with blood. The ordinary streams of industry were dried up; the commerce of the world was paralysed, so that the horrors of famine and disease greatly aggravated the common miseries of war. The peace of Ryswick (A.D. 1697) arrested the work of destruction for a time. Louis, by this treaty, obtained Strasburg, one of the chief keys of the Rhine, on which his celebrated engineer, Vauban, exhausted all the resources of his art.

The last war in which Louis engaged was still more disastrous to France. It is known as the "War of the Spanish Succession." Charles II. of Spain, dying in 1700, left the crown by his will to Philip, Duke of Anjou, the second son of the dauphin, and Louis was resolved to maintain the claims of his grandson by force of arms. The emperor, who claimed the Spanish crown for his second son, declared war against France; and William III., who was always ready to aim a blow at his old antagonist, entered into an alliance with the emperor. The reader of English history is familiar with the series of brilliant victories gained by the allies under the command of Marlborough and Prince Eugene, beginning at Blenheim (A.D. 1704), and ending at Malplaquet (A.D. 1709). In Spain, however, the arms of Louis were crowned with victory. The treaty of Utrecht (A.D. 1713) left his grandson, Philip V., on the throne of Spain, on the express understanding that the crowns of France and Spain should be for ever separate.

DOMESTIC AFFAIRS.

When Louis began to govern by himself, he evidently desired, as Voltaire says, "to reform his kingdom, to embellish his court, and to bring the arts to perfection." He wisely made choice of Colbert as his chief minister. By the wise policy of this minister and his royal master, commerce and manufactures were vastly extended and improved. The Gulf of Lyons and the Bay of Biscay were united by the canal of Languedoc, a gigantic work which had been projected in the time of the Romans, and again contemplated in the reign of Charlemagne. It employed 12,000 men under the direction of the most able engineers for seventeen years. Meanwhile, considerable progress was made in manufactures. Colbert, who was desirous that the French should excel all other people in handicrafts, invited over from Italy and the Netherlands some of the best workmen in steel, iron, plate-glass, etc. He also established the celebrated manufacture called Gobelin's tapestry, and introduced stocking-weaving from England. The French lace and silks became famous.

France had become rich and powerful, when Louis's ambition imperilled the welfare of his country, as we have shown, by drawing the sword to extend its boundaries. A still more fatal mistake was his persecution of the Huguenots, which had the effect of driving from France thousands of skilful artisans. Many took refuge in England, where they made great improvements in several of the arts, particularly in silk and ribbon weaving, the construction of clocks and watches, the making of surgical instruments and cutlery of all kinds. Instead of encouraging the industrious Protestants to remain in France by securing to them their religious liberty, Louis threatened with the severest penalties all who attempted to leave the kingdom; and, as a last act of folly, revoked the famous edict of Nantes (A.D. 1685), which, under certain restrictions, had put their religion under the protection of the law.

The reign of Louis XIV. is the golden age of French literature. Molière wrote many clever comedies; Corneille and Racine produced some great tragedies; Bossuet, Bourdaloue, and Massillon were eloquent preachers; Boileau and La Fontaine distinguished themselves as poets; Des Cartes was an eminent mathematician; Pascal is celebrated for his *Pensées;* and Fénélon is well known as the author of a poetic romance entitled *Télémaque.* Louis was the patron of all these eminent men except La Fontaine, whose extreme simplicity had no charm for *Le Grand Monarque.* For the encouragement of science and art the king instituted the academy of sciences, of belles-lettres, of painting, of sculpture, and of architecture; he also built an observatory. He gave pensions and rewards to men of genius, both French and foreign, and induced some of the latter to leave their own country and reside in France. The age of Louis is remarkable for the progress made in natural philosophy, especially in England. "It is," says Voltaire, "especially in philosophy that the English have been the masters of other nations." Bacon taught the right method of studying nature; and Newton, "the glory of the human race," was the first to discover and demonstrate the universal law of nature that holds the planets in their course.

GENERAL CONDITION OF THE PEOPLE.

The reign of Louis, though in many respects brilliant, was by no means conducive to the general happiness of the nation. The vain monarch sacrificed the prosperity and well-being of his subjects in the attempt to raise France to the first place among the nations, and himself to the highest pinnacle of glory among the crowned heads of the world.

Whilst the king was building his gorgeous palaces, and laying out his beautiful gardens, and feting his gay nobles, his poor subjects were burdened with excessive taxes to pay for all this grandeur. Whilst the king was making war to satisfy his ambition, his impoverished people often knew not where to turn for bread to satisfy their hunger.

Not only were the taxes enormous, but they were unjustly distributed. Thus the land-tax was paid only by a third of those who held land; the nobles, the clergy, and those in the service of the government were exempt. Take the following as a picture of the times. The tax-collectors of a certain district meet at a tavern to distribute the tax imposed on their district among the inhabitants who are liable. They go their rounds in a body for mutual protection, raising in their passage along the streets a multitude of cries and curses. On arriving at the end of their journey, they have pocketed nothing but insults. Bailiffs and constables are then sent; the wretched people try to gain time by bribing and treating these officials. At length, the day of final reckoning is come; the cattle are seized and sold; the miserable furniture is put up to auction; even the doors and window shutters are unhinged; nay, the cabin itself is demolished for the bricks and timber, if no other means are found of raising the amount required. But of all the imposts the most detested was the *gabelle* or salt-tax. The government monopolised the trade in salt, and accordingly it put on this necessary article any price it pleased. Every householder was compelled to purchase a certain quantity, fixed for him by the authorities, whether he had need of it or not. Further, the quantity differed in the several provinces, and there were provinces that were entirely free from the gabelle.

Such arbitrary and unequal measures as these were the seeds of the Great Revolution. Such monarchs as Louis XIV. sowed the wind, their descendants reaped the whirlwind. Signs of the coming storm were visible before Louis ended his gilded reign. Fénélon thus wrote to his majesty: "Your people die of hunger. The culture of the fields is almost abandoned; the towns and villages are depopulated; all the trades languish. Instead of drawing money from this poor people, one ought to supply them with the means of subsistence. The whole of France is as a great hospital without resources. Popular tumults are becoming common; you are reduced to the deplorable extremity of allowing sedition to go unpunished, or of killing people who are driven to despair, and whose ranks are daily thinned by famine and disease."

Such was the wretched state of France in the latter part of this reign. Louis had the unhappiness of outliving his fame, his friends, his children, and his hopes. He died in 1715, leaving the crown to his great-grandson, Louis XV., then a boy of five years.

CHAPTER XIX.

GREAT MONARCHS OF THE EIGHTEENTH CENTURY.

Great wars formed a marked feature of the eighteenth century. In every European state of any importance a large standing army was now kept. It was still considered the great business of a king to lead his armies in battle. That king was reckoned the greatest who most excelled in the art of war. Among the most renowned generals of the age were **Charles XII.** of Sweden, and **Frederick II.** of Prussia. But a greater prince than either of these, when judged by the beneficial results of his reign, was **Peter the Great** of Russia. It is the design of this chapter to give the character and chief exploits of these three famous monarchs. As the reign of Charles XII. is intimately connected with that of Peter the Great, it will be most convenient to interweave the history of these two rivals, after giving an account of

THE CZAR'S TRAVELS AND REFORMS.

Peter the Great ascended the throne of Muscovy, or Russia, in 1682, when a boy ten years of age. His sister, Sophia, who was regent, thought to keep the sovereignty in her own hands, by letting the boy grow up in ignorance and vice. But he soon became aware of his own ignorance, and evinced the most ardent thirst for knowledge. At the age of seventeen he assumed the reins of government, and being an absolute monarch, he soon showed his resolution to effect a thorough reform in the manners of his subjects, and to raise his country to a high place among the nations of Europe.

When Peter began to reign, Russia was but a poor half-civilized country, without political influence, without manufactures, without a navy, and with only Archangel for a seaport. The Russians are of the Sclavonic race, and at that time retained the long flowing robes and customs of the Asiatics. They had nominally embraced Christianity in the tenth century, but the truth of the Gospel was still, to a great extent, hidden amid the darkness of ignorance and superstition.

As the first step in working out his plans, Peter began to form an army, drilled and accoutred like the best European regiments. In this task he was greatly aided by Lefort, a Swiss, and Patrick Gordon, a Scotchman. The Czar, being determined to learn the military art thoroughly, entered his first regiment as a drummer, and gained promotion from one step to another, as he became proficient. Meanwhile, he studied the art of shipbuilding, and began to construct a navy.

Having spent seven years in laying the foundation of his country's future greatness, he resolved on visiting foreign countries, to gain the knowledge indispensable for carrying on the work he had begun. At the same time he sent several young Russians to Italy, Germany, and Holland, to acquire information of various kinds, especially that relating to naval and military matters. In the same spirit that he had entered the army as a drummer, he engaged himself to a shipbuilder, at Saardam, in Holland; and here he might have been seen in red woollen shirt and duck trousers, plying his adze as a ship carpenter. For seven weeks he lived in a little shingle cottage, rose early, made his bed, and cooked his breakfast. He passed nine months in Holland, and during that time mastered the Dutch language, acquired a clear insight into the construction of a ship, and examined carefully all the factories and institutions of Amsterdam.

From Holland he passed over to England, where he was received with great honour by William III. Peter's main object was to examine the dockyards of England, and for that purpose he occupied a house at Deptford, after he had seen the chief places of interest in London. He spent most of the day, when not in the dockyard, in sailing or rowing on the Thames; he became as expert in managing vessels as an able seaman, and quite as fond as a sailor, when the day's work was over, of retiring to a tavern for grog and tobacco. Peter was so much delighted with the British navy, that he was wont to declare, that if he were not Czar of Russia, he would like to be Admiral of England. Towards the end of the year (A.D. 1698), on taking leave of King William, Peter presented him with a ruby of the value of £10,000, which he drew from his waistcoat pocket, wrapped up in a bit of brown paper.

From England the Czar went to Vienna, to see the soldiers of the emperor, whose dress and discipline were then accounted the model for Europe. His stay at the Austrian capital was cut short by alarming news from Moscow. The *Strelitz*, the old body-guard, had rebelled. On Peter's arrival, he found that General Gordon had put an end to the mutiny. The rebels were brought to trial, and for weeks the cord, the axe, and the wheel were furnished with numerous victims daily.

The great Czar now turned himself in good earnest to the work of social reform. He made war against the long dresses and long beards of the men; he stationed tailors and barbers at the gates of Moscow, to clip the beard and whiskers of every man who passed in or out, and "to cut his petticoats all round about." Such was the outcry raised, that the autocrat had to be satisfied with imposing a tax on long beards and robes, leaving the change to the gradual work of time and the influence of his own example. Hitherto the women of rank had, according to the oriental custom, been kept in seclusion; but now they were encouraged to mix in the society of gentlemen, and to take part in the conversation at table, and in the amusements of the evening. Peter, also, had the Bible translated into the Russian tongue, set up printing-presses, founded hospitals and almshouses, erected linen and paper factories, introduced flocks of Saxony sheep, and encouraged skilful mechanics, of all nations and trades, to settle in his empire.

PETER THE GREAT AND CHARLES XII.

At the time of Peter's accession, Russia was so hemmed in by neighbouring states, that it had no access to the great ocean highway for its commerce except through Archangel, whose port, the greater part of the year, was blocked up with ice. The Black Sea was commanded by the Turks and the Baltic by the Swedes, at that time two of the most powerful nations of Europe. The Czar was convinced that his country could never be great and prosperous till seaports were wrested from them. Before leaving Russia on his tour in the west, he had seized Azov, and thus opened up a communication with the Black Sea. And now on his return he entered into a war with Sweden in the hope of gaining a footing on the coast of the Baltic; for the Swedes were not only masters of Finland, but also of the provinces between the Gulf of Finland and the Gulf of Riga. By the treaty of Westphalia, it should also be remembered, the Swedes had acquired a large part of the Baltic coast now belonging to Prussia. Accordingly, Peter entered into an alliance with the kings of Denmark and Poland (A.D. 1700); and invading Ingria, a province on the north of the Gulf of Finland, with 60,000 men, laid siege to Narva.

Sweden, assailed on three sides by her triple foe, seemed in a perilous condition, especially when it was considered that her ruler, Charles XII., was only a gay, inexperienced youth. This untried prince, however, turned out a military genius. "I am resolved," said the spirited king, "to attack the first that shall declare war against me in such a way as to strike terror into the rest;" and well he kept his word. Henceforth Charles devoted himself to war, which became his sole delight and all-absorbing passion. Whilst Peter regarded war as the necessary means to the great end he had in view, his rival revelled in it as the only employment worthy of a king. Charles loved war for its own sake; Peter delighted in war only so far as it promoted his designs for the elevation of his people.

In a campaign of six weeks, Charles brought Denmark to his feet. He then fought his way to Narva, which was hard pressed by the Russians. With his gallant force of only 9000 men, Charles stormed the entrenchments of the besiegers, whilst favoured by a snow storm that drove its flakes into the eyes of the enemy. In three hours the camp was won, and 30,000 Russians were made prisoners of war. When the Czar, who was absent, was informed of this ignominious defeat, he replied, "I know very well that the Swedes will have the advantage over us for some time; but they will teach us at length to beat them." Charles now turned his arms against Frederick Augustus, King of Poland and Elector of Saxony; and thus gave his rival time to recruit his forces for the renewal of the contest.

The notes of military preparation resounded throughout Russia. The Czar strained every nerve to create an effective army; he even melted down the church bells of Moscow to found cannon. Yet amid all this military activity, Peter steadily carried on those peaceful projects by which he hoped to regenerate the nation. Whilst the Swedish king was engaged in Poland, Peter was slowly but steadily ousting the Swedes from the banks of the Neva, and thus acquiring a site for a great commercial city. On New Year's Day, 1702, the Russian troops gained a decisive victory. "We have at last," said Peter, "beaten the Swedes when two to one against them; we shall, by and bye, be able to face them man to man." The same year he built the fortress of St. Petersburg on an island near the mouth of the Neva; and still lower down the river the impregnable fortress of Cronstadt, which commands its entrance. The country around the citadel of St. Petersburg was a morass. Here, however, the Czar resolved to build a new city. In the course of a twelvemonth the city of St. Petersburg arose as if by magic. Peter being an autocrat, he could not only collect thousands upon thousands of workmen to drain and build, but he could compel them to persevere with their labours, though they perished by thousands from toil, privation, and the pestilential air of the marshes. Under the marvellous energies of the founder, St. Petersburg soon became a fine city, and a place of great commercial importance. Peter made it his capital, and its subsequent growth and prosperity have justified his choice.

Charles XII. looked with careless indifference upon the gigantic labours of his rival, and merely remarked, "that the Czar might amuse himself in setting up his wooden houses, but they would serve only as firewood in the hands of his soldiers." Meanwhile, Peter was gradually gaining ground, and in 1704 the province of Ingria was annexed to his empire. The government of this new province was entrusted to Prince Menzikoff, a man of extraordinary abilities, who in his boyhood sold cakes and patties in the streets of Moscow. A still greater elevation of rank and fortune awaited an orphan maiden, named Catharine, who was taken captive at Marienburg, and received into the service of Prince Menzikoff. While handing round fruits and wines to the Prince's guests, she attracted the Czar's attention, who was so pleased with her beauty, intelligence, and character, that he made her his wife. This poor stranger, who had been discovered amidst the ruins of a plundered town, not only became the wife of the Czar, but on his death the absolute sovereign of his empire.

It was not until 1707 that Charles had finished his war with Frederick Augustus of Saxony and Poland. Having wrested from him the crown of Poland, Charles might have placed it upon his own head; but this singular monarch was fonder of winning crowns than of wearing them. Having nominated a prince for the vacant throne of Poland, Charles invaded Russia with his veteran troops (A.D. 1708). "Nowhere," said the great warrior, "will I treat with Peter but at Moscow." On this Peter remarked, "My brother Charles wishes to act the part of Alexander, but he shall not find a Darius in me." The Czar with his army retreated slowly before the advancing enemy, thus drawing them on step by step into the heart of a barren country, where they were overtaken by the snows of winter. After the loss of thousands of his men from cold, hunger, and disease, the king entered the Ukraine, and with 20,000 frost-bitten, ill-clad, ill-fed soldiers, besieged the small but strongly fortified town of Pultowa.

The day was now fast approaching when the two rivals were, for the first and last time, to measure their strength, and to fight a great decisive battle. Peter appeared before Pultowa with an army of 60,000 men (15th June, 1709). The two monarchs headed their respective forces. Charles, who had been previously wounded in the foot, was carried on a litter from rank to rank. The litter was shattered in pieces by a cannon ball, but the king was not struck. Peter narrowly escaped, his hat being shot through. After two hours of incessant fighting, the Swedes gave way and fell into confusion. The rout now became general and the slaughter dreadful. More than a half of the Swedish army remained bleeding or dead upon the battle-field. Charles escaped to Turkey with the fragments of his forces, and prevailed upon the sultan to declare war against Russia.

Peter, crossing the Pruth to attack his enemies in their own country, was surrounded by a Turkish army 200,000 strong. For three days the Russians kept their foes at bay, but as their ammunition was now expended, they could resist no longer. At the suggestion of Catharine, who had accompanied her husband to the seat of war, a present of her jewels was sent to the Turkish vizier with a proposal of peace. A treaty was signed and the Russian army was saved (A.D. 1711).

Charles had taken up his abode at Benaer, 60 miles from the spot where his rival was entrapped by the Turkish army. On hearing of the treaty, and the return of the Russians to their own country, his fury knew no bounds. Indeed, since the battle of Pultowa he had behaved like a madman. Instead of returning to Sweden he lingered on at Bender. Whilst the truant king was playing the part of a lunatic in Turkey, his enemies were stripping the Swedes of all their conquests; Frederick Augustus recovered the crown of Poland; Peter made himself master of the provinces on both sides of the Gulf of Finland; the kings of Prussia and Denmark laid violent hands on the Swedish dominions south of the Baltic. At length the Turks, being heartily tired of their troublesome guest, sent a body of troops to remove him. The heroic madman armed his servants, barricaded his house, and killed, it is said, twenty of the assailants with his own hand before hurling his sword into the air. Early on a November morning in 1714, Charles in disguise reached Stralsund, almost the only town his enemies had left him in Pomerania.

The return of Charles made no change in the fortune of war. Even Stralsund was compelled to surrender before the close of the year 1717. Charles had previously contrived to make his escape in a small boat at midnight. He reached a Swedish vessel that carried him to his ruined country, both prince and people being broken in fortune but not in spirit. His last mad exploit was an attempt to snatch Norway out of the grasp of the Danes, by climbing the snow-clad mountains of that rugged country with an army of 25,000 men in winter. So inured was he to cold, that he slept in the open air on a bed of straw, covered only with his cloak, whilst his sentinels were often frozen to death at their posts. Whilst besieging Fredericshall, he was killed by a ball from the fortress (A.D. 1718).

The king that had dazzled all Europe with his prowess passed away without leaving a token of his greatness. His career was like that of a bright meteor that flashes through the sky and is lost in darkness. The death of Charles was the signal for peace. Sweden was shorn of most of her former conquests. She has never regained the proud position she occupied before the reign of her great warrior.

Peter the Great gained a large portion of what Charles had lost. Two years before the death of his rival, the

Czar, feeling that his empire had nothing to fear from Sweden, undertook a second tour through Europe, accompanied by Catharine. On his arrival at the gay city of Paris, the king wished to lodge him in splendid style at the Louvre; but Peter preferred to stay at a small hotel, where he could live in his own simple frugal way. "I am a soldier," he said; "a little bread and beer satisfy me; I prefer few friends to many, and small rooms to large ones." He made a point of seeing, while at Paris, all that was remarkable for magnificence, ingenuity, or utility. He visited the splendid tomb of Cardinal Richelieu; and after looking attentively at his image, he exclaimed, "Great man! I would have given thee one half of my dominions to learn of thee how to govern the other half."

Peter spent the remaining years of his life in useful reforms and patriotic labours. In 1724, Peter, being now at peace with all the world, celebrated by a grand naval review the creation of the Russian navy, which now comprised 41 ships of the line, carrying 2106 cannons, and manned by 14,960 seamen. The little skiff, in which he had paddled when a boy, was exhibited on this occasion, under the name of the *Little Grandsire,* as the ancestor of the Russian fleet. The great Czar died of fever (A.D. 1725), caught by wading up to his knees in water to aid in rescuing a boat, full of soldiers and sailors, that had struck upon a rock. Peter found Russia a semi-barbarous country, convulsed by disorders, and weak from disunion; without a ship, with hardly a seaport; he left it one of the great powers of Europe, freed in great measure from its barbarous customs; he created a new capital on the shores of the Baltic, and a powerful fleet to protect its commerce; in a word, he laid the foundation of Russian prosperity and grandeur. He was succeeded by his beloved consort Catharine.

FREDERICK THE GREAT.

Prussia is now one of the most powerful states in the world; its greatness, however, is of recent date. This important kingdom originated in the little state of Brandenburg, which, four centuries ago, was bestowed by the Emperor Sigismund upon the noble house of Hohenzollern. In the seventeenth century the Elector of Brandenburg obtained from the king of Poland the investiture of the duchy of Prussia, a province in the north-east corner of the present kingdom of Prussia. Frederick William, the "Great Elector," acquired for Prussia, by the treaty of Westphalia, the rich city and district of Magdeburg, and other valuable possessions; and he left to his son Frederick a principality as considerable as any not called a kingdom. Frederick preferred to be a little king rather than a great elector like his father, and in the year 1700 assumed the royal title. His successor, named Frederick William after the great elector, made it the great object of his life to form an army that should surpass the best troops of Europe. Macaulay observes that "his feeling about his troops resembled a miser's feeling about his money." He loved to collect them, to count them, to review them, but they were too precious in his eyes to be thrown away upon the battle-field. He was very fond of sham fights, but took care to avoid all real warfare. The great military machine, however, which he had brought to rare perfection, was destined to accomplish great results in the hands of his famous son.

Frederick II., surnamed the Great, was born a prince, but was treated worse than a beggar's son. Kicked and cuffed about by his tyrannical father, often fed upon coarse bread and water, snubbed by the king whenever he betrayed a desire to learn anything not bearing directly upon a soldier's profession, the boy grew up with an aversion to his father, and at length tried to escape from his ill treatment. The fugitive was discovered, brought back, and condemned to death as a deserter from the army, and only saved from the scaffold by the intercession of half the crowned heads of Europe. The prince was fortunately for himself kept in prison for a long time. He could now read his favourite authors without being kicked, and play on the lute without having it broken upon his head.

Frederick succeeded his unamiable father in 1740. A few months later Charles VI. of Germany died, leaving his dominions to his daughter, Maria Theresa, according to a law of succession called the "Pragmatic Sanction," which had been promulgated nearly thirty years before, and solemnly guaranteed by all the European powers. Foremost among the princes that, in spite of treaties, took arms against Maria Theresa was Frederick of Prussia. His own words are: "Ambition, interest, the desire of making people talk about me, carried the day; and I decided for war." He poured his troops into Silesia in the depth of winter. No enemy ventured to encounter him in the field, and before January 1741, he returned to Berlin with the keys of most of the Silesian towns and fortresses at his command.

This successful robbery tempted other princes to draw the sword, and carve out, if possible, a slice of the Austrian territory for themselves. Two French armies invaded Germany; and the Elector of Bavaria, who claimed the imperial crown, marched within eight miles of Vienna. The queen fled to Hungary, and threw herself on the devotion of her subjects in that part of her dominions. At the first sitting of the Diet she appeared clad in mourning for her father, with the crown of St. Stephen on her head, and implored her people to redress her wrongs. The nobles and deputies sprang to their feet, half drew their sabres, and vowed to stand by her with life and fortune. And when she held up before them her little infant son, the old hall rang with the cry, "Let us die for our sovereign, Maria Theresa." The echoes of that war-cry resounded throughout Europe.

Frederick, the royal robber, was now ready to betray the queen's enemies with whom he had been in league. His policy was simply this: first, to rob the queen of Hungary; secondly, to permit no one else to rob her. Accordingly, he made peace with Maria upon her recognition of his claim to Silesia (A.D. 1742).

The queen was soon everywhere triumphant. The retreat of the French army from Bohemia, in the depth of a severe winter, could be traced by the corpses of thousands who died of cold, hunger, and fatigue. Bavaria was overrun, and the elector, driven from his dominions, was hurried by shame and remorse to an untimely end. An English army appeared in the heart of Germany and defeated the French at Dettingen. The French, however, took their revenge for this defeat, at Fontenoy, two years later. The treaty of Aix-la-Chapelle (A.D. 1748) restored peace to Europe. Of all the powers that had taken part in the war, the only gainer was the perfidious king of Prussia.

The combatants separated, and spent the next eight years in sharpening their swords for a deadlier struggle. This breathing time was spent by Frederick to the good of his country. He was not content with being, like Louis XIV., his own prime minister; he would be his own sole minister. The highest officers under his government were mere clerks. Macaulay gives an interesting account of the life of this active ruler and statesman at this period: "At Potsdam, his ordinary residence, he rose at three in summer and four in winter. A page soon appeared, with a large basket full of all the letters which had arrived for the king by the last courier, despatches from ambassadors, reports from officers of revenue, plans of buildings, proposals for draining marshes, complaints from persons who thought themselves aggrieved, applications from persons who wanted titles, military commissions, and civil situations. He examined the seals with a keen eye; for he was never for a moment free from the suspicion that some fraud might be practised on him. Then he read the letters, divided them into several packets, and signified his pleasure, generally by a mark, often by two or three words, now and then by some cutting epigram. By eight he had generally finished this part of his task. The adjutant-general was then in attendance, and received instructions for the day as to all the military arrangements of the kingdom. Then the king went to review his guards, not as kings ordinarily review their guards, but with the minute attention and severity of an old drill-sergeant. In the meantime the four cabinet secretaries had been employed in answering the letters on which the king had that morning signified his will. The king, always on his guard against treachery, took from the heap a handful of letters at random, and looked into them to see whether his instructions had been exactly followed. Frederick then signed the replies, and all were sent off the same evening."

The national revenue was spent chiefly on the army and on buildings. In all other respects the king was parsimonious. His wardrobe consisted of one gala dress that lasted all his life; of two or three old thread-bare coats; of yellow waistcoats soiled with snuff, and of huge boots embrowned by time. He governed as an absolute monarch. His people, however, enjoyed the blessings of order, security, and speedy justice. All religions were tolerated; but little praise is due to Frederick on this account, as his apparent liberality of spirit was due to his religious indifference.

The empress-queen, as Maria Theresa may be styled, had never for a moment forgiven the wrong which she had received from Frederick. To recover Silesia, to humble the King of Prussia to the dust, was the darling object of her life; at last she succeeded in securing the co-operation of Russia, France, Sweden, and Saxony. England, as usual, took the side opposed to France, and allied herself with Prussia. The gigantic war that began in 1756 is known as *The Seven Years' War.* It raged in almost every quarter of the globe. England and France measured their strength chiefly in America and India. Their quarrel involved the natives of these lands; black men fought on the coast of Coromandel, and red men scalped each other on the shores of the Great American Lakes.

To the astonishment of Europe, the king of Prussia proved a match for all the forces arrayed against him. As often as his cause seemed desperate, by some marvellous victory he repaired his fortune. The heroism of this king never shone so brightly as in the darkest hour of his misfortunes. At the beginning of 1757, the net seemed to have closed completely around him. The Russians were spreading devastation through the eastern provinces; Silesia was overrun by the Austrians; a great French army, after defeating the English and Hanoverians, was advancing from the west; and Berlin was in the hands of the Croatians. But in thirty days the whole face of the war was changed. At Rosbach, Frederick defeated the French, though they were two to one (Nov. 5). Victorious in the west, the king turned his arms towards Silesia, where everything seemed lost. Here he defeated the Austrians in the great battle of Leuthen (Dec. 5). "That battle," said Napoleon, "was a masterpiece. Of itself, it is sufficient to entitle Frederick to a place in the first rank among generals." But it was not sufficient to put an end to the war. Many a hard-fought battle was lost and won before the peace of Hubertsburg was signed (A.D. 1763). Frederick ceded nothing. The whole Continent in arms had proved unable to tear Silesia from his iron grasp.

Prussia was still further enlarged in the reign of this monarch by the annexation of a part of Poland. The Poles had, in the previous century, laid Europe under an obligation by the bold front they presented to the Turks. A Mohammedan army of 200,000 men was on the eve of taking Vienna, when John Sobieski, King of Poland, at the head of an allied army of Austrians, Bavarians, Saxons, and Poles, came to the rescue, and gained one of the most signal victories in the history of war (A.D. 1683). But the bravery of the Poles could not long avert the ruin of their nation. That unhappy kingdom, on the death of Sobieski, fell into incurable disorders, and by her own divisions fell an easy prey to her powerful neighbours, Prussia, Russia, and Austria. The first partition of Poland between these three powers was carried into effect in 1772, and this was succeeded in 1794 by a final partition. Thus perished the eldest born of the European family of nations, just after Prussia, the youngest of the same family, had taken its place among the foremost nations of the Continent. The high position assumed by Prussia was due mainly to the genius, brave perseverance, and unscrupulous ambition of the monarch, whom her sons, in grateful admiration, call Frederick the Great. After a reign of nearly forty-seven years, gout and asthma, ending in dropsy, brought Frederick to his death-bed (A.D. 1786).

CHAPTER XX.

RISE OF THE UNITED STATES.

America was discovered in 1492. But more than a hundred years elapsed before the English began to make those settlements on the coast of the Atlantic which afterwards became the United States. In the meantime, various nations of Europe, particularly Spain, England, and France, took part in exploring the coasts of North America.

COLONIZATION OF NORTH AMERICA.

The Spaniards, under Cortes and others, planted their flag in the southern part of the continent. The wealthy empire of Mexico, with its rich gold mines, became a province of Spain in 1521, and so remained for three centuries. Florida was occupied by the Spaniards in 1565, and St. Augustine, the oldest city in the United States, was then founded. This province passed into the hands of the British, by the treaty of Paris, in 1763.

The French were first drawn to the coasts of North America by the fisheries on the banks of Newfoundland. Champlain and other Frenchmen explored the neighbouring coasts. About the beginning of the seventeenth century, the French had effected settlements at Quebec in Canada, and at Port Royal in Acadia (Nova Scotia). The principal French explorers were Jesuit missionaries; in 1634 these zealous men had established missions as far westward as Lake Huron. The French also sailed down the Mississippi, and took possession of the country near its mouth, which they called Louisiana in honour of Louis XIV.

Meanwhile, the English settled in much larger numbers along the coasts of the Atlantic, between Canada and Florida. At the outbreak of the War of Independence, thirteen colonies had been established in these regions; and from them the Republic of the United States was formed.

The first permanent English settlement in North America was that of Jamestown, founded on the shores of Chesapeake Bay in the reign of King James (A.D. 1607). The whole country was then a wilderness in which the Indians roamed in pursuit of wild animals for the sake of their flesh and fur. It was believed to be rich in precious metals. The first company of immigrants, accordingly, did not intend to settle in the country; but hoped soon to grow rich, by successful mining or a lucrative trade with the Indians, and then return home. After suffering grievous disappointment in their search for gold, and famine and disease by their neglect to plough and sow, the adventurers, driven by necessity, became *settlers*, and began to plant and build. Other immigrants continued to arrive, and the colony of **Virginia**, with Jamestown as its capital, became a flourishing settlement. But in 1622 the Indians fell suddenly upon all the outlying settlements, and murdered 360 persons. This led to a bloody struggle, in which the red savages were taught to respect the prowess of the white man, and the terrible weapon at his command. Indian warfare, however, became a disagreeable feature of colonial life in America. These savages resisted all attempts made to civilise them: they acquired the vices of the settlers with facility, but in other respects learnt from them but little. They receded farther and farther from the settlements of the whites, and their numbers gradually dwindled away. As the natives could not be made to work for the colonists, negro slaves were purchased on the coasts of Africa, and being found useful as labourers on the tobacco plantations, this abominable traffic rapidly increased, and slavery became a legal institution in our English colonies of America. The first cargo of slaves was brought into James river by a Dutch trading vessel in 1620.

Whilst Virginia was growing into importance, a new set of colonies, called **New England,** sprung up farther north. The settlers here were for the most part Puritans, who had expatriated themselves for the sake of enjoying that freedom, religious and civil, which was denied to them at home. In 1620, the *Mayflower*, with 101 passengers, known as the Pilgrim Fathers, set sail from Plymouth in Devonshire, and landed on the coast of Massachusetts, at a place since called Plymouth. The summer of 1630 brought to Massachusetts a fleet of thirteen vessels, having on board nearly 1500 Puritan settlers. The new-comers founded the city of Boston. It is worthy of remark, that the Puritans who had sailed to the New World, to enjoy full liberty of conscience, would tolerate no difference of religion within the borders of their province. Four Quakers, who had been banished on account of their religion, were put to death for daring to return.

New York, now the first of all the States in wealth and population, was settled by the Dutch. In 1623, a company of Dutch emigrants landed on the island of Manhattan and founded New Amsterdam. This was the beginning of the great city of New York. In 1660, the Dutch colony could show a population of ten thousand. The English had all this time regarded the Dutch as interlopers, and when Charles II. became king, he resolved to make good his claim to the land they occupied. Accordingly, Charles granted their province to his brother the Duke of York, who sent out a sufficient force to take possession (A.D. 1664). New Amsterdam henceforth received the name of New York.

Pennsylvania was intended as an asylum for the persecuted English Quakers, a religious society, calling themselves Friends, which arose in England about the year 1650. This colony was founded by the celebrated William Penn, who was a member of this sect. The English government owed Penn's father, who had been an admiral in the English navy, a large sum of money. Penn, in payment, took a grant of some large unoccupied lands west of the river Delaware (A.D. 1681). It was Penn's devout wish to reconcile the Indians to his settlement in the territory granted to him by his sovereign. "I desire," he says to them, "to enjoy it with your love and consent, that we may always live together as neighbours and friends." He then offered to purchase of the Indians his right to live among them. The Indian chiefs pledged themselves "to live in love with William Penn and his children, as long as sun and moon should endure." The bargain thus struck was the only compact between savages and Christians that was never broken. As long as the Quaker control of the colony lasted, which was seventy years, there was unbroken harmony between the whites and the red men. Appropriately was the new capital called, by Penn its founder, Philadelphia (brotherly love). Unlike the Pilgrim Fathers, this noble Quaker secured to every person in his province the right "to worship God in such a way as each one shall in conscience believe is most acceptable to God."

Maryland was colonised by Roman Catholics from England in the reign of Charles I., and so called in honour of the Queen, Henrietta Maria.

In 1663, Charles II. gave Lord Clarendon and others a grant of all the land between Virginia and Florida. This territory received the name of **Carolina**, the Latin form of the king's name being *Carolus*. It was afterwards divided into North and South Carolina. Charlestown, the capital of South Carolina, also received its name from Charles II. This southern State became a famous rice-growing country, and so many slaves were employed on the rice plantations, that at the end of forty years they outnumbered the whites in this colony as five to one.

Thirteen colonies were founded by the English within the territory of the United States before the outbreak of the war between them and the mother country. **Georgia** was the last of these colonies. It was founded by a company of benevolent gentlemen, as a refuge for the destitute, in the reign of George II., from whom it derived its name. Large bands of thrifty and intelligent Scots, Swiss, and Germans, were attracted by the liberal grants of land offered to the poor and industrious.

REVOLT OF THE AMERICAN COLONIES.

The attachment of the American Colonies to the mother country was never stronger than at the close of the French War in 1763, when, by the treaty of Paris, Canada, Cape Breton, and Florida, were ceded to England. The colonists were proud of their descent from British ancestors, and gloried in belonging to a nation so renowned for its achievements. The Americans loved the land of their forefathers, and still spoke of England as "home," though they had never by the payment of taxes enriched the English treasury, yet by the quantity of British manufactures which they imported, they brought much wealth to our nation. But the bond which united the two great parts of the English race was about to be broken for ever.

The triumphs gained by the English in the Seven Year's War with the French (A.D. 1756-1763), was attended by a great increase of the national debt. As the war had been undertaken partly in defence of the colonies, it was thought not unreasonable to call upon the colonists to bear part of the expense that had been incurred. Accordingly, in 1765, it was proposed to levy a tax on them; and an Act of Parliament, called the *Stamp Act*, was passed, by which all legal contracts were to be drawn up on stamped paper. The Americans were resolved not to pay any tax imposed by the British Parliament: they contended that, according to the constitution of this realm, Englishmen could not be taxed except by their representatives, and that as the colonists were not represented in Parliament, they could not be taxed by that assembly.

When the Act of Parliament imposing the stamp duty was taken to America, it was reprinted with a skull and crossbones in place of the royal arms, and then carried on a pole through the streets of New York, with a scroll bearing this inscription, "England's Folly and America's Ruin." The Act itself was publicly and ignominiously burnt. The stamps on arriving were stowed away as waste paper. Some of those who had been appointed agents for selling them were hanged in effigy, and all of them publicly renounced the perilous office. The day when the Act was to come into operation was ushered in with portentous solemnities. At Boston the vessels in the harbour hoisted their colours half-mast high, the muffled bells of the churches tolled out a death-knell, and there was a grand *auto-da-fé*, in which the promoters of the Act were paraded and burnt in effigy. When news of this bold conduct reached England, the nation began to awake to the vast importance of this question of colonial taxation. It was at length decided to repeal the obnoxious measure, but to accompany this concession with a declaration of the right of Great Britain to impose taxes on her colonies. Most of the colonists were still loyal to the old country, and the news of the repeal was received by them with great joy and satisfaction, for they regarded the accompanying declaration only as a salve for the injured honour of the government.

Two years afterwards, however, the Parliament acted upon their assumed right to tax the colonies, by laying a duty upon tea, glass, paper, and painter's colours, imported into the American provinces. It was thought that the colonists could not object to taxation in this shape, but the new burdens were met with the same spirited opposition as before. The Puritan State of Massachusetts continued to be the focus of what the ministerialists termed sedition. Even the loyal Virginians, who had descended in great measure from the old Cavaliers, were found in the van of the opposition. The merchants of the principal cities agreed to import no more goods from Great Britain till the duties were removed. Families denied themselves the use of all foreign luxuries, and the trade with England was almost entirely stopped.

The English cabinet deemed it prudent to repeal all the taxes lately imposed, except that on tea, which was retained by way of asserting the right of the British Legislature to tax the colonies. It was hoped, that as the tax was only threepence on the pound of tea, that the colonists would quietly submit. As the people of America were contending for principles of liberty, not mere pecuniary interests, this tea tax left the dispute still open, and chilled the feeling of gratitude, which the entire repeal would have inspired. Accordingly, this small duty on tea met with a more determined resistance than ever. Rather than pay the tax, man, woman, and child, would abstain wholly from tea-drinking. No less than seventeen million pounds of tea lay hoarded up in the London warehouses of the East India Company. The British merchants, finding their trade with America thus interrupted, induced the government to make an arrangement, by which they could sell the taxed tea as cheap as they had formerly sold the untaxed tea. It was now confidently expected that the stubborn colonists would at last buy tea and drink it with every friendly feeling towards the old country. Many vessels freighted with tea, accordingly, were soon sailing across the Atlantic.

The approach of these vessels excited the Americans in a manner wholly unlooked for in England. At New York and Philadelphia, the ships were not permitted to unload. At Charleston the cargoes were landed, and stowed away in damp, musty cellars. The head of the revolt, however, was at Boston. This old Puritan town set itself in an attitude of defiance. The ships anchored in the harbour. The captains were ordered by the Bostonians to take their taxed tea back to England again. They would gladly have obeyed, but they could not obtain a passport from the governor to clear the fort. At length the citizens could not endure the sight of these hated vessels any longer in the harbour. Under cover of the darkness of a December evening, a number of armed men, disguised as Mohawks, boarded the ships, hoisted out 340 chests, knocked out their ends, and discharged their contents into the sea. This was not the rash act of a thoughtless mob, but the well considered, though resolute act of sober, respectable citizens. These "Sons of Liberty" returned quietly and grimly to their homes that night, with the consciousness that they would have to give account for their deeds that day upon the battle-field.

AMERICAN WAR OF INDEPENDENCE.

When the tea was tossed into the sea at Boston, war was virtually declared against England. The wrath of the government was concentrated on Boston, and a bill was passed to close the port. All the colonies except Georgia banded themselves together to resist the British government in any attempt to carry this bill into effect. Twelve colonies sent delegates to a General Congress, held at Philadelphia (A.D. 1744). Virginia sent two of the foremost men of the day, Patrick Henry, a celebrated orator, and **George Washington**, destined to lead the armies of America to victory, and to shape her destinies with wise and disinterested patriotism. A deep earnestness pervaded the assembly; the session each morning was opened by divine service. They drew up "a declaration of colonial rights," stating their grievances as colonists, and their rights as Englishmen. They also agreed to suspend all trade with the mother country till the justice of their demands was acknowledged; and to prepare a loyal address to his majesty. The state papers issued by Congress, in conformity with these resolutions, called forth the admiration of the Earl of Chatham: "When your lordships," said he in the House of Lords, "consider their decency, firmness, and wisdom, you cannot but respect their cause, and wish to make it your own." In vain did Chatham, Burke, and Fox, three of the greatest statesmen and orators of the day, warn their countrymen of the danger of persisting in their aggressive policy towards the colonies; the nation was bent on reducing the colonists to submission by force of arms. Henceforth, every proposal from America was treated with proud silence on the part of the British monarch and his advisers.

Blood first flowed at Lexington, near Concord (A.D. 1775). The British soldiers having fought their way into Concord, destroyed many barrels of flour, sowed the bed of the river with bullets, and spiked the cannons. Having thus rendered useless a part of the stores which the Americans had been collecting in anticipation of war, the soldiers, though jaded with their night march and their morning's toil, prepared to return without delay to Boston. The way back led through woody defiles, or along roads skirted with fences and stone walls, where men, long accustomed to the hunter's rifle, could in safety to themselves take a deadly aim upon the retreating enemy. The ranks of the unfortunate soldiers were thinned continually as they hastened back, leaving behind them a long trail of the dead and dying. Thus the sword was drawn, and the scabbard thrown away, and the *American War of Independence* begun.

A second Congress now assembled at Philadelphia. A federal union was here formed of the thirteen colonies, leaving to each colony the right of regulating its own internal affairs, but vesting in Congress the power of legislating on all matters affecting the whole community. They wisely appointed George Washington as their commander-in-chief. To his justice, prudence, perseverance, ability, and disinterestedness, the Americans are chiefly indebted for the success which finally crowned their arms.

The war now began in earnest around Boston. The British troops in this city were hemmed in by what they contemptuously termed "a rustic rout with calico frocks and fowling-pieces." The patriotic army was indeed composed mainly of hasty levies of yeomanry, many of whom had seized their rifles and hurried to the scene of action in their homespun dress. They knew but little of military discipline and tactics, but they were familiar with the use of fire-arms in hunting or in "bush-fighting" with the Indians. The first regular engagement was fought at Bunker's Hill, near Boston, which the Americans had seized and fortified under the cover of night.

The colonists twice repulsed the British before being driven out of their rude earthworks. It was a dear bought victory; for the loss of the victors was about double that of the vanquished. The Americans were justly proud of such a defeat; for they had proved to themselves and the world at large, that their contest with regular troops was far from being a hopeless one.

Washington joined the troops before Boston, soon after their defeat at Bunker's Hill. He strained every nerve to form his raw levies into a well-disciplined army. His difficulties were gigantic. The men mistook insubordination for independence, and those from one colony refused to serve under officers from another. There was also for some time a great dearth of powder in the American camp. Washington's situation, from the want of military supplies, was such that "I was often obliged," he writes to a friend, "to conceal it from my own officers." For several months the siege of Boston went on without any decisive step on either side. Washington's inaction caused great dissatisfaction among his countrymen; but he could not justify himself, as he afterwards explained, without exposing the weakness of his army to the enemy, by declaring his lamentable deficiency of ammunition and military accoutrements. At length, after eight months spent in shaping and equipping his army, Washington secretly, by night, occupied and fortified the Dorchester Heights commanding the city. The British commander, General Howe, found it necessary to evacuate Boston as soon as possible, and take to his ships (March, 1776). Thus by the eminent services of Washington, and his admirable management, an undisciplined band of husbandmen in a few months became soldiers, and were enabled to invest, for nearly a year, and finally to expel a brave army of veterans, commanded by the most experienced generals.

The Americans now resolved formally to separate from the mother country, and to form an independent republic. A formal document was drawn up, called a Declaration of Independence, in which the thirteen colonies were declared to be free and independent states. In this celebrated document it is maintained as indisputable: "That all men are created equal; that they are endowed by their Creator with certain unalienable rights; that among these are life, liberty, and the pursuit of happiness. That, to secure these rights, governments are instituted among men, deriving their just powers from the consent of the governed; that whenever any government becomes destructive of these ends, it is the right of the people to alter or to abolish it, and to institute a new government, laying its foundation on such principles, and organising its power in such form as to them shall seem most likely to effect their safety and happiness. Prudence, indeed, will dictate that governments long established should not be changed for light and transient causes; and accordingly all experience hath shown that mankind are more disposed to suffer while evils are sufferable, than to right themselves by abolishing the forms to which they are accustomed. But when a long train of abuses and usurpations, pursuing invariably the same object, evinces a design to reduce them under absolute despotism, it is their right, it is their duty, to throw off such government, and to provide new guards for their future security. Such has been the patient suffering of these colonies; and such is now the necessity which constrains them to alter their former system of government." The solemn document was adopted by the American Congress, July 4, 1776, and promulgated to an expectant world. When the news reached New York, the leaden statue of George III. was pulled down amid the shouts of an excited crowd, and broken up to be melted into bullets, "to be used in the cause of independence."

The first great success that rewarded the patriotism of the Americans, after their declaration of independence, was the surrender of General Burgoyne's army of 6000 men at Saratoga (Dec. 1777). Within their earthen entrenchments at this place the English soldiers resisted the pangs of hunger and the overwhelming masses of the enemy for five days, in the hope of relief from General Clinton. The spirit of the troops was manly and noble to the last; but as all the provisions were exhausted, it became absolutely necessary to surrender. By this surrender the Americans gained 42 pieces of brass artillery, 4600 muskets, and an immense quantity of military stores. It had also the effect of filling up Washington's thin ranks by reviving the hopes of the Americans.

The campaigns of 1778 and the two following years were not marked by any decisive battle. The tide of victory ebbed and flowed, but the war consisted for the most part of skirmishes, sieges, marches, and counter-marches, each general trying to outwit his opponent. At length, Lord Cornwallis, an English general of high reputation, became hemmed in by a force twice as numerous as his own, at Yorktown. Washington brought 100 pieces of artillery to bear upon the British works. Cornwallis, however, stood the siege for three weeks, his men presenting a gallant front to hunger, disease, and cannon-shot. Finding his situation hopeless, he surrendered to Washington with all his military stores and his 7000 famished soldiers (A.D. 1781). This event virtually closed the war.

Early in 1782, the House of Commons decided in favour of peace; and in the following year a treaty was signed acknowledging the independence of the United States. The war by which this great result was attained had not been one of daring achievements and brilliant exploits; it was a cool, cautious, defensive war, in which patience and steady perseverance were the qualities most essential. Before the end of the year 1783, the last red coat had disappeared from the United States, and the American army disbanded.

The Americans had now to devise a federal form of government, that should give the states the strength of a united nation, without trenching on the independent action of each state in its own internal affairs. In 1787, deputies from the states met at Philadelphia and drew up a new constitution, according to which the legislative power was vested in a Congress of the United States, consisting of a Senate and a House of Representatives; whilst the executive power was intrusted to a President, who should hold his office for a term of four years. Washington was unanimously elected the first President (A.D. 1789).

CHAPTER XXI.

THE FRENCH REVOLUTION.

France has in the course of the last hundred years passed through many revolutions, and made trial of many different forms of government. This instability has arisen from the mighty shock given to the whole fabric of society in France by the great revolution of 1789. This great catastrophe was the result of an unjust code of laws, of an oppressive system of taxation, and of a corrupt court, the evils of which had been accumulating for centuries, and had at length attained such fearful dimensions, that nothing short of a thorough revolution seemed capable of securing to the nation the conditions of liberty and prosperity.

Some of the evils under which the French people groaned, have been already depicted in the history of the reign of Louis XIV. After his death, France sunk deeper and deeper into the mire of misery, under the increasing weight of taxation, whilst the Court revelled in every form of costly luxury and shameful debauchery, under the presidency of Madame de Pompadour, and of Madame du Barry, her successor. The extravagant expenditure of the Court was supported chiefly by taxes wrung from the peasantry, who, it is calculated, had to pay two-thirds of their earnings in one form or another into the royal treasury, whilst the nobility and the clergy—the great landholders of the nation—were altogether exempt from taxation. The old voluptuary, Louis XV., foresaw that some fearful catastrophe would, after his death, befall France: *Après nous le déluge* was his oft-repeated saying.

THE REIGN OF LOUIS XVI.

Louis XVI. succeeded his grandfather, Louis XV., in 1774. Though only twenty years of age, he had married four years previously Marie Antoinette, the beautiful daughter of the Empress Maria Theresa. At the moment when they became king and queen, they sank upon their knees, and exclaimed with streaming eyes, "O God! guide us, protect us; we are too young to reign." The new sovereign was an amiable man, of good intentions, and pure morality; but wanting that grasp of intellect, and firmness of temper, which the circumstances of his reign demanded.

Revolution could only be averted by a just distribution of the national burdens over all classes of the community. The attempt was made by Turgot in the beginning of this reign, but the opposition of the privileged classes was too strong, and the support of the king too weak, for him to effect any real reform. Necker, who succeeded him as financial minister, then tried to ward off national bankruptcy by prudent management and economy. All his efforts, however, were rendered fruitless by the unwise intervention of France in the quarrel between Great Britain and her American colonies. At the end of this expensive war with England, Necker gave up the national purse to Calonne, who tried to meet the increased demands upon it by the common expedient among spendthrifts of borrowing without a thought as to the means of repayment. When the nation was on the very verge of bankruptcy, Necker was reinstated (A.D. 1788). His recall gave so much satisfaction to the populace of Paris, that they shouted all day and all night, "Vive le Roi!" "Vive Necker!" But it was not in his power to fill the empty coffers with gold, nor the exhausted granaries with corn. In this extremity the king convoked the *States-General*—an assembly similar to our English Parliament, which had not met since the time Richelieu took the helm of state in 1614.

The despotism established by this minister was now

about to be overthrown by a down-trodden people, clamouring for bread, and thinking it might be found if only *liberty, equality, and fraternity* could be established. The poor famished people of France, in their ignorance, naturally thought that an escape from all the calamities they had so long endured, could best be effected by an entire subversion of the ancient régime.

The States-General met at Versailles (5th May, 1789). The assembly consisted of 1145 members, belonging to three different orders—the nobility, the clergy, and the commons or deputies of the people. The latter, called the *Tiers Etat,* outnumbered the other two combined. In ancient times these three orders had assembled in different chambers and voted separately; but now the Tiers Etat was resolved to override the privileged orders, by insisting on the three orders forming one assembly and voting as one body. Many of the clergy assented to this proposal and joined the commons, but the nobles stood aloof. After some weeks had been spent in inaction, the commons assumed the title of the *National Assembly,* and proceeded to legislate for the nation without regard to the king or the nobility, like the Long Parliament of Charles I. Louis sent his grand-master of the ceremonies to order the deputies to adjourn. Mirabeau, the most prominent among the deputies by his great abilities and commanding influence, rose and said, "Return and tell your master, that we are here by the power of the people, and that nothing short of bayonets shall drive us out." The king was too timid and too irresolute to employ such vigorous measures against the usurpation of the third estate; he merely tried to keep it in check by requesting the nobles and clergy to join that body.

Whilst noisy debates resounded through the hall in which the Assembly met, all Paris was in a ferment on account of the military preparations made by the king to overawe the capital. The shopkeepers, the artisans, and citizens of all ranks enrolled themselves, under the title of the *National Guard,* to resist the royal troops. Every place was ransacked for fire-arms, and in two days 50,000 pikes were manufactured by willing hands and distributed among the ranks of the citizen-soldiers. A fierce mob then attacked the Bastile, a strongly fortified prison, in the dungeons of which many an innocent man had been consigned in the previous reign, by a royal warrant, called *une lettre de cachet.* After a conflict of five hours, the Bastile fell before the cannon and hatchets of the rioters (July 14), whilst the royal troops looked on with folded arms. Louis now became aware that he had only his Swiss body-guard to depend upon; and never did a body of men prove their fidelity more nobly than these men, in their endeavour to shield the king from the dangers which were thronging around him.

The fall of the Bastile was the signal for riots throughout France; everywhere the spirit of lawlessness broke loose, and madly ranged throughout the land. The *chateaux* of the nobles were pillaged and burnt to the ground. The royal standard, emblazoned with the *fleur de Lis* on a white ground, was trampled in the dust, and the *tricolour*, as the emblem of liberty, equality, and fraternity, was uplifted in its place.

In the autumn a mad mob, headed by a band of frantic women, shrieking out "Bread! give bread!" proceeded to Versailles to make their wants known to the king and the National Assembly. That night they encamped by the side of large fires in the open streets. Before daylight a party of rioters gained access to the royal palace, and penetrated with horrid menaces to the door of the queen's apartment. The palace soon became the scene of indescribable tumult and bloodshed. The resolute stand made by the faithful body-guard, and the timely arrival of La Fayette at the head of the national guard, saved the royal family; but Louis was obliged to accompany the rabble to Paris, and take up his residence at the Tuilleries (Oct. 6th). Here the king found himself in a prison rather than a palace, and in the position of a criminal rather than a king.

The National Assembly also transferred its sittings to

the capital, and remodelled the constitution. On the anniversary of the fall of the Bastile (14th July, 1790), the celebrated *National Federation* took place, when a countless host assembled in the Champs de Mars to witness the king, his ministers, the deputies, and the public functionaries, take the oath to the new constitution. The people, finding that the new constitution did not at once relieve them from the miseries of famine and destitution, thought they had not yet found the true remedy for their woes, and became as lawless as ever. The bull had been unloosed, and he still persisted in rushing madly about and using his horns. By the end of the year many of the nobles had emigrated, and a few months later the king tried to make his escape, but he was discovered and brought back. Louis was treated as a deserter; he was suspended from his kingly functions, and a guard placed over his person.

THE REIGN OF TERROR.

The sovereigns of Austria and Prussia now resolved to interfere on behalf of the unfortunate king. But the efforts they made to avert the fate that threatened him only served to hasten his execution. The presence of a foreign army on the frontiers of France raised the spirit of the revolutionists throughout the land to the highest pitch of enthusiasm; and placed the chief power in the hands of the most violent demagogues. At Paris the supreme direction of affairs fell into the hands of the Red Republicans or Jacobins, under whose auspices the *Reign of Terror* was inaugurated. It was their belief that France could only be cured by copious bleeding; that at least 260,000 heads must fall before freedom could be assured, and above all that the king's head must be sacrificed to the cause of "liberty, equality, and fraternity."

The Reign of Terror commenced on the 10th of August, 1792, when a savage mob attacked the Tuilleries, whose halls and corridors were soon strewed with the bleeding bodies of the brave Swiss guards. The king and his family had placed themselves under the ægis of the

Assembly. Louis was now deposed, and sent with the queen and the royal children as prisoners to the gloomy palace of the Temple. The sanguinary work of the 10th of August was surpassed by that of the 2nd of September, when an indiscriminate slaughter took place of at least 2000 persons, who had been thrown into the prisons of Paris on suspicion of being unfavourable to the revolution. Before the end of the year the king was brought to trial, and on the 23rd of January, 1793, he was led to the scaffold where the guillotine stood ready for its royal victim. The fallen monarch attempted to address the surging crowd, but his faltering voice was drowned by an incessant rattle of drums, and in a few moments more his tongue was silent in death.

This murder sent a thrill of indignation and horror throughout Europe. The regicides gloried in their bloody work, and offered to do for any other land, that wished to "recover its freedom," what they had already done for their own country. No other nation, however, seemed anxious to share in the blessings of a revolution which only produced irreligion and anarchy, making life and property equally insecure. On the contrary, all Europe regarded the French as their common enemy, and formed a coalition against them.

To meet the new dangers that threatened France, a Committee of Safety was appointed, with Danton, **Robespierre**, and Marat as its leading members. This committee was empowered to take whatever measures might appear necessary to the welfare of the republic. The guillotine was the great national safeguard in the eyes of these men. The executions became one of the public amusements. About fifty victims were brought to the guillotine daily in Paris. Bands of heartless women seated themselves round the scaffold, and whiled away the time between the acts of the tragedy in knitting. Marie Antoinette was among the victims. She died with the calm heroism of a martyr on the spot where her husband was executed nine months before. Not only the friends of the late king forfeited their lives, but even some of those who had been most instrumental in bringing on the revolution, because they were in favour of a limited monarchy. The guillotine, which could not kill above one a minute, was found in some places to be too slow an engine of destruction. Couthon, at Lyons, destroyed whole crowds of unhappy royalists by the shot of cannon; and the not less infamous Carrier, at Nantes, packed large boats with men, women, and children, and had them towed out into the deep water of the Loire, where they were scuttled, and left to sink with all their shrieking freight.

The more moderate republicans began to recoil from the bloody work. Even Danton, one of the three ruling Jacobines in the Committee of Safety, tried to check the bloody torrent; but he only lost his own head for his humanity. Marat, another member of the notorious triumvirate, had already yielded his life to the sure hand of Charlotte Corday, who had come from Caen to plunge a knife into the breast of the miscreant. When brought for trial before the Revolutionary Tribunal, she boldly avowed, "It is I that killed Marat." By whose instigation? "By no one's!" What tempted you then? "His crimes." "I killed one man," added she, "to save a hundred thousand; a villain to save the innocent; a savage wild beast to give repose to my country." The doom is death as a murderess. On the same evening, therefore, the fatal cart brings its fair burden to the black scaffold. By the death of Danton and Marat, Robespierre was left sole dictator of France. When he had "purged society" by killing all the royalists of note, he hoped to purify it still more by the destruction of the leaders of the moderate republicans; at length, "he felt as if, to get things to his mind, the whole human race except himself would require to be annihilated." Having sent to the guillotine many of his associates, he was himself dragged to the place of execution, and there tasted the bitterness of death amid the yells and curses of the savage spectators, who had until that moment applauded his extraordinary method of regenerating society by means of the guillotine. With the death of Robespierre ended the Reign of Terror (29th July, 1794).

During this dark period of intestine struggle, the armies of the republic maintained their ground against the European coalition with a gallantry, skill, and persevering resolution, which created universal astonishment. They not only held France against all comers, but even annexed Belgium. And soon it became evident that a great military genius had arisen among them. This was Napoleon Bonaparte, who had already gained distinction, at the siege of Toulon, as an artillery officer.

NAPOLEON BONAPARTE.

Napoleon Bonaparte was born at Corsica in 1769. He married Josephine, widow of Count Beauharnais. Twelve days after his marriage he set out from Paris to take the command of the French army in Italy (A.D. 1796). At Lodi and at Rivoli he defeated the Austrians, who, in consequence, ceded to the French, by the treaty of Campo Formio, both Lombardy and the Netherlands (A.D. 1797). Such was the result of the *first* Austrian war with France. The republic of Venice, the Queen of the Adriatic, was in the same year extinguished, and its territory occupied by the French.

An army was now assembled at Boulogne for the invasion of England; but, owing to the shattered condition of the French navy, the project was abandoned. By the advice of Napoleon, it was resolved, instead, to deal England an indirect blow by the conquest of Egypt, as the first step towards the invasion of British India, and the most effectual way of crippling her commerce with that distant dependency. The battle of the Pyramids, fought near Cairo, gave Bonaparte immediate possession of that city, and virtually decided the conquest of Egypt. Ten days later, by the destruction of the French fleet in the Bay of Aboukir, the victorious army was cut off from France. The executive power, in France, had soon after the fall of Robespierre been vested in a *Directory* consisting of five members. Their manifest incompetency tempted Napoleon suddenly to withdraw from the army in Egypt and return to Paris. His military renown had gained for him such popularity, that he was able with the applause of the entire nation to transfer the supreme power from the Directory to himself, with the title of the *First Consul.* Napoleon now resided at the Tuilleries, and was soon surrounded by a court formed very much upon the ancient regal pattern (A.D. 1800).

During Napoleon's absence in Egypt, Austria, in alliance with Russia, had renewed the war with France, and redeemed the greater part of Italy. But his return changed everything. His army climbed the Alps, and by a famous victory at Marengo regained Italy. A few months later, Moreau, by the equally great victory of Hohenlinden, opened to the French the way to Vienna. The treaty of Luneville (A.D. 1801) closed the *second* Austrian war.

There was now a lull in this great European war. Bonaparte was desirous of peace to consolidate his power. The treaty of peace with England, signed at Amiens, was in reality a truce, giving a breathing-time to the combatants. This time was well spent by the First Consul in devising measures for redeeming France from the state of anarchy and chaos into which it had been cast by the violent throes of the revolution. French industry and trade revived in consequence of his wise and sagacious policy. The cathedrals and churches which had been shut up during the mad days of the revolution were reopened, and a suitable maintenance was provided for the clergy. The *Code Napoléon*, a systematic digest of French laws, is a lasting monument of his wisdom and zeal, as chief ruler of the French nation. After the morning inspection of his troops, he would preside over a council, formed of his ablest lawyers, and there he would sit from mid-day till five in the afternoon, never inattentive, never weary, marking out clearly, without passion and without prejudice, the best foundation on which property, commerce, marriage, in short all the complicated relations of life, were thereafter to repose. As a warrior, this great man became, from his inordinate ambition, the curse of France and the scourge of Europe; but as a legislator he was the benefactor of his countrymen. The French, in grateful recognition of his services, declared him Consul for life; and two years later (A.D. 1804) he was proclaimed Emperor of the French, with the right of transmitting the crown to his heir. The emperor and his wife, Josephine, were crowned by the Pope in the cathedral of Notre Dame. He was also crowned King of Italy at Milan, the celebrated iron crown of the ancient Lombard princes being used on the occasion.

A coalition between England, Russia, and Austria was now formed against the emperor. His navy was annihilated by Nelson at Trafalgar (A.D. 1805), and all his hopes of invading England perished. On the Continent, however, he was everywhere successful. On the day before the battle of Trafalgar, the Austrian general, Mack, capitulated with 30,000 men at Ulm. A month more sufficed to bring his legions to the gates of Vienna, which he entered in triumph. The campaign was brought to a successful close at Austerlitz (2nd Dec., 1805), where, by marvellous strategy, he gained a most splendid victory over the combined forces of Austria and Russia. The allied emperors, who had watched from a neighbouring height the destruction of their armies, only saved themselves by a hasty flight. The treaty of Presburg closed this *third* war with Austria.

The great conqueror now began to give kingdoms to his brothers. To his brother Joseph he gave the crown of Naples; and to his brother Louis the crown of Holland. He now turned his arms against Prussia, and by the decisive battle of Jena (A.D. 1806), deprived that country of her army, her capital, and her fortresses. The victor made a triumphal entry into Berlin, and issued against England the famous *Berlin decree*, in which all the nations of Europe were ordered to shut their ports against British merchandise. Russia was the only great power on the Continent that dared to oppose his will. Against that country the conqueror next advanced, and, after a drawn battle at Eylau, gave the Russian army at Friedland a total overthrow. Alexander, the Russian emperor, met the victor at Tilsit, on a raft moored in the middle of the river Niemen, and arranged terms of peace (A.D. 1807).

The amazing successes of Napoleon caused him to dream of Europe as an empire, with Napoleon as its emperor, and Paris as its capital. He now expelled the royal family from Portugal, and having induced the imbecile King of Spain to abdicate his throne, obliged his brother Joseph to exchange the crown of Naples for that of Spain. The story of the Peninsular War, which followed this act of aggression, belongs to English history, and is here omitted. Though Napoleon's generals were often defeated at the hands of Wellington in the Peninsula, the emperor himself still pursued his career of victory elsewhere, until his fatal retreat from Moscow.

In 1809, Austria, for the *fourth* time, entered the lists against France. In an incredibly short time the French army was filing through the streets of Vienna. But the chief fighting had yet to be done. The decisive battle of Wagram compelled Austria to sheathe her reluctant sword. The treaty of peace was sealed by marriage. The empress Josephine, having brought no children to the emperor, was divorced; and Maria Louisa, daughter of the Austrian emperor, became the wife of the imperial *parvenu*, who hoped by this alliance with the ancient house of Hapsburg to found a new dynasty in France, which would command the respect of Europe. A son was born as the fruit of his marriage, but he was not destined to reign.

The astonishing series of victories gained by Napoleon had raised him to the highest pinnacle of power ever attained by man, but such was the dizzy height to which he had climbed that he became giddy and fell. In defiance of the advice of his old and sage counsellors, he resolved on the invasion of Russia, as the Czar Alexander had dared to disregard his Berlin decree, and open his ports to British goods. "My destiny," he presumptuously said, "is not yet accomplished—my present situation is but a sketch of a picture which I must finish." It was, however, not finished in the way that he anticipated. The Russian campaign of 1812 is the most disastrous in the annals of history. The army of invasion amounted to 400,000 men, drawn partly from France and partly from all the European states that lay at the feet of the conqueror. The Russians retreated before the invaders, whose goal was Moscow. At Borodino, 70 miles from Moscow, the Russians made a stand, and there was fought one of the most sanguinary battles on record. After their dear-bought victory, the French were able to resume their march to Moscow.

On the 14th of September, Napoleon entered the ancient capital of Russia in the expectation of dictating terms of peace to Alexander; but to his chagrin and astonishment he found the streets silent and deserted, and only the dregs of the population left. He had, at any rate, as he supposed, found comfortable winter quarters for his army. But in this he was doomed to disappointment. In six days the city was in ashes, Russian incendiaries having contrived to set fire to the city in several places at once, with the determination of rendering the invaders homeless, and of compelling them to retreat in the midst of winter. That retreat was the saddest tragedy ever acted in real life. Early in November that year a most severe winter set in with heavy snow-storms, and unrelenting frosts. Thousands dropped down and found a grave in the snow. The Russians hung upon the rear of the retreating army, and cut off thousands that had survived both cold and hunger. The most appalling scene was presented at the passage of the Beresina. One of the two wooden bridges, constructed by the French, broke down under the excessive weight; the other was blown up on the approach of the Russians, leaving an untold number at the mercy of the enemy. When the ice was dissolved in the following spring, 12,000 dead bodies were found upon the shore. The Niemen was reached on the 12th of December by the fragments of the "Grand Army;" out of 400,000 men in the prime of health and strength that had crossed the Niemen six months before, not more than 25,000 famished and frost-bitten fugitives now recrossed it on their way home again. Of the main army nearly a third had perished in battle; about a third had died of cold, hunger, and fatigue; and the remainder had been made prisoners.

Napoleon reached Paris before the news of the terrible fate of his army was publicly known. He immediately gave orders for a new army of 300,000 men; and such was the amazing hold which he had upon the heart of France, that in four months he was at the head of 350,000 soldiers ready to risk life and limb in his service. He was now like a lion at bay, conscious that he was being encircled by his enemies and in danger of being encaged for life. The eventful year, 1813, brought the English and their Peninsular allies to the south of France, while the Russians and their German allies advanced to the eastern frontiers of that unhappy country. Many a sanguinary battle was fought before the chain was drawn around the bleeding sides of France. Napoleon made his last stand at Leipsic; for two days he held his ground against the allied armies, but on the third day he began to fall back upon the Rhine with a dispirited and disordered force. He crossed the Rhine with only 75,000 men, and arrived in Paris one evening in November, still haughty and defiant. The allies crossed the frontier of France, and slowly forced their way to Paris, which they entered and occupied, until a treaty of peace was signed (4th April, 1814). By this treaty France was stripped of all the territory she had gained; and Napoleon, instead of becoming Emperor of Europe, was obliged to accept the little isle of Elba for his empire.

Whilst Napoleon retired to Elba to brood over his fallen fortunes and dream of a brighter day, representatives from the European powers concerned in the late war met at Vienna to draw up a new map of Europe. The Bourbon dynasty was now restored in the person of Louis XVIII., brother of the unfortunate Louis XVI. The new king soon showed that he "had learnt nothing and forgotten nothing." He thought to rule France as his ancestors had ruled before the Revolution. Frenchmen began to talk of the violets of next spring, and a certain Corporal Violet was often mentioned as likely to return when the winter had passed. Ladies who longed for his coming wore the innocent little flower in their bonnets. The veteran troops of the emperor, who had returned to their homes, could not forget the victories they had won under his command. It was evident that the fallen emperor was still the idol of the French nation.

In March, 1815, all Europe was startled with the intelligence that the lion encaged at Elba had contrived to escape, and was now at large in France. He was received by his countrymen with open arms, and by the 1st of June was ready to take the field with a large army. At Waterloo, Napoleon and Wellington met in battle for the first and last time (18th June). During the whole of that summer day the French made heroic but unsuccessful efforts to break through the British lines. At four o'clock in the afternoon, the boom of distant cannon announced the approach of a Prussian army under Blucher. Napoleon, knowing that the time had now come for one grand final attack, ordered the "Old Guard," which had been kept in reserve, to advance under the command of Marshal Ney, "the bravest of the brave." The British Guards met them with a murderous volley at fifty yards, and then with a ringing cheer burst down the slope to encounter the "Invincibles" of France. "They are hopelessly mixed," cried the fallen Bonaparte, as he rode away to the rear. "Let the whole line advance," was Wellington's final order. The whole French army broke up like a frozen river under the influence of a sudden thaw; its fragments, some jammed together, and some loosely scattered, went rushing on in one headlong stream back to their own country.

Napoleon now ceased to be the central figure in the civilised world. He was banished to the island of St. Helena in the South Atlantic, and there he died in 1821.

CHAPTER XXII.

CHIEF EVENTS SINCE 1815.

THE Congress of Vienna, in 1815, rearranged the map of Europe, which had undergone many alterations since the French Revolution, and restored the dethroned princes to their respective states. Peace of unusual duration was the happy result of the fall of Napoleon. There was no war between the Great Powers of Europe until 1854, when England and France took up arms against Russia in defence of Turkey. The intervening period of peace was one of extraordinary progress in science, and in the arts and conveniences of life. Hardly a year passed without the invention of many useful and wonderful machines. Steam has been applied to purposes of locomotion both on land and water. The wires of the electric telegraph have almost brought the ends of the world within speaking distance. While the lightning has been converted into a messenger almost as swift as thought, the sun has been turned to account as an artist, in producing sun-pictures or photographs. The gas in our streets has almost turned night into day, whilst the lucifer-match enables us at any moment to call light out of darkness. The nineteenth century will probably be long remembered as the great period of scientific progress and invention.

REVOLUTIONS IN FRANCE.

The period of this long international peace, thus distinguished by ingenious inventions and marvellous discoveries, was not free from civil wars and revolutions. France, more particularly, has been the scene of civil strife. After the fall of Napoleon I., the Bourbons were restored to the throne of France. Louis XVIII., and his brother Charles X., reigned in succession; but their government was by no means popular. In 1830, the people of Paris rose against King Charles; and his cousin, Louis Philippe, Duke of Orleans, was made king in his place. In 1848, the French compelled Louis Philippe to sign his abdication, and established a republic with Louis Napoleon, a nephew of Napoleon the Great, as president. The president and the National Assembly did not work harmoniously together. At length it became evident that one of the two must fall, as the government had come to a dead lock. When the Parisians awoke on the morning of December 2, 1851, they found the walls placarded with an "Appeal to the People," and signed "Louis Napoleon Bonaparte." The news soon spread that the obnoxious members of the Assembly had been seized by the President's orders during the night, and were now in prison. Such was the celebrated *coup d'état* by which the reins of government were secured by Napoleon. The French nation, voting by ballot, responded to the President's appeal by registering an overwhelming majority in his favour; and before the end of another year, by the same means, showed their willingness to accept him as emperor.

When Louis Napoleon became emperor, he declared that the empire was the guarantee of peace in Europe —"The empire is peace;" but however much he may have personally desired peace, Europe has often since been the theatre of great wars. The two most important results of these recent wars are a united and free Italy, and a consolidated German empire, with the King of Prussia as emperor. France, under Louis Napoleon has, directly or indirectly, been greatly instrumental in producing these results.

UNION OF ITALY.

In 1859, Napoleon landed with an army in the north of Italy to assist Victor Emmanuel, King of Sardinia, in driving the Austrians out of Italy. At that time Italy was but a geographical term. The country so called consisted of a number of states under a variety of rulers, the chief of whom were the Austrian Emperor and the Pope, the King of Sardinia and the King of the Two Sicilies. Freedom was unknown throughout the Peninsula, except in Piedmont, which was under the government of Victor Emmanuel, who, by steadily keeping his word to all parties, had won for himself the honourable nickname of *the honest king*. Though he had won the confidence of the Italians, there was no hope that they would ever be able to unite under his rule, unless some foreign power would help them to rise from under the iron heel of Austria. The Austrian emperor not only ruled his Italian provinces of Lombardy and Venetia as an absolute monarch, but encouraged the other rulers of Italy to govern in the same spirit. A brighter day dawned for this unhappy nation, when Napoleon took the field in Northern Italy as the champion of the oppressed. Having gained the battles of Magenta and Solferino, and driven the Austrians across the Mincio, Napoleon entered into a treaty with Francis Joseph of Austria, at Villafranca (A.D. 1859), by which Lombardy was added to the dominions of Victor Emmanuel. Four of the smaller states in the centre of Italy were also by their own desire annexed to his kingdom.

Napoleon had thus, in a short campaign, accomplished much for Italy; but the work was only half done. To the astonishment of Europe that work was almost completed in the course of the following year (A.D. 1860), by the sublime daring and enthusiasm of Garibaldi. This patriot set sail from Genoa (May 5), with 2000 volunteers, to give freedom to Naples and Sicily, that had long groaned under the tyranny of Ferdinand II., who, from bombarding his own cities to terrify his subjects, had won for himself the nickname of *King Bomba.* His son, Francis II., had just begun his reign, when Garibaldi landed his troops in Sicily, and found all the people ripe for revolt. The royal troops were everywhere defeated. Francis fled from his capital (Sep. 7), and on the next day Garibaldi entered it. In February, 1861, the first Italian Parliament was held at Turin, in a wooden building erected for the purpose, and there Victor Emmanuel was declared *King of Italy.*

Still Venetia was subject to the Austrian emperor and Rome to the pope. But events were fast hastening on, by which these blots were removed from the new page of Italian history. In 1866, a war broke out between Austria and Prussia. Victor Emmanuel entered into an alliance with Frederick William of Prussia, and attacked the Austrians in Italy, but without success. Austria, however, was completely humbled by Prussia in a great battle at Sadowa. By the treaty which terminated this *Seven Weeks' War,* Venetia was ceded to the King of Italy, whilst Hanover became a part of Prussia.

Italy was now a kingdom without a capital. Rome was still in the hands of the pope, Pius the Ninth; and it could not be wrested from him, as it was occupied by French troops. At length, in 1870, that impediment was removed by the exigencies of France in the great war with Prussia. The Prussians crossed the French frontier in July, and in the following month the last French soldier left Rome for the defence of his own country. The troops of the Italian king soon afterwards marched into Rome, and on the last day of the year the king himself entered his new capital.

UNION OF GERMANY.

Meanwhile, a series of memorable victories, gained by the Prussians and their German allies in France, were fast binding in one brotherhood all the German states under the headship of Prussia. On the 2nd of September Napoleon surrendered with his army at Sedan. Marshal

Bazaine, who had taken refuge in the strong fortress of Metz, also capitulated with a large army. Strasburg, after a gallant defence, was compelled to open its gates. Paris sustained for some months all the miseries of famine, but her fate was sealed after her devoted sons had made in vain two desperate attempts to break through the lines of the besiegers.

While the siege was going on, King William of Prussia, being in the grand hall of the Grand Monarque at Versailles, received the title of *German Emperor* from the kings and princes of the states of Germany. Paris was soon afterwards obliged to admit the conqueror. As all further resistance on the part of France would have been madness, a treaty was signed, by which France agreed to pay an enormous sum of money, besides giving up nearly all Alsace, together with that part of Lorraine where German is spoken. Thus all Germany, except the German dominions of the House of Austria, has become consolidated into one empire—all the German states, except the Austrian, forming one confederation, with a common constitution, under the presidency of the King of Prussia, as Emperor of Germany.

AMERICAN WAR OF SECESSION.

Before Italy and Germany were thus united, the republic of the United States successfully passed though a civil war which at that time threatened its dismemberment. The *War of Secession*, as it is called, began in 1861 between the Northern and Southern States. The men of all these states are of the same language and descent; but the chief bond by which nations are united is not identity of race and speech, but community of interest. A large party in the Southern States contended that they would enjoy greater prosperity if they seceded from their brethren in the Northern States; whilst the former drew their wealth chiefly from their cotton, sugar, and tobacco plantations, by the aid of slave labour, the latter derived theirs chiefly from their manufactures in which free men only were employed. The war of secession ended in the complete triumph of the unionists (A.D. 1865). One important result of the war has been the suppression of slavery throughout North America; and there is reason to hope from the efforts now being made in Africa and elsewhere, that the time is not far distant when slavery will be abolished throughout the world.

INDEX.

WILLIAM COLLINS & COMPANY, PRINTERS, GLASGOW.

www.ingramcontent.com/pod-product-compliance
Lightning Source LLC
LaVergne TN
LVHW010238110826
845151LV00004B/1325
* 9 7 8 1 4 2 5 5 2 4 5 6 2 *